Asymmetry in Morphology

Linguistic Inquiry Monographs
Samuel Jay Keyser, general editor

Asymmetry in Morphology   Anna Maria Di Sciullo

The MIT Press
Cambridge, Massachusetts
London, England

© 2005 Massachusetts Institute of Technology

MIT Press books may be purchased at special quantity discounts for business or sales promotional use. For information, please e-mail special_sales@mitpress .mit.edu or write to Special Sales Department, The MIT Press, 55 Hayward St., Cambridge, MA 02142.

This book was set in Times New Roman on 3B2 by Asco Typesetters, Hong Kong.
Printed and bound in the United States of America.

Library of Congress Cataloging-in-Publication Data

Di Sciullo, Anna Maria.
Asymmetry in morphology / Anna Maria Di Sciullo.
    p.   cm. — (Linguistic inquiry monographs ; 46)
Includes bibliographical references and index.
ISBN 0-262-04229-0 (alk. paper) — ISBN 0-262-54184-X (pbk. : alk. paper)
1. Grammar, Comparative and general—Morphology. 2. Asymmetry (Linguistics) I. Title. II. Series.
P241.D52   2005
415′.9—dc22   2005047873

10 9 8 7 6 5 4 3 2 1

A Vincent e Piera
"Gradite questi pensieri che, con
tutto l'affetto, vi mando."

Contents

Series Foreword

We are pleased to present the forty-sixth in the series *Linguistic Inquiry Monographs*. These monographs present new and original research beyond the scope of the article. We hope they will benefit our field by bringing to it perspectives that will stimulate further research and insight.

Originally published in a limited edition, the *Linguistic Inquiry Monographs* are now more widely available. This change is due to the great interest engendered by the series and by the needs of a growing readership. The editors thank the readers for their support and welcome suggestions about future directions for the series.

Samuel Jay Keyser
for the Editorial Board

Acknowledgments

Asymmetry Theory is a theory of grammatical relations and their interpretation by the external systems. It targets a central property of the symbolic representations of the language faculty: asymmetry. I investigate the pervasiveness of this property in morphological objects.

The radical hypothesis presented here, the Asymmetry Hypothesis, and its explanatory power in morphology could not have existed without the current work in the Minimalist Program (Chomsky 1995; Uriagereka 1999) and in the Antisymmetry framework (Kayne 1994; Moro 2000), as well as the ongoing controversy on the relative autonomy of morphological and syntactic objects (Williams 1981a, 1981b; Selkirk 1982; Di Sciullo and Williams 1987; Baker 1988; Chomsky 1970, 1995, 2001; Halle and Marantz 1993; Bach 1996; Brody 2000; Koopman and Szabolcsi 2000; Hale and Keyser 2002).

I first presented the Asymmetry Hypothesis in 1998 at the 24th GLOW Colloquium at the University of Athens, in 1999 at MIT at the Penn/MIT Round Table on the Lexicon, as well as in courses I taught at the 1999 GLOW International Summer School in Thermi. Parts of the ideas formulated in the work were presented at the Cognitive Syntax and Semantics Conference in Dubrovnik in August 2000, at the Twelfth European Summer School in Logic, Language and Information at the University of Birmingham in July 2000, at the University of Paris V in April 2000, at the University of Massachusetts at Amherst in February 2000, at the 20th Incontro di Grammatica Generativa in Trieste in March 2001, at the Asymmetry Conference at UQAM in May 2001, at the Third International Conference of Morphology at the University of Barcelona in September 2001, at the Language, Brain, and Computation Conference at the University of Venice in October 2002, and at the Asymmetry at the Interfaces Conference at UQAM in October 2003. I thank these audiences for their comments.

Special thanks to Calixto Aguero, Manuela Ambar, Emmon Bach, Greg Carlson, Gennaro Chierchia, Noam Chomsky, Guglielmo Cinque, Roberto De Almeida, Manuel Español-Echevarría, Abdelkader Fassi Fehri, Sandiway Fong, Alessandra Giorgi, Jacqueline Guéron, Ken Hale, Henk Harkema, Irene Heim, Jim Higginbotham, Richie Kayne, Jay Keyser, David Lebeau, David Lightfoot, Giuseppe Longobardi, Alec Marantz, Andrea Moro, Marcin Morzycki, Marina Nespor, David Pesetsky, Jean-Yves Pollock, James Pustejovsky, Angela Ralli, Eric Reuland, Gemma Rigau, Tom Roeper, Sergio Scalise, Peggy Speas, Carol Tenny, Harry van Der Hulst, and Edwin Williams.

I also thank the coresearchers of the Asymmetry Project—Réjean Canac-Marquis, Rose-Marie Déchaine, Manuel Español-Echeverria, Philippe Gabrini, Mohamed Guerssel, Mark Hale, Virginia Hill, Charles Reiss, Yves Roberge, and Mireille Tremblay—for their contributions to this project.

Many thanks to Olga Zavitnevich-Beaulac for the data in Russian, to Edit Jakab for the data in Hungarian, to Grace Masagbor for the data in Yekhee, to Dana Isac and Stanca Somesfalean for the data in Romanian, and to Marcin Morzycki for the data in Polish. I also thank Francine Tessier and Marcin Morzycki for proofreading the manuscript. Finally, I thank Tom Stone, Elizabeth Judd, and Sandra Minkkinen from the MIT Press for their perseverance through the process of turning my manuscript into a book.

This work is supported in part by funding from the Social Sciences and Humanities Research Council of Canada to the Major Collaborative Research Project on Asymmetries in Natural Languages and Their Treatment by the Performance Systems (Grant no. 412-97-0016).

Introduction

In this book, I focus on a property of structural relations that has been shown to be essential for the understanding of linguistic phenomena. This property is asymmetry—that is, the irreversibility of two elements in a structured set. My contention is that asymmetry is a hardwired property of morphological relations. I raise the question of whether asymmetry is the only basic property of grammatical relations, and take symmetry as well as antisymmetry also to be available properties of relations in grammar. Typically, asymmetric relations yield restrictions in acceptability/grammaticality and interface legibility (interpretation). In contrast, symmetric relations do not give rise to the same restrictions. While it has been shown that asymmetry is basic in the description and the explanation of syntactic and phonological phenomena, its centrality in derivational morphology, or morphosyntax, if correct, would make morphological objects regular objects of the grammar.

My view contrasts with the traditional assumption that morphology, in particular derivational morphology, is irregular and thus immune to basic hardwired regularities of form and interpretation. According to Jackendoff (1975), all words of a language are listed in the lexicon. The rules of morphology are conceived as redundancy rules, by means of which the "cost" of a lexical item is computed. Those that are totally predictable will have no cost. Derivational morphology, as opposed to inflectional morphology and syntax, is traditionally considered the domain of exceptions (Fabb 1984, 38). In many languages, including English and the Romance languages, gaps have been observed in the merger of affixes and roots, such that some affixation processes have been identified as less productive than others (Aronoff 1976, 1983; Scalise 1984, 1994). Selkirk (1982) proposes that productive compounds are derived in syntax and that unproductive or idiosyncratic ones are listed in the lexicon. Semantics is generally assumed to be noncompositional or not entirely compositional in word structure, unlike the semantics of phrase structure (Chierchia and McConnell-Ginet 1990). Derivational morphology has often been contrasted with inflectional morphology. The lexicon (the locus of exceptions) has been proposed as the location of the former, while the syntax (the locus of regularity) has been proposed as the location of the latter (Chomsky 1970).

I focus here on morphological regularities, and take the asymmetric property of morphological relations to be a specific instance of the basic property of the relations of the language faculty. To illustrate this point, I formulate a theory of grammar where generic operations have specific instantiations in parallel derivations of the computational space. I call this theory *Asymmetry Theory*. I define the main features of this fully parallel model, in which the derivations proceed in separate planes of the computational space, with limited interactions between the derivations. The dynamic parallelism of the model allows for the expression of typical similarities between the derivations, as well as typical differences. I posit that morphological and syntactic relations share a property, asymmetry, while they diverge with respect to other properties of their primitives, operations and interface conditions. Asymmetry Theory holds that morphology combines and manipulates asymmetric relations only; symmetry and antisymmetry give rise to morphological gibberish.

Current theories of morphology do not approach the properties of morphological relations in these terms. Instead, they focus on the similarities and the differences between morphological and syntactic objects in terms of notions such as "morphological relatedness" and "derivational autonomy." For example, in Distributed Morphology (Halle and Marantz 1993; Marantz 1997, 2003), the derivation of morphological objects is performed in the syntactic and the phonological components. This is not the case in A-Morphous Morphology (Anderson 1992), where morphological derivations are independent from syntactic derivations. These theories also differ with respect to the nature of the operations deriving morphological objects. Morphological operations are assumed to be different from syntactic operations in A-Morphous Morphology, while they coincide with syntactic operations in Distributed Morphology. Furthermore, in Distributed Morphology, the notion of root is central and is the key to morphological relatedness; however, in A-Morphous Morphology, roots—and more generally morphemes—are not basic. Morphological theories also differ with respect to the role attributed to the lexicon. The lexicon is in play in Lexeme-based morphology (Anderson 1992; Aronoff 1994; Beard 1988, 1995), whereas it does not have any role in Distributed

Morphology. Moreover, linear and nonlinear models have been proposed regarding the articulation of the morphological component in the grammar. In most theories, there is a linear ordering of the morphological module with respect to the other modules of the grammar, whether the morphology precedes syntax or follows it, and whether it precedes the lexicon or follows it (Jackendoff 1975; Kiparsky 1982; Di Sciullo and Williams 1987; Anderson 1992; Aronoff 1994).

I take a different approach to the understanding of the parallelism and the differences between morphological and syntactic objects. In effect, by focusing on consistent crosslinguistic evidence of the regularity of form and interpretation of morphological objects, new knowledge can be found on the properties of morphological relations. Under this view, the questions of determining the autonomy or nonautonomy of morphology, and the question of identifying the key to morphological relatedness, are subsumed under the more basic question of determining how the properties of morphological relations are instances of the basic properties of the grammar.

Asymmetry Theory holds that the structural relations generated by the grammar are asymmetric as early as possible in the derivations and that morphological derivations start with asymmetric relations. The fact that mirror structures in the sense of Moro (2000) are not observed in morphological objects constitutes an argument for the strict asymmetry of morphological relations. A further argument pointing to the same direction is that inverse scope is not found in morphological objects. These facts also lead to the conclusion that the properties of morphological relations do not coincide with the properties of syntactic relations. My proposal brings additional evidence supporting and further articulating the relative autonomy of syntax and morphology, argued for in Di Sciullo and Williams 1987.

I show that the form of morphological objects is more restricted than the form of syntactic objects. I bring evidence from a variety of languages to show that the minimal morphological domain—what I call the *M-Shell*—is a formal object including two layers of asymmetric relations. This excludes nonbranching projections, as well as *n*-ary branching projections, from the set of possible morphological proper forms. I show that the M-Shell imposes severe restrictions on the form and interpretation of morphological objects.

While the Linear Correspondence Axiom (Kayne 1994) brings together the precedence and the dominance relations, Asymmetry Theory establishes a connection between the structural relations and the operations of the grammar. In current theoretical frameworks, the operations of grammar have independent justifications. Thus, the merger of syntactic objects is subject to formal requirements (Hale and Keyser 1998, 2002; Chomsky 1995, 2000a, 2000b, 2001) and movement is triggered by uninterpretable feature checking (Chomsky 1995, 2000a, 2000b, 2001). I suggest that structural relations and operations are related. More specifically, I propose that the operations of the grammar are triggered by the necessity of obtaining asymmetric relations as soon as possible in the derivations. In the case of morphology, the derivations start with asymmetric relations; syntax does not see the full asymmetry of morphological relations, and must generate its own, destroying points of symmetry as soon as they arise. There is a basic justification to such grammatical computation. The operations of the grammar must derive asymmetric relations to ensure linearization of the constituents for phonetic legibility, on the one hand, and semantic legibility of argument structure, aspect, and operator-variable relations, on the other hand. Linear order, scope, and the other semantic relations are optimally legible in asymmetric relations at the interfaces.

I base the architecture of Asymmetry Theory on my previous work on the modularity of the grammar (Di Sciullo 1996c), and on the Derivation by Phase Model (Chomsky 2001). To illustrate the empirical coverage of the theory, I extend my previous works on the morphology of the Romance, Slavic, modern Greek, and English languages. Furthermore, I add new empirical evidence from these languages, and from Russian, Hungarian, Turkish, and Yekhee, a poorly studied north-central Edoid language from the Niger-Congo family.

This book is organized as follows. Chapter 1 points out the central role of asymmetry as a property of the relations in grammar and its manifestations in morphological objects. Chapter 2 defines Asymmetry Theory. Chapter 3 details the properties of morphological domains in terms of the M-Shell, and shows that the M-Shell is close to Chomsky's notion of phase. Chapters 4 to 6 consider some empirical predictions of the M-Shell Hypothesis. Chapter 7 discusses the interaction of asymmetric relations and the legibility conditions imposed by the external systems. I show that severe restrictions on scope hold in morphological objects, which are not observed in syntactic objects, and suggest a way to account for this semantic interface (LF) difference between the two sorts of objects. I justify the existence of a phonetic interface (PF) operation that is required by tractability considerations. This operation affects specific layers of the M-Shell, bringing additional support to the M-Shell Hypothesis and to the Strict Asymmetry of Morphology. Chapter 8 discusses linguistic variation with respect to the linear order and the PF legibility of the parts of morphological objects and provides evidence that, given independent properties of individual languages, asymmetric relations are preserved under variation. In the concluding remarks, I relate asymmetry to the Global Economy of the grammar.

Chapter 1

Asymmetric Relations

The notion of asymmetry has more than one use in linguistic theory.[1] I use *asymmetry* to refer to a property of a relation between two elements in a set.

In a tree a relation is asymmetric if for any two nodes A and B, it holds from A to B and not from B to A. The relations of precedence, dominance, and sister-containment (asymmetric c-command) are the only basic relations in a tree that are asymmetric (see (1)).

(1) a. [A B]   b. A   c.

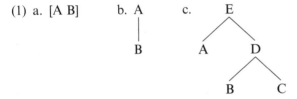

In a set of ordered pairs, a relation is asymmetric if the set contains no pairs the coordinates of which are inverted (see (2)). A relation is symmetric if the set includes pairs such as $\langle A, B \rangle$ and $\langle A, B \rangle$. An antisymmetric relation is an asymmetric relation that may also include reflexive pairs such as $\langle A, A \rangle$ and $\langle B, B \rangle$.[2]

(2) a. {A, B, C}
    b. {$\langle A, B \rangle$, $\langle B, C \rangle$, $\langle A, C \rangle$}

I focus on configurational asymmetry, and in particular, on the sister-contain relation in the derivation of morphological objects—that is, the objects generated by the morphological components of the grammar. I will generally use trees or bracketed structures to represent morphological relations and, in some cases, I will use the set theoretical notation.

I begin with the Asymmetry Hypothesis, which I substantiate on linguistic and experimental grounds. I then consider current proposals related to the idea that asymmetry plays a role in grammar with respect to linearization (Kayne 1994) and movement (Moro 2000), and I raise some issues related to the derivation and the linearization of morphological objects. I propose that asymmetry is the characteristic property of morphological relations.

1.1 The Asymmetry Hypothesis

In the Minimalist Program (Chomsky 2000b), the language design is the best solution to the interface legibility conditions. The Asymmetry Hypothesis (see (3)) further explores the idea that grammar is perfect.[3]

(3) *The Asymmetry Hypothesis*
   Asymmetric relations are core relations of the language faculty.

Language is a perfect solution to interface legibility conditions because it makes maximal use of asymmetric relations in the derivations and at the interfaces. Under standard assumptions, the lack of asymmetry would make linguistic expressions impossible to linearize at PF, assuming that if they are not asymmetrically related, two elements fail to linearize (Kayne 1994 and related works). The absence of asymmetry would also make linguistic expressions impossible to interpret at LF, because scope relations are legible under asymmetry (Fox 2000, among other works).[4] The asymmetric property of syntactic relations can be illustrated as follows.

Given the set theoretical definition of asymmetry, if an ordered pair $\langle A, B \rangle$ is part of an asymmetric relation, say a set S_1, then the ordered pair $\langle B, A \rangle$ is not part of S_1. An asymmetric relation is noncommutative. In other words, the members of the ordered pairs that constitute the relation cannot be inverted without destroying the property of the relation—that is, asymmetry. My contention is that this property helps make grammar perfect. Now consider what would be the case if symmetry were the core property of grammatical relations. By definition, a symmetric relation is commutative. If $\langle A, B \rangle$ is part of a symmetric relation, say the set S_2, then $\langle B, A \rangle$ would be also in S_2. Such relations are clearly not characteristic of natural language. In a linguistic expression, if an element A both precedes and follows an element B, the two instances of A cannot be identical. Consider the examples in (4), where the sentences are described in terms of relations—that is, sets of ordered pairs, the members of the ordered pairs being "minimally" the terminal elements of the sentences.

(4) a. John saw John.   {⟨John, saw⟩, ⟨saw, John⟩, ⟨John, John⟩}
    b. John saw JOHN.   {⟨John, saw⟩, ⟨saw, JOHN⟩,
                           ⟨John, JOHN⟩}
    c. John saw himself. {⟨John, saw⟩, ⟨saw, himself⟩,
                           ⟨John, himself⟩}
    d. John arrived ~~John~~ {⟨John, arrived⟩, ⟨arrived, ~~John~~⟩,
                           ⟨John, ~~John~~⟩}

In (4a), the first and second occurrences of *John* cannot refer to the same individual. In (4b), *John* and *JOHN* do not denote the same individual at LF since one occurrence of *John* is focused and the other is not; they are not identical objects at PF. In (4c), *John* and *himself* denote the same individual; however, they are not identical grammatical objects, because *himself* is an anaphor and *John* is not. In (4d), assuming the copy theory of movement, the copy of *John* is not identical to *John* at PF, since unlike the latter, the former has no PF legible features.[5] The examples in (4) illustrate that the terminal elements of syntactic expressions are part of asymmetric relations. Thus, the same element cannot both precede and follow another element in a sentence. However, scope ambiguity is observed in syntactic expressions (see (5)). With the narrow-scope interpretation of *someone* (see (5b)), the asymmetric c-command relations of (5a) are preserved, whereas with the wide-scope interpretation of *someone* (see (5c)), they are not.[6] Thus, differences in asymmetric relations give rise to differences in semantic interpretation.

(5) a. Everyone saw someone.
    b. Everyone saw a potentially different person. $\forall y \mid \exists x$ y saw x
    c. There is someone that everyone saw. $\exists x \mid \forall y$ y saw x

Typically, in syntactic expressions, asymmetric relations are attested on the basis of the restrictions they bring about on the distribution of constituents and their interpretation. If two constituents A and B are in an asymmetric relation, they cannot be inverted without giving rise to a difference in interpretation (see (5)) or, in some cases, to syntactic gibberish (see note 1 on extraction asymmetries).

Asymmetry is a core notion in generative grammar. It is part of the Standard Theory in the discussion on constraints on movement (Chomsky 1965, 1975; Ross 1967). In the Government and Binding Theory (Chomsky 1981, 1982, 1986; Higginbotham 1985; Reinhart 1983), asymmetry is part of the definition of the Binding Theory. As a property of linguistic relations, asymmetry has been shown to be determinant in the analysis of a variety of phenomena, including constituency, displacements, binding, linear order, and scope. In the minimalist framework (Chomsky 1995, 2000a, 2000b, 2001; Uriagereka 1999), it is part of the definition of the operations of the grammar and of the units of the computation. That asymmetry is determinant in syntactic relations has been shown in various recent works in generative syntax (see Boeckx 2003, on resumption), as well as in generative phonology (see Raimy 2000a, 2000b, 2003, on backcopying and reduplication; see also Dresher 2003; Hulst 2002; Hulst and Ritter 2003; Piggott 2003), generative morphology (see Roeper and Keyser 1992; Keyser and Roeper 1997, on compounds) and L-syntax (see Hale and Keyser 2002). Given the Asymmetry Hypothesis (see (1)), the fact that asymmetric relations are in play across the board in grammar does not come as a surprise. The pervasiveness of this property of relations suggests that asymmetry is hardwired in grammar. The idea that the operations of the grammar are defined in terms of asymmetric and symmetric relations emerges with the Minimalist Program (Chomsky 2000b, 2001) where Merge can be symmetric (i.e., set-Merge) or asymmetric (i.e., pair-Merge). The Agree Operation requires that the agreeing terms be in an asymmetric c-command relation. The Defective Intervention Constraint (Chomsky 2000b) is also based on asymmetric relations. In a broader perspective, Chomsky (personal communication and 2001, 8) notes that the principle determining that the Specifier precedes the head in a syntactic constituent might be a reflection of a more general property that holds at other levels too. Syllable structure—C-VC, rather than CV-C (see (7))—may reduce to more general cognitive principles.[7]

(6)

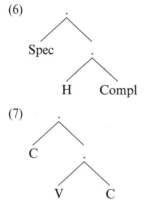

(7)

The fact that syntactic as well as morphological and phonological asymmetries are widely attested in natural languages suggests that this property of relations is basic in grammar. According to the Asymmetry Hypothesis, asymmetry is a core property of the relations of the language faculty. Recent results from psycholinguistics provide experimental evidence for the view that asymmetric relations contribute to the optimality of human perception and processing of linguistic expressions.

Experimental results from De Almeida and Tesolin (2004) on the processing of verb-argument (noun) relations show no difference in priming effects when verb primes are followed by purely syntactic (i.e., nonsemantic) targets (e.g., close-MOON) and when verbs are followed by semantically related targets (e.g., close-DOOR) at short presentation times (e.g., 40 milliseconds). Differences between these prime-target pairs appear only at longer prime presentation times (e.g., 120 milliseconds). These results suggest that humans are predisposed to perceive the pure syntactic properties of argument structure independently of the semantics of that relation. Furthermore, the processing of prefixed verbal structures provides evidence that the external systems are sensitive to the asymmetry of morphological expressions. Experimental data from Tsapkini, Jarema, and Di Sciullo (2004) on the processing of French prefixed verbs, such as *refermer* 'to close again', *enfermer* 'to enclose', and *réenfermer* 'to enclose again', show a difference in the priming of sequential prefixes, like the iterative prefix *re-* versus spatial prefixes—for example, the locative prefix *en-* 'in'. These results are expected if there is structural asymmetry between the two sorts of affixal relations expressing in one case the sequential relations and in the other case the spatial relations. Moreover, experiments motivated by the asymmetric structure of syllables consisting of an onset (initial consonant or cluster) and a rime (vowel and any following consonants) can be found in Rebecca Treiman's work. Treiman (1985) reports experiments providing behavioral support for this syllable structure, showing that 8-year-olds more easily learned word games that treated onsets and rimes as units than games that did not. Other experiments support the cohesiveness of the onset: 4- and 5-year-olds less easily recognized a spoken or printed consonant target when it was the first phoneme of a cluster than when it was a singleton. Yet another experiment on the reading of printed words shows that a consonant-consonant-vowel nonsense syllable is more difficult for beginning readers to decode than consonant-vowel-consonant syllables.

Jointly, these theoretical hypotheses and the corroboration of these hypotheses by experimental data suggest that asymmetry is basic in grammar. It might be the case that asymmetry is a part of the biological endowment enabling humans to develop the grammar of the language to which they are exposed, so that they can quickly generate and interpret the expressions of their language in a relatively short period.

1.2 Morphological Relations

I posit that asymmetry is the characteristic property of morphological relations that contributes to their legibility by the external systems. The asymmetry of morphological relations follows from the basic asymmetry of relations in grammar.

It has been shown on the basis of English and other languages that asymmetric relations give rise to restrictions on the merger, agreement, and linking of syntactic constituents. If morphological relations are asymmetric, similar restrictions are predicted to be observed for morphological constituents. Actually, stronger restrictions are predicted in morphological objects than in syntactic objects, if asymmetry is the characteristic property of morphological relations, as opposed to being one of the properties of syntactic relations. Consider the following.

If A and B are two elements of a morphological object, they cannot be inverted without giving rise to morphological gibberish, indicated as (#) (see (8a, b)). Furthermore, a given element A cannot both precede and follow another element B, (8c). In (8d), the first occurrence of the affix *en-* (en_1) has directional features and the second occurrence of the affix (en_2) has event (verbal) features. Moreover, (8e) is not possible, with the second occurrence of A as a copy of the first, as if movement had taken place within the morphological object. If the second occurrence of *-en* (*-en$_2$*) had verbal event features, as is the case in (8d), tense would wrongly be predicted to occur to the left of the root in English.

(8) a. write-er-s   {⟨write, -er⟩, ⟨-er, -s⟩, ⟨write, -s⟩}
    b. #er-write-s   {⟨-er, write ⟩, ⟨-write, -s⟩, ⟨er-, -s⟩}
    c. #er-write-er {⟨-er, write⟩, ⟨write, -er⟩, ⟨-er, -er⟩}
    d. en-light-en {⟨en$_1$-, light⟩, ⟨light, -en$_2$⟩, ⟨-en$_1$, -en$_2$⟩}
    e. #en-light-~~en~~ {⟨en-, light⟩, ⟨light, -~~en~~⟩, ⟨-en, -~~en~~⟩}

These facts suggest that morphological relations are asymmetric. In a morphological object, the same element, (say, an affix), cannot both follow and precede another element, (say, a root). Consider now the following examples with compounds, which also point in the same direction.

(9) a. the taxi driver / #the driver taxi
    b. the taxi's driver / the driver of the taxi

    c. the dollhouse / #the house-doll
    d. the doll*'s* house / the house of the doll

(10) a. the expert-tested software. / #the tested-expert software
      b. Expert*s have* tested the software. / The software was tested by
         experts.
      c. wind-blown hair / #the blown-wind hair
      d. The wind *has* blown her hair. / Her hair was blown by the wind.

In English deverbal compounds, the nonhead precedes the head, even though in cases such as (9a, c) it is related to the complement position. Its position cannot be the result of a movement operation, because the bare nonhead may not occupy the complement position.[8] In the absence of an active functional element, such as the possessive, a complement does not typically precede a noun in a syntactic expression (see (9b, d)). Similarly, with compounds including subjects (see (10)), the precedence relations are not identical to the ones obtained in related syntactic expressions. An intervening functional element must be present in the syntactic expressions, but not in the compounds. These facts also indicate that the properties of morphological relations cannot be equated with the properties of syntactic relations.[9]

Moreover, there is no scope ambiguity in morphological objects, as there can be in syntactic objects (see (5)). Suppose that the affix *un-* can be the spell-out of negation and that the affix *-able* is the spell-out of modality (in this case possibility) in morphological objects. The interaction of negation and modality is strict in morphology. For example in (11a), the negation scopes over the modal, as does the likely paraphrase in (11b); the modal does not scope over the negation, since (11c) is not a likely paraphrase (≠) of (11a). The absence of scope ambiguity in morphological objects also points to the conclusion that morphological relations are asymmetric only.

(11) a.   This is unpredictable.   NEG > MOD
      b.   It is not possible to predict this.   NEG > MOD
      c.   ≠It is possible not to predict this.   MOD > NEG

Asymmetry is hardwired in morphological relations. I use the term *asymmetry* to refer to the property of morphological relations, to the exclusion of symmetry and antisymmetry. *Antisymmetry* is used in Kayne 1994 to express the property of syntactic relations with respect to linearization.[10] Symmetry and asymmetry are used in Moro 2000 to express the properties of syntactic relations with respect to movement. The following

paragraphs consider Kayne's and Moro's hypotheses and their consequences for the derivation of morphological expressions.

1.3 Asymmetry and Linearization

According to Kayne's (1994) Linear Correspondence Axiom, the linear
ordering of terminals is a function of the asymmetric c-command relation
between all the ordered pairs of preterminals (see (12), (13)).[11] Because
the precedence relation is asymmetric, transitive, and total, the LCA is
calculated over all the ordered pairs of the preterminals in a tree. The precedence relation is asymmetric and irreflexive since an element can never
precede itself. A well-formed tree cannot contain two nonterminal nodes
symmetrically c-commanding each other, unless at most one of the two
nonterminal nodes contains at least one other nonterminal node. If this
requirement is not met, the terminal nodes will fail to linearize.[12]

(12) *Linear Correspondence Axiom*
     d(A) in a linear ordering of T. (Kayne 1994, 6)

(13) Let X, Y be nonterminals and x, y terminals such that X dominates
     x and Y dominates y. Then, if X asymmetrically c-commands Y, x
     precedes y. (Kayne 1994, 33)

(14) *C-command*
     X c-commands Y iff *X and Y are categories* and X excludes Y, and
     every category that dominates X dominates Y. (Kayne 1994, 16)

(15) *Asymmetric c-command*
     X asymmetrically c-commands Y, if X c-commands Y and Y does
     not c-command X. (Kayne 1994, 4)

Consider the phrase marker in (16).

(16)

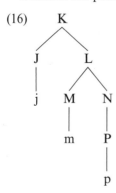

The set of all the pairs of nonterminal nodes such that the first asymmetrically c-commands the other is the set A in (17), and d(A) in (18). The three ordered elements in (19) constitute a linear ordering of the set in (16). Assuming that transitivity holds, antisymmetry is respected and the ordering is total.

(17) A = {⟨J, M⟩, ⟨J, N⟩, ⟨J, P⟩, ⟨M, P⟩}

(18) d(A) = {⟨j, m⟩, ⟨j, p⟩, ⟨m, p⟩}

(19) {j, m, p}

According to Kayne, the LCA applies at all levels of representation. It applies to internal levels of representation, including D-structure and S-structure, and it applies also to the PF interface for linearization. It derives the basic properties of X-bar structure, see (20). It allows only a single type of constituent, the one represented in (21), in which a head projects only one level of complement, with only one more level of expansion, because in the antisymmetry framework, subjects and adjuncts are formally nondistinct.[13]

(20) a. A constituent must have a head.
      b. A constituent has one and only one head.
      c. A head has only one complement.
      d. A head cannot take another head as its complement.

(21)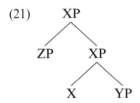

The LCA imposes strict ordering relations. Given the Universal Base Hypothesis, the order of the base constituents is universally specifier-head-complement, crosslinguistic variation in word order being a consequence of movement.

Kayne (1994, 38–41) suggests, on the basis of the properties of English and Romance compounds such as *overturn* and *ouvre-boîte* 'can opener', that the LCA extends under the word level. In doing so, he assumes that the structure of compounds is more complex than what appears prima facie, because the LCA must apply to structural descriptions where there is asymmetric c-command between all pairs of preterminals. This is the case for the head-adjunction structure in (22), where J adjoins to K.

(22)

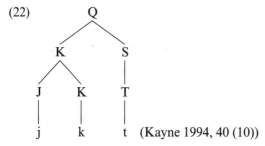

j   k   t   (Kayne 1994, 40 (10))

Kayne (1994, 40) proposes that the complex verb *overturn* is derived by head movement (see Baker 1988; Travis 1984), *over* adjoining to *turn* (see (23)).

(23)

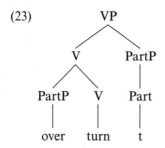

Head movement is part of the derivation of Part-V compounds, and XP movement is also part of the derivation of deverbal compounds. Kayne (1994, 41) suggests that a possible analysis of *can opener* might be "'er [open [NP [N can]]]', *open* adjoining to *-er* and the NP [NP [N can]] moving to the specifier of the *-er* projection" (see (24)).

(24)

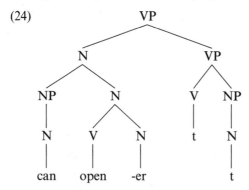

Even though linearization may technically be achieved by head movement, this rule, and more generally sister adjunction, introduces symmetry in the derivation and it may alter scope relations, which may in some cases alter the semantic interpretation (see chapter 7). The asymmetric relations can be kept constant in a model where the morphological derivation takes place in a separate plane from the syntactic derivation. In such a model, nothing requires linearization in morphology to be obtained by head movement or XP movement. The linearization of the morphological constituents may be achieved by an operation that applies only in the phonology and that does not introduce symmetry in the derivation, as discussed in chapters 2 and 7.

1.4 Movement as Symmetry Breaking

Moro (2000) developed a weak version of Kayne's (1994) Antisymmetry Theory and argued that movement is asymmetry breaking. Points of symmetry are derived when the LCA is violated, as in (25a) for small clauses, (25b) for multiple-specifier constructions, and (25c) for clitic structures, from Moro (2000, 32).

(25)

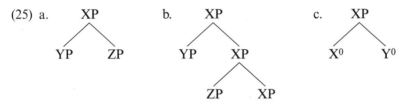

According to Moro (2000), movement is forced by the requirement of eliminating symmetric relations or "points of symmetry" generated in the course of the derivation. Points of symmetry are postulated on the basis of "mirror structures" found in syntax across categories (among others, see Den Dikken 1997; Kayne 1994; Moro 1997; Zamparelli 1995). The examples in (26) illustrate this phenomenon in the IP, the DP, and the AP domains.

(26) a. a picture of the wall is [t the cause of the riot] / the cause of the riot is [a picture of the wall t]
   b. John bought [books of [t this type]] / John bought [this type of [books t]]
   c. you are [t kind] / it's [kind of [you t]]

In each case, two phrases can alternatively move to derive the correct output given that there are two distinct ways to neutralize a point of symmetry. According to Moro, if movement were considered a way to delete the uninterpretable features of one element, the existence of such "mirror structures" would be hard to understand. In each pair, the two displaced elements are linked by one and the same relation, namely predication;

Moro (2000), following Williams (1980), analyzes predication as a symmetric structure. According to Williams (1980), predication is a mutual
m-command between two maximal projections, a subject YP and the
predicate ZP (see (27)).[14]

(27)   XP

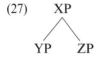

    YP   ZP

If points of symmetry consist of two elements X and Y and movement
is a way to neutralize points of symmetry, then potentially, whenever it is
observed that X moves, it should also be possible to observe an associated
structure where Y moves. This prediction appears to be borne out in XP
structure with cases of canonical versus inverse copular structures discussed in (26).

In morphology, such an alternation is not observed, which indicates
that points of symmetry are not derived in morphology, and thus that
movement does not take place to eliminate them. If the derivation of
morphological objects gave rise to mirror structures, alternations such as
the ones in (28) in derivation and in (29) in compounding would be
expected to occur, contrary to fact.

(28) a.   [write -er]
     b.   [write [-er t]]
     c.   #[-er [write [t t]]]

(29) a.   [man walk]
     b.   [walk [man t]]
     c.   #[man [walk [t t]]]

The example in (28) shows that the relation between an affix and a
root is not symmetric; the affix and the root are not sisters. If this
were the case, mirror structures could be created by the displacement of
either the affix or the root, thus destroying the point of symmetry. This
is not the case, notwithstanding the fact that a predication relation could
be assumed to hold between the "agentive" nominal affix -er and the
predicative root *writ-* before movement would take place (see (30)).

(30)   X

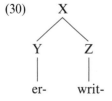

   Y   Z

   er-   writ-

Compounds such as *walk-man*, with a predication (subject-verb) relation, even though less common than compounds with a verb-object
relation, are found in a variety of languages, including Romance (e.g.,
scorri-mano, run hand, 'stairway'), and German (e.g., *Vogel sprech*, speak
bird, 'talking-bird'). Here again, the constituents cannot be sisters before
movement takes place (see (31)), because mirror structures cannot be created without giving rise to morphological gibberish (see (29c)). Thus,
there is no evidence that points of symmetry are introduced in the derivation of deverbal compounds based on predication.

(31)

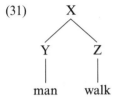

The facts in (28) and (29) suggest that points of symmetry are not found
in morphology. I posit that points of symmetry are never created in the morphological derivations precisely because morphology combines and manipulates asymmetric relations only; symmetric relations are irrelevant in
morphology. This is apparently not the case for syntax, under the assumption that points of symmetry can be derived in syntactic derivations.[15]

1.5   The Strict Asymmetry of Morphology

Morphology and syntax differ with respect to the choice of properties of
relations made available by the grammar. Morphology picks asymmetry
only. This is why morphology is more restricted than syntax. I state my
proposal as follows:

(32)   *The Strict Asymmetry of Morphology*
       Morphology combines and manipulates asymmetric relations only.

The severe restrictions on the linear ordering and the scope of the
constituents in morphological objects provide evidence that morphology
manipulates asymmetric relations only. The hypothesis in (32) makes the
following predictions for English:
• Affixes and roots cannot be inverted:

(33)   a. writ- er / #er- write
       b. re-writ-ing / #ing-write-re
       c. en-trap-ment / #ment-trap-en

• Inversion is impossible among affixes:

(34) a. compute, comput-able, comput-er, comput-er-ize, comput-er-iz-able / #comput-ize-er, #comput-er-able, #comput-able-ize

   b. re-en-trap / #en-retrap, re-en-capsul-ate / #en-re-capsul-ate
      re-dis-connect / #dis-re-connect

• The constituents of compounds cannot be inverted either. The nonhead precedes the head in deverbal compounds (35a), in root compounds (35c), as well as in compounds including modifier-head relations (35e, g):

(35) a. paper cutter / #cutter-paper
   b. teacup / #cup-tea
   c. Sunday driver / #driver-Sunday
   d. elephant man / #man-elephant

• Recursivity does not affect the precedence relations. In English compounds, recursivity is to the left, expanding the nonhead constituent (see (36)):

(36) a. paper cutter / tick-paper-cutter / #paper-tick-cutter
   b. teacup / English-teacup / #tea-English-cup
   c. Sunday driver / Easter-Sunday-driver / #Sunday-Easter-driver

It is generally the case that affixes cannot be reordered in word structure. However, there are two cases where reordering is possible: (1) diminutive clusters in Italian and (2) causative-reflexive affixation in Ecuadorian Quechua, reported in Muysken 1981. As predicted, different orderings of the affixes yield systematic differences in interpretation.

(37)   dim1 > dim2; dim2 > dim1
       -ino: descriptive; *-etto*: evaluative
   a. tavolo, tavolino, tavoletto   (It)
      'table', 'small table', 'funny small table'
   b. tavolinetto, tavolettino
      'small funny table', 'funny small table'

(38)   CAUSE > REC; REC > CAUSE
   a. verb CAUSE *-chi* REC *-naku*   (EQ)
      maqa- chi   naku- rka- n
      beat   CAUSE REC pl.   3
      'They let each other be beaten.'
   b. verb REC *-naku* CAUSE *-chi*   (Qu)
      maqa- naku- ya-   chi-   n
      beat   REC DUR CAUSE 3
      'He is causing them to beat each other.'   (Muysken 1981)

The inversion of affixes in morphological expressions give rise to a difference in semantic interpretation, whereas the inversion of two constituents in syntactic expressions may also give rise to a difference in information structure, including focus—as illustrated in (39) with locative inversion, and in (40) with quotative inversion—as well as to a difference in inference structure—as illustrated in (41) with passives and in (42) with middles.

(39) a. John rolled down the hill.
     b. Down the hill rolled John.

(40) a. "I am so happy" Mary thought.
     b. "I am so happy" thought Mary.

(41) a. Beavers build dams.
        (One property of beavers is that they build dams.)
     b. Dams are built by beavers.
        (It is a property of dams to be built by beavers.)

(42) a. It is easy (for John) to wash this shirt.
     b. This shirt washes easily (for anybody).

The Strict Asymmetry of Morphology also predicts that inverse scope is not possible, as illustrated in (11) above with NEG and MOD affixes, other than with a difference interpretation for the affixes. This can be seen with the affix *un-*, which may be the spell-out of negative or inverse semantic features.

With a root that does not denote an activity, *un-* may only be the spell-out of the negative feature (see (43)). With a root that does denote an activity, both options (negative and inverse) are available (see (44b, c)). Notwithstanding the two interpretations for *-un*, inverse scope does not arise, since (44d) is not a likely paraphrase of (44a).

(43) a. This situation is unbearable.
     b. It is not possible to bear this situation.
     c. #It is possible not to bear this situation.

(44) a. This shoe is untieable.
     b. It is not possible to tie this shoe.   (negative *un-*)
     c. It is possible to untie this shoe.   (inverse *un-*)
     d. #It is possible not to tie this shoe.

Thus, parts of morphological expressions cannot be inverted without giving rise to gibberish or a difference in interpretation, which is not a difference in information structure, as is the case when inversion occurs in narrow syntax (see (39)–(42)).

If asymmetry is a core property of grammatical relations, the asymmetry of morphology is an instance of a core property of relations of the grammar; it is not an instance of a property of syntactic relations. There is crosslinguistic evidence that morphology manipulates asymmetric relations, whereas it might be the case that symmetric and antisymmetric relations are also derived by syntax. Findings reported in Moro et al. 2001 in functional imaging on the neurological correlates of the syntactic and morphological components of the language faculty reveal the relative autonomy of these components. This provides neurophysiological evidence for my argument that while asymmetry is a basic property of relations in grammar and thus part of syntax and morphology, morphological relations cannot be equated with syntactic relations. However, parallelisms are observed between morphology and syntax—for example with respect to the "head of" relation, and with respect to Agree, as discussed in chapter 3.

If syntax cannot be equated with morphology, how can the operations of the grammar ensure that both syntactic and morphological derivations generate asymmetric relations? I consider this question in the next chapter from the perspective of Minimalism and formulate the Asymmetry Theory.

Appendix: Sets, Pairs, and Relations

Current generative grammar, in particular the Minimalist Program, operates a number of theoretical notions such as *set*, *pair*, *ordered pair*, *relation*, *symmetry*, and *asymmetry*. These notions are extensively used by linguistic theories (e.g., the Antisymmetry framework and the Dynamic Antisymmetry framework). In the following paragraphs I will briefly define these set theoretical notions (for further details see Partee, Ter Meulen, and Wall 1990).

A *set* is an aggregation of discrete individuals regarded as a whole. The individuals that are part of a set constitute its members. A finite set consisting of the positive integers 1, 2 can be denoted by listing the names of its members, as in {1, 2}. This so-called list notation of a set specification differs from the predicate notation that specifies some property typical/ characteristic of all and only its members—for example, {x | x is a positive integer less than 3} reads "the set of all x such that x is positive integer less than 3." The list notation is widely applied in current syntactic theory. For instance, Chomsky (2001, 10) uses it to define the set of expressions Exp derived by the computational procedure. Thus, Exp is the set of interface representations ⟨PF, LF⟩, where PF is the phonetic interface and LF is the semantic interface.

The members of a set can either be in unordered or in ordered relation. In the former case, given two sets, the order of the members of the sets does not affect their equivalence. Thus, the set {1, 2} could be equivalently denoted as {2, 1}, because there is no order or precedence relation specified for the members. More complex mathematical structures can be built if the notion of order is defined over the members of a set.

An *ordered pair* with a as the first coordinate and b as the second coordinate is denoted ⟨a, b⟩, where the elements of the set are in angle brackets. Given the two sets A and B, the set, whose members are all the possible ordered pairs with the first coordinate from A and the second coordinate from B, is called the Cartesian product of A and B and is represented as A × B. For example, if A = {a, b} and B = {1, 2}, then the configurations A × B = {⟨a, 1⟩, ⟨a, 2⟩, ⟨b, 1⟩, ⟨b, 2⟩} and B × A = {⟨1, a⟩, ⟨1, b⟩, ⟨2, a⟩, ⟨2, b⟩} are obtained.

Ordered pairs are used to express asymmetric relations between all the pairs of nonterminal symbols in a phrase marker in Kayne 1994. Chomsky (2000b, 133) uses the difference between sets and pairs to define the operations of the grammar—in particular in the definition of Pair-Merge, or the adjunction operation, as opposed to Set-Merge, or the substitution operation.

A *relation* is a set of ordered pairs in a given domain. For example, given a domain of discourse I, containing all human beings, the Cartesian product I × I is formed. The predicate "x is the mother of y" is true for certain ordered pairs in I × I, and false for the others. If the set of ordered pairs for which "x is the mother of y" is true, the extension of the predicate can be called the relation of motherhood. Thus, any subset of a Cartesian product is a relation holding between the first and the second coordinates of each ordered pair. If R is a relation and ⟨a, b⟩ is an ordered pair in R, a stands in a relation R to b, which can be written aRb.

Given the two sets A and B, if all the members of A are also the members of B, then A forms a *subset* of B. The subset relation is expressed by ⊆ or ⊇, the open side of the symbol pointing away from the subset, as in {1, 2} ⊆ {1, 2, 3}, {1, 2, 3} ⊇ {1, 2}. To avoid the possibility of identical sets, the term *proper subset* is used. A is a proper subset of B or is properly included in B whenever A is a subset of B but not equal to B. Proper inclusion is denoted by ⊂ and ⊃—for example, {1, 2, 3} ⊆ {1, 2, 3} and {1, 2} ⊂ {1, 2, 3}. A (binary) relation R that is a subset of A × B is said to be a relation "from A to B." Relations between sets are crucial in the definition of the building blocks of grammar, as discussed in section 1.5.

The relations in a set are characterized by a number of properties such as symmetry, asymmetry, and antisymmetry.

(1) If $R \subseteq A \times A$, then R is symmetric iff
$$(\forall x\ y)\ (\langle x, y \rangle \in R \rightarrow \langle y, x \rangle \in R).$$

A relation R in a set A is *asymmetric* if and only if for any $\langle x, y \rangle$ in R, it is never the case that $\langle y, x \rangle$ is also in R.

(2) If $R \subseteq A \times A$, then R is asymmetric iff
$$(\forall x\ y)\ (\langle x, y \rangle \in R \rightarrow \langle y, x \rangle \notin R).$$

Here are some examples of asymmetric relations in the set $A = \{a, b, c, d\}$: $\{\langle a, b \rangle, \langle d, c \rangle\}$, $\{\langle b, a \rangle, \langle e, c \rangle, \langle k, f \rangle\}$.

A relation that is otherwise asymmetric but may include pairs of the form $\langle x, x \rangle$ is antisymmetric. An *antisymmetric* relation is an asymmetric relation with the additional property that the set may include reflexive relations:

(3) If $R \subseteq A \times A$, then R is antisymmetric iff
$$(\forall x, y)\ (\langle x, y \rangle \in R \wedge \langle y, x \rangle \in R \rightarrow x = y).$$

Examples of antisymmetric relations in $A = \{a, b, c, d\}$ are: $\{\langle b, a \rangle, \langle a, a \rangle\}$, $\{\langle b, b \rangle, \langle a, b \rangle, \langle d, c \rangle\}$, $\{\langle b, a \rangle, \langle e, c \rangle, \langle k, f \rangle\}$.

Consequently, every asymmetric relation is also antisymmetric, but not the converse.

Symmetry is the property of relations in a set such that for every pair $\langle x, y \rangle$ in the set, the pair $\langle y, x \rangle$ is also part of that set.

An asymmetric relation is irreflexive. A relation R in a set A is reflexive if and only if all the ordered pairs of the form $\langle x, x \rangle$ are in R for every x in A.

(4) If $R \subseteq A \times A$, then R is reflexive iff
$$(\forall x \in A)\ \langle x, x \rangle \in R.$$

(5) If $R \subseteq A \times A$, then R is irreflexive iff
$$(\forall x \in A)\ \langle x, x \rangle \notin R.$$

For example, given the set $B = \{a, b, c\}$, the relation $R_1 = \{\langle a, a \rangle, \langle a, b \rangle, \langle b, b \rangle, \langle b, c \rangle, \langle c, c \rangle\}$ is reflexive because it contains the ordered pairs $\langle a, a \rangle$, $\langle b, b \rangle$, $\langle c, c \rangle$, whereas the relation $R_2 = \{\langle a, a \rangle, \langle a, b \rangle, \langle b, b \rangle, \langle b, c \rangle\}$ is nonreflexive because the ordered pair $\langle c, c \rangle$ is lacking. The relation $R_3 = \{\langle a, b \rangle, \langle b, c \rangle, \langle a, c \rangle\}$ is irreflexive because it contains neither $\langle a, a \rangle$ nor $\langle b, b \rangle$ nor $\langle c, c \rangle$, whereas the relation

$R_4 = \{\langle a, b\rangle, \langle b, c\rangle, \langle a, a\rangle\}$ is not irreflexive because the pair $\langle a, a\rangle$ is present.

Thus, in set theory, asymmetry is the property of sets of ordered pairs such that for any pair $\langle x, y\rangle$, there cannot be a pair $\langle y, x\rangle$ or $\langle y, y\rangle$ or $\langle x, x\rangle$ in that set. The members of the pairs are ordered unidirectionally. Asymmetry and antisymmetry differ with respect to ordering relations. Asymmetry manipulates only strict ordering relations; in contrast, the antisymmetry theory permits weak ordering relations. In a strict ordering relation, no element precedes itself; whereas in nonstrict orderings, every element precedes itself. Partial orders are transitive relations that are either antisymmetric and reflexive, or asymmetric and irreflexive. Total orders are partial orders that in addition are said to be connected.

The set theoretical properties of relations apply to mathematical configurations—that is, to structures composed of one or more sets together with one or more relations in these sets. A tree diagram is an oriented mathematical configuration, the properties of which can be defined in terms of ordered pairs of nodes connecting branches.

The relations of dominance, precedence, sister, and c-command between pairs of nodes in a tree such as (6) can be formulated as follows: node x_1 *dominates* node x_2 if there is a connected sequence of branches extending downward from x_1 to x_2 in the tree. In (6) x_1 dominates x_2, and that x_2 dominates x_3.

(6)

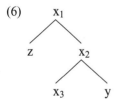

Given a tree, and assuming that x dominates y ($\langle x, y\rangle$), the set of all ordered pairs $\langle x, y\rangle$ for that tree constitutes the dominance relation for the tree. Dominance is asymmetric. It defines a strict ordering of the nodes in a tree. Two nodes are ordered in a "left-to-right" direction just in case they are not ordered by dominance. Given a tree, the set of all the ordered pairs $\langle x, y\rangle$ such that x precedes y (x is to the left of y) is said to define the precedence relation of that tree. Precedence is irreflexive. If x precedes y, then y cannot precede x, and thus this relation is asymmetric. Precedence determines the strict partial order over the nodes of a tree.

Distinct nodes immediately dominated by the same node are called "sisters." The relation "sister of" is symmetric—that is, if x is the sister of y, y is also the sister of x. If x c-commands y, then x and y do not dominate each other and all the categories that dominate x dominate y. If x asymmetrically c-commands y, then x c-commands y and y does not c-command x. In the tree in (6), sisterhood holds for the pairs $\langle z, x_2 \rangle$ and $\langle x_3, y \rangle$, whereas asymmetric c-command holds for the pairs $\langle z, x_3 \rangle$ and $\langle z, y \rangle$.

It has been proposed that c-command is not an elementary relation but can be derived from the properties of derivations (Epstein 1995; Frank, Vijay-Shanker, and Chen 1996; Reuland 1998). Asymmetric c-command falls out in a natural way from the operations of the grammar in the minimalist framework (Chomsky 2000a). This relation is subsumed under the more elementary "sister" and "contain" relations derived by the operation Merge. In Chomsky 2000b, 116, c-command is a relation that falls out from the computational process. Thus, the operation Merge takes two elements α and β and forms a more complex one K incorporating both α, β. Merge provides two relations: sisterhood, which holds for (α, β), and immediate contain, which holds for (K, α) and (K, β). By composition of relations, two new relations are derived: the relation *contain* and the relation *c-command* (sister-contain). Thus, K contains α if K immediately contains α, or K immediately contains L, which immediately contains α; conversely α is a term of K if K contains α. And α c-commands β if α is the sister of K that contains β. See Chomsky 2000a for discussion.

Chapter 2

Asymmetry Theory

Asymmetry Theory is a theory of the relations generated by the grammar and their legibility by the external systems. The theory incorporates the hypotheses that asymmetry is a basic property of the relations of the language faculty and that morphology manipulates asymmetric relations only. It offers an answer to the question of why asymmetric relations are part of morphological as well as syntactic derivations, even though morphological and syntactic objects cannot be equated. The components of the grammar share basic properties and differ with respect to their primitives, operations, and conditions. Thus, the Atomicity Thesis, according to which words are atomic with respect to phrasal syntax and phrasal semantics (Di Sciullo and Williams 1987; Lapointe 1979), is preserved and the parallelism between morphology and syntax follows from the architecture of the grammar. In this chapter, I define the basic elements of Asymmetry Theory and the morphological component in a minimalist perspective.[1]

2.1 Asymmetry Theory and the Architecture of the Grammar

I assume the basic properties of the Minimalist Program (Chomsky 2001) and define a fully parallel model of grammar according to which morphological and syntactic derivations proceed in parallel. The architecture of Asymmetry Theory is an implementation of the Modularity of Computational Space Hypothesis (Di Sciullo 1996c), according to which the computational space is partitioned in parallel planes of computations with limited interactions between the derivations.[2] This hypothesis is compatible with the Derivation by Phase Model (Chomsky 2001; Uriagereka 1999). Asymmetry Theory extends the Derivation by Phase model into a fully parallel model. The representation in (1) illustrates, with great oversimplification, the components, M, S, Φ, Σ, the parallel D_M/D_S, derivations, and the resulting domains of computation, $domain_1$ ... $domain_n$, which are interpreted at LF and PF.

(1) Φ $domain_1$ ... $domain_n$
                                                                    $\rightarrow$ LF
    Lex(LA)   M   S D_M/D_S D_M/D_S
                                                                    $\rightarrow$ PF
                   Σ $domain_1$ ... $domain_n$

Thus, there are four sorts of derivations, morphological (D_M), syntactic (D_S), phonological (D_Φ), and semantic (D_Σ). The computation maps a lexical array (LA, or numeration) to D_M and D_S, and the units of the computation (phases) are transferred to the phonological component (Φ), which maps the outcome of D_S to PF for phonetic interpretation, and to the semantic component (Σ), which maps the outcome of D_S to LF for semantic interpretation, cyclically and in parallel. Lexical insertion must occur before PF and LF, at a point in the derivation determined by the featural properties of the elements in the LA and the requirement that they be inserted in a derivation D only if their features are active in D.[3]

In Asymmetry Theory, the morphological component D_M derives the morphological relations between affixes and roots. The morphological domains are transferred to the semantic derivation (D_Σ) and to phonological derivation (D_Φ). The scope relations along with the other morphological relations are legible at LF, and linear precedence relations between affixes and roots are derived in D_Φ and are legible at PF.

The components of the grammar need not be ordered with respect to each other, because their interaction follows from the architecture of the grammar and their own individual properties. Full parallelism does not prevent D_M from having precedence over D_S. Asymmetry Theory holds that both M and S have access to Lex, which is a repository of underivable vocabulary items, including affixes and roots. M has access to affixes and roots, which must form complete morphological units in D_M before being transferred to D_S. If S does not have access to affixes and roots, the morphological derivations will be derivationally prior to the syntactic derivations. D_M and D_S have precedence over D_Φ and D_Σ, because the inputs of D_Φ and D_Σ are complete morphological and syntactic domains.

Moreover, parts of D_S can be transferred to D_M, and conversely, parts of D_M can be transferred to D_S. The derivation of syntactic words, (see Di Sciullo and Williams 1987) is an example of the former.[4] The derivation of discontinuous constituents is an example of the latter.[5] In both cases transfer is possible only if the constituent has independence—that is, is isolable—at the interfaces.

A derivation D_1 is transferred to a derivation D_2 in order to be interpretable by the external systems. In Chomsky (2001, 5), Transfer hands D_{NS} over to Φ and Σ. In the fully parallel model of Asymmetry Theory, Transfer also hands D_M over to Φ and Σ. Moreover, D_M and D_S may exchange domains. Lexical insertion may also be thought of as a case of Transfer from LA, to D_M or D_S. Thus, for an expression to be interpreted by the external systems, its parts must transfer from LA to $D_1, \ldots, D_n$ to Φ and Σ. Asymmetry Theory articulates further the Derivation by Phase Model, according to which the computation maps an LA to the interface expressions cyclically.

In the next section, I radically depart from standard assumptions, and I define generic and component-specific properties of the grammar within Asymmetry Theory.

2.2   Minimal Trees and Homogeneous Projections

The relations of precedence, dominance, and sister-contain are the main basic asymmetric relations of the grammar. The precedence relation is crucial at PF, where the linear order of constituents is legible, and the sister-contain relation is crucial at LF, where the scope and the other morphological relations are legible.

One way to implement the strict asymmetry of morphology is to take affixes and roots to be part of the asymmetric relations of (2) at the initial point of D_M. I will refer to this structure as the *minimal tree*, define it in (3), and take it to be the configurational primitive of M.

(2)

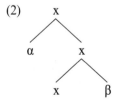

(3) *Minimal tree*

T is a minimal tree iff T has exactly one head, one specifier, and one complement.

In a minimal tree, all the terminals are part of an asymmetric sister-contain relation. For example, in the tree in (2), α sister-contains x and β. The hierarchy of the constituents in (2) is determined by the Universal

Base Hypothesis (Kayne 1994).[6] Thus in (2), α, the specifier, precedes x, the head, and is followed by β, the complement of x. The minimal tree contributes to the strict asymmetry of morphology, and it provides the minimal structure for the representations of the morphological features.

The primitives of S do not include the morphological minimal tree, and the syntactic operations apply to objects the morphological structure of which is not available. Because the primitives of M include the minimal tree, asymmetry is a basic property of morphological relations. The minimal tree is not part of the primitives of S, and the properties of syntactic relations are not limited to asymmetric relations; symmetry and antisymmetry are also available in S. Thus, though the asymmetric property of relations is available to all the components, it is the characteristic property of the primitive relations of M only.

The linear order of the morphophonological constituents is legible at PF, and is derived by an operation applying at D_Φ (see section 2.4). In Asymmetry Theory, the descriptive notions of prefix and suffix are not part of the primitives of M. The linear order of affixes with respect to roots is not stipulated but is a consequence of the operations of the grammar in conjunction with language-specific properties (see chapter 8).

The morphological relations, including scope, aspect, and argument structure, are legible at LF. In a minimal tree, the argument features are distributed on the nonheads; the modifier features and the operator-variable features are in the specifier-head relation.[7] All affixes are part of predicate-argument, aspect, and operator-variable relations; however, their morphologically salient feature determines their position in a minimal tree. Three sorts of affixes can be distinguished in this perspective: predicate affixes, modifier affixes, and operator-variable affixes, each one with two subsorts, as described below.

The predicate affixes determine the semantic type—for example, $\langle et \rangle$, $\langle e, \langle et \rangle \rangle$, $\langle\!\langle et \rangle, \langle et \rangle\!\rangle$—of the morphological object of which they are part.[8] Predicate affixes also affect the argument structure of their complement, a root or another morphological object; for example, the nominalizer -er affects the external argument of the root or the morphological object to which it applies (e.g., *Chomsky wrote "On wh-movement," the writer of "On wh-movement"* (**by Chomsky*)). This is the case for the secondary predicate affixes, such as -able and -ly (*students read these books, these books are readable (by students)*). Because they determine the semantic type of the derived morphological object and affect argument structure, predicate affixes head their minimal tree.

The modifier affixes bring aspectual modification to a morphological object without affecting its semantic type. They subdivide into internal aspectual modifiers, such as the external aspectual modifier affixes (e.g., the sequential affixes *re-* and *dis-*, as in *discharge* and *recharge*), and the internal modifier affixes (e.g., the locational *en-* in *entrap*, and the directional *a-* in *await*). Because they do not determine the semantic type of the derived morphological object, modifier affixes are located in the specifier of their minimal tree. Privative affixes, such as *a-* in *asocial*, and negative affixes, such as *in-* and *non-*, are also part of this set, along with numeral affixes, such as *bi-*, *tri-*, and *quadri-*.

Finally, the operator affixes are the morphological spell-out of an operator feature or a variable feature that is bound by an operator. The *wh*-morpheme of *wh*-words and the *th*-morpheme of the determiners and complementizers are examples of the first case; inflectional affixes, such as the plural morpheme *-s* and the past-tense morpheme *-ed*, are examples of the second case. Because the first sort of affixes link a variable in D_M, they are located in the specifier of their minimal tree; because the second sort of affixes are linked outside of D_M, they head their minimal tree.

Thus, the head of a minimal tree may be filled with a predicate affix or an operator-bound affix; the specifier of a minimal tree may be filled with a modifier affix, or with an operator affix (see (4)).

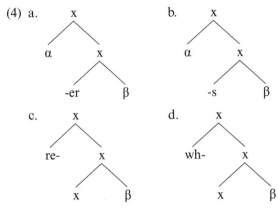

(4) a., b., c., d.

The distribution of affixes within minimal trees is parallel to the distribution of constituents in syntactic projections, where primary predicates are heads, and modifiers and operators occupy the specifier position of functional (F) projections, which are superior to lexical (L) projections. Functional heads identify the upper bound of a computational domain (see Grimshaw 1991; Speas 1990; Van Riemsdijk 1989), and they are generated exclusively in the functional projections sister-containing lexical projections (see Cinque 1999; Carlson 2003; Kayne 2001, 2003; Sportiche 2002). I will refer to this hypothesis as the *Hierarchy of Homogeneous Projections* (see (5)).

(5) *The Hierarchy of Homogeneous Projections Hypothesis*
   Only functional elements head functional projections and sister-contain lexical projections.

Homogeneity is a property of the basic projections generated by the grammar; it is part of the properties shared by M and S. I will assume further that there are three main semantic layers of projection. The top layer is the operator layer, the intermediate layer is the modifier layer, and the lower layer is the predicate-argument layer (see (6)). These three semantic layers correspond to the three morphological domains: the A-Shell, the Asp-Shell, and the Op-Shell.

(6)

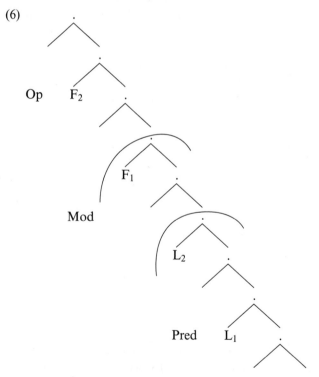

The Hierarchy of Homogeneous Projections has consequences for both D_S and D_M. One consequence for D_S is that clitic pronouns, being functional elements, are generated in the functional projection only.[9] One

consequence for D_M is that affixes that contribute to aspectual modification are generated in the F-projections, and they sister-contain the affixes
generated in the L-projections (see chapter 5). Another consequence of
the hypothesis for D_M is that infixes with semantic features are generated
in the Hierarchy of Homogeneous Projections according to their semantic
contribution and scope properties, which are legible at LF; their surface
linear order is legible only at PF.[10]

The difference in the choice of the primitive relations available in the
grammar is determinant in the derivation of morphological expressions
as opposed to syntactic expressions. The vocabulary items of M are part
of minimal trees, which is not the case in S; however, their position in the
basic morphological projection line is parallel to their position in the syntactic projection line. The parallelism and differences between S and M
are expressed with a minimum of theoretical apparatus, and follow from
the architecture of the grammar.

2.3   Features, Interpretable and Uninterpretable

The grammar includes a set of features, interpretable and uninterpretable.[11] Uninterpretable features must be checked and deleted in the
course of the derivations. The interpretable features are phonetic and semantic features that must be legible at the interfaces by the external systems. The phonetic features are legible by the sensorimotor system at PF,
whereas the semantic features are legible by the conceptual-intentional
system at LF.

The components differ with respect to the choice of features available
to the grammar. In particular, M and S differ with respect to their uninterpretable and interpretable features.[12] Assuming that movement is related to the checking of the uninterpretable EPP feature, this feature is
not part of the uninterpretable features of M, since there is no evidence
of overt movement and that expletives are not found word internally.
However, unvalued features are part of D_M, such as the nonargument
feature [−A] (the negative value standing for the absence of argument
feature), and must be eliminated by a [+A] feature, which values it. The
uninterpretable features of M are [−A] (argument) and [−pred] (predicate), [−F_E] (external aspect) and [−F_I] (internal aspect), [−X] (variable),
and [−Re] (restrictor). Each pair is part of a different layer of the morphological projection—that is, the predicate-argument layer, the modifier
layer, and the operator-variable layer (see chapters 4 through 6). The

[−Xφ] feature is also part of the unvalued features of roots and is checked by the [+Xφ] feature of inflectional affixes (see chapter 3).

Uninterpretable features that must be checked and deleted in the course of D_S do not coincide with the uninterpretable features that must be checked and deleted in the course of D_M. This is expected given the architecture of the grammar in Asymmetry Theory, because D_M and D_S are parts of different planes of the computational space. Being different components, their feature systems differ. The morphological interpretable features are accessible to D_S, and are part of the shared features of M and S. However, the interpretable features of M and S do not coincide. Assuming that categorial features like N and V are interpretable, they are part of D_S only. D_M is category-free; it does not include categorial features such as N and V. This must be the case if roots are not specified for categorial features, as proposed in Chomsky 1970, a position also adopted in Hale and Marantz 1993. Affixes are also unspecified for categorial features. For example, the affix *-er* is either nominal (e.g., *produce, producer*), or has no categorial features at all when used in a derived comparative (e.g., *smart, smarter*). I take the categorial feature of a morphological object to be determined in D_S by its closest functional sister-containing head.

Assuming that asymmetry is a generic property of relations in grammar, it must also be a property of the Lex relations. The features of the underivable items are stored in Lex, in terms of minimal trees (see (7)).

(7) a.

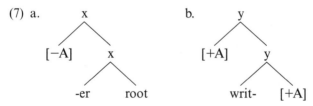

In (7a), the affix *-er* heads the minimal tree because it has predicate properties. The affix has an uninterpretable [−A] feature in its specifier position. It does not have a [+A] feature in its specifier position because it is not a causative affix. Furthermore, it asymmetrically selects a root with an interpretable [+A] feature in its specifier, as is the case for *writ-* in (7b). Derivational affixes differ in selectional restrictions; their features are part of Lex and must be learned, except for the fact that they are part of asymmetric relations. Asymmetric relations make lexical specifications learnable (see Di Sciullo et al. 2003a).

Thus, M and S have both interpretable and uninterpretable features, and they differ with respect to the choice of specific features.

2.4   Operations, Generic and Component-Specific

The grammar includes generic and component-specific operations. The generic operations are instantiated in M and S in different ways.[13] By distinguishing generic from component-specific operations, the parallelism and the differences between morphological objects and syntactic objects follow from the architecture of the grammar.

2.4.1   Generic

The grammar includes generic operations: Shift derives complex objects on the basis of more elementary ones, Link relates features objects, and Flip derives a mirror image of a minimal tree and contributes to linearization. The generic operations have specific implementations in M and S (see (8), (9)).[14]

(8) *Shift* (α, β)
Given two objects α, β, Shift (α, β) derives a new object δ projected from α.

(9) *Link* (α, β)
Given two objects α and β, α sister-containing β, Link (α, β) derives the object (α, β), where α and β are featurally related.

Shift is a generic merger operation; it applies in D_S and in D_M. When applying in D_S, Shift merges two syntactic objects, without having access to their morphological structure; when applying in D_M, it merges morphological trees under asymmetric selection. That is, the head of a minimal tree selects the head of another minimal tree, with the first sister-containing the other in the derived tree. Asymmetric selection in M is parallel to the selection relation in S discussed in Collins (2002). Shift is an asymmetric operation in the sense that only one of the two objects to which it applies becomes the label of the new object. It differs from the operation Merge as defined in Chomsky 2000b, since set-Merge is a symmetric operation, in the sense that either one of the two objects undergoing Merge is equally a candidate for the label of the new object. Moreover, the uninterpretable features of heads are checked by Shift applying under Agree (see chapter 3).

Link is the generic Attract/Move/Bind operation and also applies in both D_S and D_M. It may apply to elements in specifier-head relation, as well as to two elements in head position or in nonhead position. It derives new featural relations on the basis of already existing ones. As defined in (9), Link applies to two objects in asymmetric relation. However, it may give rise to pied-piping only in D_S. Link may relate interpretable features, as is the case in anaphoric binding. Like Shift, it ensures uninterpretable feature checking under Agree.[15] Shift checks the uninterpretable features of the nonheads.

Agree is defined in terms of feature identity in Chomsky 2000b. However, it can be defined in terms of a proper inclusion relation between structured sets of features. While an uninterpretable feature is unvalued (e.g., the [−A] feature), an interpretable feature (e.g., the [+A] feature) is valued, and the relation between the checker and the checkee is a proper subset relation, since the null set is a subset of all sets.[16] Thus, the Agree relation can be defined as follows.

(10) Agree (φ_1, φ_2)

Given two sets of features φ_1 and φ_2, Agree holds between φ_1 and φ_2, iff φ_1 properly includes φ_2, and the node dominating φ_1 sister-contains the node dominating φ_2.

Viewed as proper inclusion between two sets of features, Agree is an asymmetric relation that holds from the set of features of α to the set of features of β. Agree is also asymmetric in the sense of Chomsky 2001, where, in order to check the uninterpretable feature of the goal, the probe must be phi-complete. The definition of Agree in (10) is a natural definition of the notion of a chain: a chain would be any set of nodes (whose occupants are) totally ordered by Agree. The notion of "chain" would then follow from the architecture of the grammar in a natural way.

Finally, the theory includes the operation Flip that applies in D_Φ and contributes to linearization. The generic form of this operation is the following.

(11) *Flip (T)*

Given a minimal tree T, Flip (T) is the tree obtained by creating a mirror image of T.

The operation Flip derives a mirror image of a minimal tree under different conditions, whether it applies to the outcome of D_M or D_S. Flip applies before the PF precedence relations have been established, and so it does not modify the precedence relations. Moreover, Flip does not alter the dominance relations. Flip contributes to linearization in the derivation of morphological and syntactic objects that linearize under different conditions. When applying to the outcome of D_S, Flip derives the order of "heavy" modifiers generated in the specifier of a functional projection, thus to the left of a functional head by creating a mirror image of the tree headed by that functional head at PF. When applying to the outcome of D_M, Flip derives the linear order of predicate and operator-bound affixes, which are generated in the head position of their minimal tree, given independent properties of the languages (see chapter 8). Flip derives the effect of head movement, avoiding the theoretical shortcomings of this operation (see chapter 7). It also derives the effect of remnant movement in D_M and conventions such as the Transportability convention (Keyser 1968) for the distribution of adverbs in D_S (see chapter 7).

2.4.2 M-Operations

Asymmetry is a primitive property of M, and this choice determines the definition of the operations that apply in D_M. I will refer to these operations by prefixing M to the generic operations of the grammar; thus the operations of M are the following: M-Shift, M-Link, and M-Flip.

M-Shift applies to two trees and it substitutes the second into the complement position of the first. M-Shift expands the structures upward and ensures that specifiers precede heads and that complements follow through D_M. M-Link applies to a tree and relates two positions with yet unrelated features. These operations are defined and illustrated below.

(12) *M-Shift* (T_1, T_2)
Given two trees T_1 and T_2, M-Shift (T_1, T_2) is the tree obtained by attaching T_2 to the complement of T_1.

(13) a.

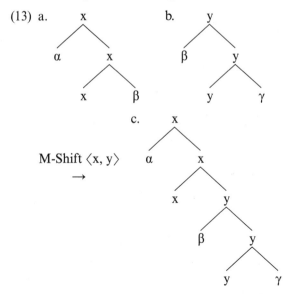

M-Shift $\langle x, y \rangle$
$\rightarrow$

(14) *M-Link (T)*

Given a tree *T* containing a position δ_1 and a position δ_2, such that δ_1 sister-contains δ_2 and δ_1 agrees with δ_2, M-Link (*T*) is the tree obtained by creating a featural relation between δ_1 and δ_2.

(15)

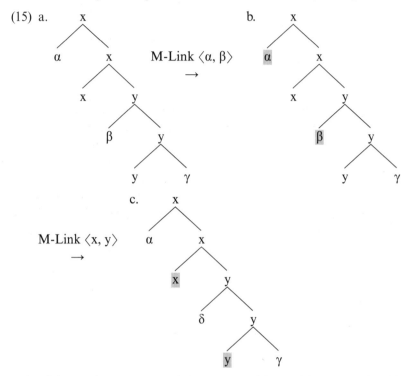

Applying under Agree, M-Link targets positions with contravalued features; it does not target covalued features. I will use shading to identify linked positions. Thus, the uninterpretable morphological features are checked and deleted, and the interpretable morphological features may be carried along as free riders. M-Link applies in local specifier-head relation, as well as in what can be viewed as morphological long-distance agreement relations, be they head positions or nonhead positions.

M-Flip applies in D$_\Phi$ and contributes to the linearization of the constituents of morphological domains. It creates a mirror image of a minimal tree, under certain conditions. This interface operation applies only if the specifier position of a minimal tree has no legible phonetic features (see (16)). Given the three sorts of affixes identified in section 2.2, M-Flip derives the position of affixes for languages such as English. Thus, predicate affixes and Op$_\Phi$ affixes follow the root; modifier and Op affixes precede the root. The effect of M-Flip is illustrated in (17).

(16) *M-Flip (T)*

Given a minimal tree T such that the Spec of T has no PF features, M-Flip (T) is the tree obtained by creating the mirror image of T.

(17) a.   b.

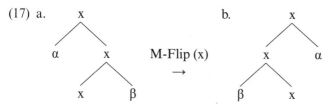

The syntactic correlate of M-Flip—that is, S-Flip—applies when the specifier of a syntactic minimal tree has phonetic features, and Flips only the specifier to the right (see chapter 7).

Thus, in Asymmetry Theory, the operations of M and S are specific instances of the generic operations of the grammar.[17] Only the operations of M apply in the derivation of morphological objects; consequently the Atomicity Thesis is preserved. Since the operations of M and S are instances of the generic operations of the grammar, parallelism is observed between morphological and syntactic objects.[18]

2.5   Conditions, Strict Asymmetry, and Legibility

Asymmetry Theory holds that the derivations are driven by the computational/conceptual necessity of obtaining strict asymmetric relations as early as possible, given the following condition.

(18) *Strict Asymmetry*

Every object {head, nonhead} introduced in a derivation must be part of an asymmetric relation with another object of the same sort {head, nonhead} as early as possible.

Strict asymmetry is obtained at the first application of M-Shift in D_M, while more than one application of S-Shift is required to satisfy this condition in S, assuming (as in Chomsky 2000a, 2001) that the operations of S apply to structurally unanalyzed objects. Strict Asymmetry contributes to the efficiency of the computation and the checking of uninterpretable features. It can be thought of as being a specific case of the Earliness Principle (Pesetsky 1989), which requires operations to be performed as quickly as possible.[19] Strict Asymmetry also contributes to the interpretation of the objects generated by the grammar at LF and PF. Given the Legibility condition (see (19)), symmetric relations are not optimally legible by the external systems.

(19) *Legibility*

    Only interpretable elements in asymmetric relations are optimally legible by the external systems.

Legibility restricts the properties of the structural relations optimally interpretable by the external systems. It provides an explanation for the fact that symmetric relations, if derived, must be eliminated before they reach the interfaces. Given (19), optimal interpretation is possible only under asymmetric relations. Strict Asymmetry is a formal factor driving the derivations. The Legibility Condition contributes to the optimality of language design. It requires that the representations derived by the grammar be minimal, in the sense that there cannot be superfluous relations in representations. This is akin to Chomsky's (1995) Full Interpretation, according to which there cannot be superfluous symbols in representations. The Legibility condition contributes to the interpretability of the interfaces by the external systems.

2.6 Summary

Asymmetry Theory is a theory of grammar that incorporates the hypothesis that asymmetric relations, such as precede, dominate, and sister-contain, are the basic asymmetric relations of the language faculty. Thus, symmetric relations, such as "sister of" and "identical to," while being available to the language faculty, are not basic to all the components. Crucially, morphology picks out asymmetry from the set of the properties of relations available in the language faculty, whereas this is not the case for syntax. Because morphology picks out a single property of relations from the set of properties of relations available in the grammar, it is more restricted than syntax. The asymmetry of morphological relations is a consequence of the basic asymmetric property of the relations of the language faculty; it is not a consequence of the asymmetry of the syntactic relations.

    Given Asymmetry Theory, morphological and syntactic objects are similar. They are derived in parallel planes of the computational space with restricted interactions between the derivations. Morphological objects are distinct from syntactic objects, given the strict asymmetry of morphological relations. They are derived by different instantiations of the generic operations of the grammar, including the operation ensuring the linearization of their parts at PF. Thus, defined from a minimalist perspective, Asymmetry Theory presents a specific hypothesis on the articulation of morphology in the architecture of the grammar.

Chapter 3

Layers and Shells

In this chapter, I focus on morphological domains. What are their properties? What makes them different from syntactic domains? How are they interpreted at the interfaces?

Asymmetry Theory holds that M and S are parallel planes of the computational space. They share the generic properties of the grammar and differ with respect to specific properties of their primitives, operations, and conditions. Chomsky (2001) proposes that the derivation proceeds by phases, which further reduces the computational burden of the grammar, a major goal in the Minimalist Program.[1] In Asymmetry Theory, the domains of the computation (phases) have specific implementations in morphology and in syntax.

This chapter is organized as follows. First I formulate a hypothesis about the properties of morphological domains, and point out how it differs from other hypotheses about the properties of these domains. Then I show that the morphological domain satisfies Chomsky's definition of the phase in a specific way.

3.1 The M-Shell Hypothesis

I will refer to a morphological domain by the term M-shell.[2] The M-Shell is a configuration consisting of two layers of asymmetric (sister-contain) relations (see (1)).

(1) a.

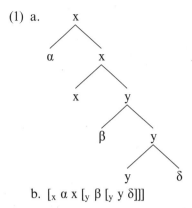

b. [$_x$ α x [$_y$ β [$_y$ y δ]]]

The M-Shell is derived by one application of M-Shift to two minimal trees and subsequent applications of M-Link to their parts. The elements of the M-Shell are placeholders for morphological features, including interpretable and uninterpretable features in head (x, y) and nonhead (α, β, δ) positions. I posit the following:

(2) *The M-Shell Hypothesis*
Morphological features enter into asymmetric relations in the domain of the M-Shell.

Extended morphological objects include more than one M-Shell, and are derived by the recursive application of M-Shift. An M-Shell$_1$ (D$_1$) is a morphological domain, and an M-Shell$_2$ (D$_2$) can be derived by the application of M-Shift to a minimal tree and to the previously derived M-Shell$_1$. Thus, whether simplex or complex, a morphological object is formed of subunits with constant formal properties. Once derived, an M-Shell may only be affected by operations that do not affect its integrity; it is a strongly impenetrable unit of the computation, as discussed in section 3.4.2. An M-Shell may only be affected by operations that extends it up to a certain limit (e.g., *constitut-ion, constitute-ion-nal, constitute-ion-nal-ity, anti-constitute-ion-nal-ity, #th-anti-constitut-ion-al-ity; form-al, form-al-ize, form-al-ize-able, un-form-al-ize-able, un-form-al-ize-able-ity #wh-un-form-al-ize-able-ity*).

A morphological object has a lower and an upper bound. The lower bound of a morphological object is determined by the M-Shell, where Strict Asymmetry holds: every element of an M-Shell is in asymmetric relation with another element of the same sort. The upper bound of a morphological object is determined by a central difference between syntactic domains and morphological domains—that is, a syntactic domain is propositional, whereas a morphological domain is not.

Consider the representations in (3), where morphological projections, like syntactic projections, are modeled on the basis of canonical hierarchical projections, each projection with its semantic correlate, as discussed in chapter 2 in terms of the Hierarchy of Homogeneous Projections.

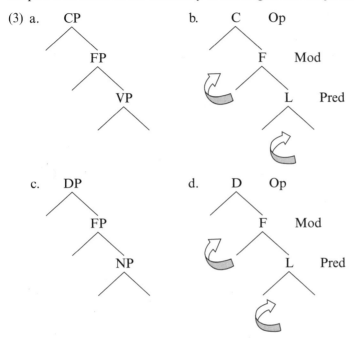

(3) a. CP
b. C Op
c. DP
d. D Op

Syntactic domains are propositional (see Chomsky 2001); they extend at least up to the CP projection (see (3a)). They are also argumental (see Adger 2003); they extend up to the DP projection (see (3c)). A morphological domain, however, is neither propositional nor argumental—even though complementizers (C) and determiners (D) are derived in D_M; a morphological domain cannot extend from the L-projection up to the topmost projection (C or D). Consequently a morphological domain can grow within a given layer, and grow up at most to its next superior layer (see (3b,d)). Thus, lexical (L) derivations occur (e.g., *write, writer*; *child, childhood*), as well as intermediate functional (F) derivations (e.g., *unfold, reunfold*), and closing functional (C, D) derivations (e.g., *at, what*; *here, there*). D_M may derive an F-object on the basis of an L-object (e.g., *fold, unfold*; *write, rewrite*), but not a C or D object on the basis of an L-object (e.g., *write, #whwrite*; *child, #thchild*).

Thus, given the Hierarchy of Homogeneous Projections, the difference in the size of a morphological object versus the size of a syntactic object is a consequence of the basic divide between the properties of the syntactic and the morphological domains: syntactic domains are propositional or argumental, morphological domains are not.

3.2 On the Specificity of the M-Shell

The M-Shell excludes other possible configurations for morphological domains. Besides excluding nonbranching structures (see (4)), it also excludes bare sisterhood relations (see (5)) as well as it disallows *n*-ary branching structures (see (6)).[3]

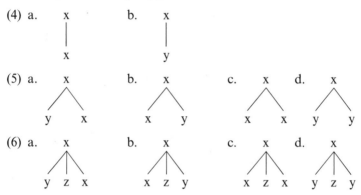

Nonbranching projections cannot be derived by the operations of the grammar, because by definition M-Shift combines two minimal trees. Ternary (and *n*-ary) branching structures cannot be derived either. The exclusion of binary branching structures from possible morphological domains—if true—is unexpected, because it is generally assumed that the relation between an affix and a root is sisterhood (see Selkirk 1982; Roeper and Siegel 1986; Di Sciullo and Williams 1987; Borer 1988, 1991).[4] It is also generally assumed that an affix has a c(ategorial)-selection feature that determines its insertion in a morphological structure. For example, the nominal affix -*er* is specified for the lexical feature]$_V$]$_N$ in Lieber 1992, 54. Thus, the affix -*er* c-selects a verb (V) as its sister node; and the affix and the V are immediately dominated by N. However, head-sister selection has empirical as well as theoretical shortcomings, as discussed in Di Sciullo 1996b. If roots are not specified for categorial features (see Chomsky 1970), c-selection is not available. Collins (2002) contrasts head-sister selection with the head-head selection, and offers support for the latter on the basis of the properties of syntactic expressions. Moreover, as seen in chapter 1, the relation between an affix and a root is asymmetric; affixes and roots cannot be inverted (e.g., *writer*, #*erwrit*). Given that the sisterhood relation is symmetric, the structure in (7) in not an appropriate structure for the affix-root relation.

(7)   af

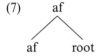

The more articulate structure in (8), where the affix is in an asymmetric head-head relation with the root, is closer to the minimal requirements. However, the structural relations in (8) are necessary but not sufficient, because affixes differ with respect to whether they have a [−A] or a [+A] feature in the specifier of their minimal tree. Causative affixes have a [+A] specifier, whereas noncausative affixes do not.

(8)   af

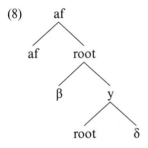

The necessary and sufficient set of structural relations constitutive of the M-Shell is the one represented in (1), repeated here in (9), where x is an affix and y is a root. This configuration satisfies Strict Asymmetry— that is, every element in the M-Shell is in asymmetric relation with another element of the same sort. It is also optimally interpretable at the interfaces, given the Legibility Condition, according to which optimal interpretation is obtained under asymmetry.

(9)   x

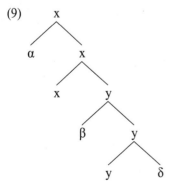

3.3 The Morphological Domain

The domain defined by an M-Shell is close to Chomsky's (2001) notion of phase—that is, a domain for cyclic interpretation and spell-out. In the following paragraphs, I consider how the diagnostic for the phase applies to the M-Shell. The facts indicate that the notion of phase has a specific implementation in D_M. This is expected in the theory developed here, since morphological and syntactic domains are derived in parallel.

The phase-based approach to derivations (Chomsky 2000b, 2001) allows for a deeper understanding of syntactic (Adger 2003; Holmberg 2001) as well as semantic (Chierchia 2001; Nissenbaum 2000) phenomena. It also contributes to our understanding of the properties of D_M, as discussed below.

3.4 The Diagnostic for the Phase

The notion of cyclic domain has been discussed in terms of Chomsky's (2001) notion of phase, Uriagereka's (1999) notion of Multiple Spell-Out, and Collins's (2002) notion of phase as a saturated constituent. A phase has the following properties.

(10) *Diagnostics for the phase*
   a. F-XP configuration
   b. Subject to Impenetrability
   c. Independence at the interfaces
   (Chomsky 2001; Legate 2003; Adger 2003; Matushansky, forthcoming; Svenonius 2003)

According to Chomsky (2000b, 2001), a phase is a propositional category (vP, CP). v*P is a strong phase and thus opaque to extraction at the CP level. The only positions from which extraction can take place are the head and the "edge" (the specifier and the adjoined positions) of a phase. Chomsky (2000b, 107) provides evidence that syntactic phases are propositional on the basis of the examples in (11), in which the lower proposition is a domain of cyclic interpretation and spell-out.

(11) a. [John [t thinks [Tom will [t win the prize]]]]
   b. [which article is there some hope [α that John will read t_h]]

It has been shown that other categories besides propositions are syntactic phases (see Adger 2003 for DPs and Legate 2003 for VP). Moreover, the syntactic properties of phases have been shown to be related to semantic properties (see Aguero 2004; McGinnis 2001; and Pylkkänen 2002 for the distribution and semantic properties of high and low applicatives). I assume that phases are not limited to propositions and that their syntactic properties are related to semantic properties. I show that the M-Shell satisfies the phasehood diagnostics in a specific way (see also Harley and Noyer 2000; Embick and Noyer 2001; Marantz 2003).[5]

3.4.1 F-XP

A syntactic phase includes an F-XP configuration, where F is a functional head and XP is its complement—for example, in a vP, a functional small v selects a complement VP. Likewise, an M-Shell includes a head-complement relation. The head of an M-Shell is an affix or a functional head F with no PF features, as in the case of modifier affixes. The head of an M-Shell qualifies as a functional category, assuming Abney's (1987) criteria. Affixes like functional categories are closed-class items; they have no descriptive content, they select only one complement, and they are inseparable from the latter. The head of an M-Shell has functional features, including uninterpretable morphological features, such as the $[-A]$ feature, as well as interpretable features, such as the $[+A]$ feature. The head of an M-Shell, a morphofunctional element, asymmetrically selects the head of its complement. The complement of the functional element is a maximal category in the sense of Chomsky (1993, 2000a), since it does not project any more. Thus, an M-Shell is a morphological F-XP configuration.

Di Sciullo and Williams 1987 point out that a morphological object may include more than one head with respect to a given feature. The notion of Head$_F$ expresses this property. The head$_F$ is a relativization of Williams's 1981b Right Hand Rule (RHR), according to which the head of a word is the rightmost constituent of that word.[6]

(12) *Definition of "head$_F$" (read: head with respect to the feature F)*
    The head F of a word is the rightmost element of the word marked for the feature F. (Di Sciullo and Williams 1987, 26)

Both the RHR and the head$_F$ are based on the linear order of affixes. In the theory developed here, the precedence relations are legible at PF and are dissociated from the morphological relations legible at LF. D_M derives the morphological relations, and D_Φ derives the linear precedence relations.[7] I propose the definition of head$_F$ in (13) that holds at LF, and is not based on linear precedence relations.

(13) *Head_F of a morphological domain*
     The head_F of a morphological domain D_i is the highest sister-
     containing head in D_i marked for the feature F.

The definition in (13) is a recursive identification of the head_F in a
model where morphological derivations proceed by phases. It also allows
a morphological domain to have more than one head with respect to the
same sort of feature, say the feature [+pred]. The derivation in (14) illustrates this point.

(14) a. Numeration
        {[[−A] -ity α]], [[−A] -ive β]], [[+A] produce [+A]]}
     b. M-Shift ⟨-ive, -produce⟩
        [_{D_1} [−A] -ive_{[+pred]} [[+A] product- [+A]]]

     c. M-Shift ⟨-ity, D_1⟩
        [_{D_2} [−A] -ity_{[+pred]} [_{D_1} [−A] ive-_{[+pred]} [[+A] produce [+A]]]]

     d.

Given the morphological numeration in (14a), M-Shift applies to the
minimal tree headed by *-ive* and the minimal tree headed by the root *produce*, and derives D_1 (14b). The morphological head_pred (read head with
respect to the feature [+pred]) of D_1 is *-ive*. M-Link applies in D_1 and
the uninterpretable [−A] feature is checked by the interpretable [+A] feature of the complement of the root. M-Shift applies to the minimal tree
headed by *-ity* and to D_1, and derives D_2 (see (14c) and (14d)). The mor-

phological head$_{pred}$ of D$_2$ is *-ity*. Thus, M-Shells and syntactic phases are parallel; they share the same asymmetric form (F-XP/head-complement).

3.4.2 Impenetrability

As mentioned above, according to Chomsky (2001), v*P is a strong phase and thus opaque to extraction at the CP level. The only position from which extraction can take place is from the head and the "edge" (the specifier and the adjoined positions) of the vP, given the Phase Impenetrability Condition (PIC).

(15) *The Phase Impenetrability Condition*
    [$_{ZP}$ Z ... [$_{HP}$ α [H YP]]]
    The domain of H is not accessible to operations at ZP; only H and its *edge* (either SPECs or elements adjoined to HP) are accessible to such operations. (Chomsky 2001, 108)

Chomsky formulates a theory of Agree that eliminates "feature movement" entirely in feature checking. Feature checking does not necessitate a specifier-head relation between the probe and the goal, but can be met via Agree (see (16)). Move is possible only if a prior Agree relation is established.

(16) *Agree*
    α > β
    └──┘
    Agree (α, β), where α is a probe and β is a matching goal, and " > " is a c-command relation. (Chomsky 2000b, 122)

Agree occurs within a phase and across phases. It is not unrestricted, however; it is only possible if the probe and the goal are in the same phase, or if the goal is at the edge of the phase immediately contained in the phase that includes the probe.[8] The elements undergoing Agree must be active—that is, they must participate in uninterpretable feature checking.

Agree and the PIC hold in D$_M$. Agree applies in D$_M$, given that the latter includes uninterpretable morphological features, such as the [−A] feature and the [−Xφ] feature.[9] The PIC holds for morphological phases, as can be seen with uninterpretable phi-feature checking. Assuming that an inflectional affix has an uninterpretable phi-feature ([−Xφ]) and that any noninflectional head with an agreement paradigm has an interpretable ([+Xφ]) feature when it leaves the morphological numeration, a [−Xφ] head may only enter into an Agree relation with the closest [+Xφ] head. The examples in (17) illustrate the accessibility of the head of an M-Shell (D$_1$) and the nonaccessibility of the complement of D$_1$.

(17) a. computer -ize -s   (computerizes)

$[_{D_2}$ ε -s$_{[-X\varphi]}$ $[_{D_1}$ α -ize$_{[+X\varphi]}$ [β computer$_{[+X\varphi]}$ γ]]]

   b. form -al -ize -s   (formalizes)

$[_{D_3}$ ε -s$_{[-X\varphi]}$ $[_{D_2}$ η -ize$_{[+X\varphi]}$ $[_{D_1}$ α -al [β form$_{[+X\varphi]}$ γ]]]]

   c. read -er -s   (readers)

$[_{D_2}$ ε -s$_{[-X\varphi]}$ $[_{D_1}$ α -er$_{[+X\varphi]}$ [β read$_{[+X\varphi]}$ γ]]]

   d. form -al -ity -s   (formalities)

$[_{D_3}$ ε -s$_{[-X\varphi]}$ $[_{D_2}$ η -ity$_{[+X\varphi]}$ $[_{D_1}$ α -al [β form$_{[+X\varphi]}$ γ]]]]

The structures in (17) include the causative-inchoative affix -ize, not analyzed in two separate heads, the variables α, β, γ, η, ε, standing for [±A] features, and the inflectional affix -s, with the unvalued feature [−Xφ]. The latter may have event (verbal) phi-features, including the tense feature, or sortal (nominal) phi-features, including the plural feature. Given the PIC, the [−Xφ] feature of the head of a higher morphological domain may not enter into an Agree relation with the [+Xφ] feature of the head of the complement of a lower morphological domain. In (17a) and (17b), the inflectional affix has event phi-features, and in (17c) and (17d), it has sortal phi-features. This follows from the fact that the edge and the head of a morphological domain are accessible to the next phase up. The PIC makes correct predictions for D_M for uninterpretable [−Xφ] features. It derives the fact that an inflectional affix agrees with its closest superior head. Thus, the examples in (17) show that, at least for uninterpretable feature checking, the PIC holds in D_M.

A morphological domain is, however, subject to a stronger impenetrability condition than the syntactic domain. The edge and the head of a morphological domain are accessible to the next phase up for uninterpretable feature checking without leading to movement, since head movement would introduce symmetry in D_M (see chapter 1).

Further evidence that the PIC applies in D_M comes from the Agree relation holding between argument features [+A] and nonargument features [−A], assuming that [+A] features are interpretable, whereas [−A] features are not, and must be eliminated in D_M. Consider the examples in (18), where the causative-inchoative affix -ize is analyzed as two separate heads, -e- spelling out the causative head and -i- spelling out the inchoative head, as argued for in Di Sciullo 1999b.

(18) a. formal -i-(z) -e   ((to) formalize)

$[_{D_2}$ [+A] -e $[_{D_1}$ [−A] -i(z)- [[+R] formal [+A]]]]

b. formal -i(z)- -er   ((a) formalizer)

$[_{D_3}$ [−A] -er $[_{D_2}$ [+A] -e $[_{D_1}$ [−A] -i(z)- [+R] formal [+A]]]]]

These examples illustrate that D_1 can be isolable from the higher morphological domains, D_2 and D_3, with respect to M-Link and uninterpretable feature checking. In (18a), the [−A] feature checking does not occur across domains. In (18b), it occurs across the two upper domains D_2 and D_3, in conformity with the PIC, since the edge of D_2, and not the complement of the head of D_2, is accessible to D_3. These examples show, on the basis of [−A] feature checking, that a morphological domain is bounded. The examples in (18), as well as the ones in (17), illustrate the incidence of the PIC in D_M.

Consider now the examples in (19), illustrating that the complement of the head in D_1 is accessible to operations outside of D_1, contravening the PIC. In (19a) and (19b), the [−A] feature of *-able* is checked by the [+A] feature, which is not at the edge of a lower adjacent domain, D_2.

(19) a. solid- i(f) -e -able   (solidifiable)

$[_{D_3}$ [−A] -able $[_{D_2}$ [+A] -e- $[_{D_1}$ [−A] -i(fy)- [[−A] solid [+A]]]]]

This is solid cement. / The cement is solid. / The cement solidifies. / They solidified the cement. / Cement is solidifiable.

b. liquid- i(f) -e -able   (liquefiable)

$[_{D_3}$ [−A] -able $[_{D_2}$ [+A] -e- $[_{D_1}$ [−A] -i(fy)- [[−A] liquid [+A]]]]]

This is liquid wax. / The wax is liquid. / The wax liquefies. / They liquefied the wax. / Wax is liquefiable.

Consider the example in (19a) with *solid* and *-able*. The [−A] feature in D_3 is checked by the [+A] feature of D_1 (which is the argument of the inchoative predicate spelled out by *-i-*), and not by the [+A] feature at the edge of D_2 (which is the external argument of the causative predicate, spelled out by *-e-*). The internal argument (*cement*) of the head of the complement of D_1 (*solid*) is the external argument of the derived construct (D_3) used predicatively (*cement is solidifiable*). The PIC does not hold in this case, which can be thought of as being an instance of morphological long-distance agreement. Derivational affixes such as *-able* (and *-ee*) impose specific linking relations on the A-features of their complement domain that may override the PIC. This is expected in the fully parallel model of Asymmetry Theory, where D_S and D_M are parallel.

Agree occurs across M-Shells, as seen above, as well as occurring within an M-Shell, as seen in (14). This can be illustrated with both [−A] and [−Xφ] feature checking. Considering [−A] feature checking, the examples in (20) and (21) illustrate the accessibility of the complement of an M-Shell. Considering the [−Xφ] feature checking, the examples in (22) show the accessibility of the head of the complement of an M-Shell.

(20) a. employ -er

　　　$[_{D_1} [\underline{-A}] \text{ -er } [[\underline{+A}] \text{ employ } [+A]]]$

　　　John employs Paul. / John is the employer of Paul. / Paul's employer / the employer of Paul (*by John)

　　b. impress -ive

　　　$[_{D_1} [\underline{-A}] \text{ -ive } [[\underline{+A}] \text{ impress } [+A]]]$

　　　The tigers impress the crowd. / The tigers are impressive (for the crowd). / The crowd saw impressive tigers.

(21) a. employ -ee

　　　$[_{D_1} [\underline{-A}] \text{ -ee } [[+A] \text{ employ } [\underline{+A}]]]$

　　　John employs Paul. / John is the employer of Paul. / John's employee / the employee of John (*by Paul)

　　b. read -able

　　　$[_{D_1} [\underline{-A}] \text{ -able } [[+A] \text{ read } [\underline{+A}]]]$

　　　Students read the *Tractatus*. / The *Tractatus* is readable by students. This book is a readable book (for students).

(22) a. read -s

　　　$[_{D_1} \alpha \text{ -s}_{[\underline{-X\varphi}]} [\beta \text{ read}_{[\underline{+X\varphi}]} \delta]]]$

　　　John reads papers on indefinites.

　　b. product -s

　　　$[_{D_1} \alpha \text{ -s}_{[\underline{-X\varphi}]} [\beta \text{ product}_{[\underline{+X\varphi}]} \delta]]]]$

　　　These are the products of modern times.

Agree occurs within and across morphological domains, as is the case for syntactic domains. As seen previously, morphological domains are subject to a stronger impenetrability condition than syntactic domains because feature checking under Agree does not lead to movement. Morphological domains are also more restricted than syntactic domains with respect to the properties of Agree, as evidenced below.

Two types of Agree are distinguished in Di Sciullo and Isac 2003: Agree-check and Agree-concord. Agree-check is a relation under which feature checking takes place, whereas Agree-concord is a relation under which no feature checking takes place. Agree-check is similar to Move, but Agree-concord has different properties.[10] Agree-check and Move can be "collapsed" regarding both the locality domains that are relevant for their application (phases) and their effect—that is, they both lead to feature checking.[11]

Agree-check, but not Agree-concord, occurs in D_M. This can be seen with case features. Agree-concord is not observed either with uninterpretable features, as is true of languages with rich morphological case, such as modern Greek and the Slavic languages, and does not take place in compounds derived in D_M (but see Ralli 1999 on ancient Greek). In modern Greek, while the genitive case (GEN) must be legible in phrases instantiating a possession relation (see (23a)), no case is part of the internal structure of compounds (see (23b)). The examples in (23c, d) from Serbo-Croatian further illustrate this fact.

(23) a. to spit-i   tis   kukl-as (MG)
        the house-NOM of the doll-GEN
        'the house of the doll'
     b. kukl-o-spit-o
        'doll-LV-house-NOM'
     c. nosač-∅   za knig-i (SC)
        holder-NOM for book-NOM/PL
        'holder for books'
     d. knig-o-nosa-č-∅
        book-LV-holder-NOM
        'book-holder'

The fact that Agree-concord is not obtained in morphological objects can be seen as a consequence of the fact that active morphological features are part of asymmetric relations. Antisymmetric relations—that is, relations that are asymmetric but that also include reflexive relations, such as ⟨case, case⟩—are not a crucial part of D_M. Thus, while Agree-check occurs within and across morphological domains, and is subject to strong Impenetrability, Agree-concord does not occur in M-Shells. This follows from Asymmetry Theory, according to which morphology manipulates asymmetric relations only.

3.4.3 Independence at the Interfaces

In the Minimalist Program, a phase is a unit of syntactic computation that is isolable at the interfaces (it can be sent to Spell-Out and to LF). A phase is transferred to the interfaces when the next higher phase is completed (see Chomsky 2001). Syntactic phases can be isolated at PF. They can be moved and can be targeted by successive cyclic operations. They are assigned phrasal stress through the Nuclear Stress Rule. Adger 2003 suggests that the Nuclear Stress Rule applies each time syntactic material is spelled out. This predicts that categories relevant to the syntactic and phonological cycles coincide. Syntactic phases can also be isolated at LF. Syntactic constituents that are interpretable at LF translate as saturated functions with bound variables, and those that are uninterpretable are either unsaturated or contain unbound variables. Call the former type "complete" and the latter "incomplete." Only "complete" constituents are visible after the operation Transfer (see Svenonius 2003). An independent X-domain is transferred to PF or LF, where it is subject to Interpret. Interpret associates the domain (configuration) with an interpretation.

3.4.3.1 Isolable of PF Evidence that M-Shells are isolable morphological domains at the PF interface comes from stress assignment.[12] Thus, a syntactic phase is assigned phrasal stress by the Nuclear Stress Rule (Chomsky and Hale 1968; Cinque 1993; Zubizarreta 1998; Arregi 2003), whereas a morphological phase is assigned stress by word-internal stress rules, including the Compound Stress Rule (Chomsky and Hale 1968; Cinque 1993; Arregi 2003). Thus, an M-Shell qualifies as an independent unit at the PF interface given the properties of stress assignment in morphological domains. Phrasal stress depends on syntactic structure. As formulated in Cinque 1993, the Nuclear Stress Rule (see (24)) is sensitive to the embedding of a word in a phrase (P). In SVO and SOV languages, sentence stress is on the object. The generalization reduces to depth of embedding in the formulation of the Nuclear Stress Rule in Zubizarreta 1998 (see (25)).

(24) *Nuclear Stress Rule* (Cinque 1993)
Nuclear stress in P is on the most deeply embedded word in P.

(25) *Nuclear Stress Rule* (Zubizarreta 1998)
α is more prominent than β iff β asymmetrically c-commands α.

Assuming Bare Phrase Structure (Chomsky 1993), Arregi (2003) argues that stress must be stated in terms of headedness and branching (see (26), (27)):

(26) *Comp generalization* (Arregi 2003)
     In a head-comp structure, comp is more prominent than the head.

(27) *Spec generalization* (Arregi 2003)
     In a X-spec structure, X is more prominent than spec.

It cannot be reduced to depth of embedding or asymmetric c-command. But in fact, word-internal stress is based on structure. This is the case for the Compound Rule (Chomsky and Halle 1968), as well as for Lieberman and Prince's (1977) Compound Stress Rule, according to which stress assignment in compounds is dependent on whether a constituent branches (see (28)). This is also the case in Cinque 1993, where stress in compounds is assigned from left to right to the nonhead. Thus, stress assignment in compounds is structure dependent.

(28) *Compound Stress Rule*
     In a configuration [$_C$ A B $_C$], if C is a lexical category,
     B is strong iff it branches. (Lieberman and Prince 1977, 257)

The question arises whether word-internal stress and phrasal stress fall under the same generalization. For Arregi (2003), the Compound Stress Rule is a subcase of the Comp generalization and the Spec generalization.

(29) a. *taxi* driver
     b. *ball* throw

(30) a. *nervous* system
     b. *public* affairs

(31) a. *easy* rider
     b. *late* departer

Arregi's analysis makes correct predictions for head-complement compounds such as the ones in (29), where the stress falls on the complement, which is more prominent according to the Comp generalization in (26). However, assuming that adjuncts are specifiers (Cinque 1999), this analysis wrongly predicts that stress falls on the head in compounds including an adjunct, such as the ones in (30) and (31), given the Spec generalization, in (27). In these compounds, the stress falls on the adjunct—that is, the specifier. Compound stress and phrasal stress do not fall under the same generalizations. Furthermore, in English-derived words, stress is assigned from left to right to the syllable before the last. Word-internal stress assignment is not subject to the rules of phrasal stress assignment, whether in compounding or in derivational morphology. The reason is that the morphological and syntactic domains do not coincide at PF. Thus, the conditions on stress assignment are different.

3.4.3.2 Isolable at LF   M-Shells are also isolable domains of interpretation at the semantic LF interface. According to the notion of compositionality (Frege [1891] 1952; Montague 1970, 1973, 1974; Heim and Kratzer 1998) the interpretation of a linguistic expression is a function of the interpretation of its parts and the way the parts are related. Given the implementation of this notion by the semantic operation of functional application, (32)—I posit that compositionality holds for the core interpretation of morphological domains, that is, M-Shells.[13]

(32) *Functional Application*
    If α is a branching node, and {β, γ} is the set of α's daughters, then α is in the domain of [ ] if both β and γ are and [β] is a function whose domain contains [γ]. In this case, [α] = [β]([γ]). (Heim and Kratzer 1998, 49)

This view is opposed to the regular practice in type-theoretical semantics according to which the semantics of derivational morphology is defined in their lexical entry, and thus is not derived by the semantic operations. I attribute the fact that the semantic interpretation of M-Shells is derived compositionally to the basic assumption that morphological objects are regular objects of the grammar.

Even though M-Shells are not propositional (they do not denote truth values), they can be isolated at LF, since they have a denotation—for example, common nouns denote sets of individuals, and are of type ⟨et⟩. M-Shells can be analyzed as semantically complete units of morphological computation at LF since they have a semantic type, which can be derived compositionally from the types of their constitutive parts.

Functional application is a semantic operation that implements the compositionality of syntactic expressions. I would like to suggest that it also applies to morphological structures. In Asymmetry Theory, the underivable properties are part of the lexicon, and morphological objects are regular objects of the grammar; they are subject to the morphological operations, M-Shift and M-Link. They are also regular objects of the grammar because their interpretation is derived compositionally from the interpretation of their parts.

The M-Shell is a semantically isolable domain at LF because it is a complete predicate. That is, an M-shell must denote a property. Therefore to say that it is complete is to say that it reached the type ⟨et⟩, and it is complete only when it reaches that type. The following example illustrates this point. If roots have no category but have the default semantic type ⟨et⟩, and if the category of nominals is also ⟨et⟩, the semantic type of an affixal nominalizer, say -er, must be the complex type ⟨⟨et⟩, ⟨et⟩⟩. Functional application derives the semantic type of a derived nominal on the basis of the semantic properties of its parts. For example in (33), the semantic type of *writ-* percolates to the root of its minimal tree. Functional application applies to the node of the affix and the root of the lower layer of the M-Shell, and the resulting type ⟨et⟩ percolates to the root of the upper layer of the M-Shell.

(33)

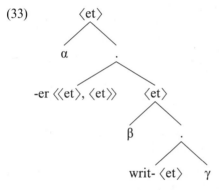

The M-Shell is a cyclic domain with respect to the morphological operations, such as M-Shift and M-Link, as well as with respect to the semantic operations, such as functional application. It is a "complete" semantic domain with respect to functional application, and is isolable at LF.

Morphological domains include operator-variable relations, one of them being the generic operator. A morphological object such as *writer*, for example, does not denote an individual in a world of interpretation, but rather denotes a set of individuals who write generally/habitually/by profession. Specific time reference is not optimal with bare nominals (see (34)).

(34) a. #A six heures, Max est écrivain.   (Fr)
        'At six, Max is (a) writer.'
    b.   Max est écrivain.
         'Max is (a) writer.'

Unlike syntactic objects, morphological objects may not contain
any specific time or individual reference. Di Sciullo and Williams 1987
provided evidence that morphological objects exhibit genericity and referential opacity. For example, the nominal constituents included in compounds are not referential arguments (see (35)). The example in (35a) is
not a contradiction, whereas (35b) is. Semantic opacity is paired with syntactic opacity, as can be seen in (35c), where it is not possible to question
a nominal expression included in a compound.

(35) a.   John is a [Nixon admirer] in every sense except that he does not
          admire Nixon.
     b.   *John admires Nixon in every sense except that he does not
          admire Nixon.
     c.   *Who is John an [t admirer]

The examples in (36) show that a pronoun cannot take as its antecedent a nominal expression that is part of a morphological domain.
These facts indicate that morphological domains are not accessible for
intrasentential and intersentential anaphora.

(36) a.   #Book-shelving is one of John's favorite activities, especially
          when they (the shelves) are tall.
     b.   #Book-shelving is one of John's favorite activities, especially
          when they (the books) are on linguistics.

Moreover, words have different interpretations whether they are in a
morphological domain or in a syntactic domain (see (37), (38)). In the
example in (37a), *what* is not part of the same morphological domain as
ever and is interpreted as a *wh*-word, whereas in (37b), *what* is part of the
same morphological domain as *ever* and may be interpreted as an indefinite (see chapter 7). The examples in (38) present another case with the
Japanese particle *ka* as a question marker (see (38a)), and as part of an
indefinite (see (38b)).

(37) a.   What did he ever do to deserve this?
     b.   He did whatever came to his mind.
     c.   He did whatever.

(38) a.   John-wa nani-o tabe-masi-ta ka?   (Ja)
          'What did John eat?'
     b.   Dare-mo ga nani-ka o tabe-te-iru.
          'Everyone is eating something.'

In Di Sciullo and Williams 1987 the semantic opacity of words follows
from the assumption that morphology is independent from syntax, and

thus the syntactic and phrasal semantic rules do not apply equally to the derivation and the interpretation of words.[14] In the theory developed here, it follows from the fact that morphological and syntactic domains are derived in parallel planes of the computational space. The parallelism between morphological and syntactic domains is a consequence of the relativization of the generic operations of the grammar to M and S.

3.5 Summary

The M-Shell is a unit of the morphological computation. It is a configuration the head$_F$ of which is the topmost head marked for F. The M-Shell is strongly impenetrable and, while Agree-check applies in the M-Shell, Agree-concord does not. The M-Shells are isolable at both interfaces and the operations that interpret them are parallel to those that interpret syntactic domains. Morphological and syntactic domains share basic properties without being coextensive, as expected in Asymmetry Theory, because they are subsections of parallel derivations. If there were no distinction between the derivations of morphological and syntactic objects, computational complexity would arise. At the initial point of the derivation, choices between structurally analyzed and unanalyzed elements and between asymmetric and symmetric selections would arise. Furthermore, two different boundedness conditions would be required at the phase-evaluation level. Moreover, further choice points would arise with respect to the bare output conditions. Computational complexity does not arise, however, if the two sorts of objects are derived in parallel (see Di Sciullo 2003a).

In the following chapters, I provide empirical evidence to show that there are systematic argument, aspect, and operator-variable feature asymmetries that can be expressed in a unified way, given the M-Shell. Restrictions are predicted to occur on the shifting and linking of morphological features. In the theory developed here, morphological and syntactic domains are parallel and not identical objects. M-Shells and syntactic phases certainly differ in the way they linearize at PF; the position of heads in these constructs do not generally coincide. They also differ with respect to the featural versus categorial properties of their parts, as well as with respect to the operations to which they are subject at the interfaces. Moreover, they may differ regarding the number of layers of which they are composed. This might be the case, considering works such as Androutsopoulou and Español Echevarria 2003, where more than two layers are required for the derivation of DPs in syntax (see also Giusti 1991; Ritter 1991; Manzini and Savoia 1999).

Chapter 4

Argument-Feature Asymmetry

In this chapter, I focus on the relations between A(rgument)-features in morphological domains. I posit that A-features are part of the asymmetric relations of the A-Shell. Predictions can be made with respect to the acceptability of morphological objects on the basis of the interaction of the operations of the grammar and what I call *argument-structure flexibility*.

I elaborate my earlier work on the argument-structure properties of affixes and articulate the regularities I described in Di Sciullo 1996b in the framework of Asymmetry Theory.[1] Evidence from English as well from other languages illustrates further that A-feature asymmetry contributes to explaining why morphology appears to be idiosyncratic. Blocking, as defined in Aronoff 1976, does not cover the cases of nonoptimal affixation for which no semantically equivalent form is already available (e.g., #*he is a departer*, #*she is a goer*).[2] The cases that are not accounted for by blocking cannot be rescued by the introduction of supplementary structure; however, nonoptimal cases of D_M can, given argument-structure flexibility (e.g., *he is an early-departer, she is an out-goer*). My contention is that both the restrictiveness and the interpretability of A-Shells follow from the properties of the operations applying in D_M in interaction with argument-structure flexibility.

Several works on argument structure point to the correctness of the hypothesis that the arguments of a predicate are in asymmetric relation. The syntactic distinction between external versus internal arguments (Williams 1980), the more articulated argument structure of L-syntax (Hale and Keyser 2002), and Chomsky's (1998) little v analysis (e.g., [$_{vP}$ SU v [$_{VP}$ OB [V O̶B̶]]]) constitute different instances of the asymmetric relations of argument structure. Thus, the external argument of a head sister-contains its internal arguments, whether it is external to the VP as in Williams 1980, internal to the VP as in Koopman and Sportiche 1991, external to the VP in the specifier of VoiceP as in Kratzer 1996, in the specifier of meaningful functional projections as in Pylkkänen 2002, or in the specifier of vP as in Chomsky 2000a.

According to Marantz (1984), the external argument of a lexical head is not a true argument of the verb, because it does not trigger special interpretations of the verb, as internal arguments do. The external argument does not seem to be selected by the verb as the internal arguments are, a fact also observed in Jackendoff 1983. In morphology, however, the external argument of an affix is semantically related to the meaning of the affix; it is "selected" by that affix. In Di Sciullo and Williams 1987, affixal heads differ with respect to the nature of the external argument, which plays a role in the derivation of the argument structure of morphological objects.[3] Since it may be selected by an affixal head and may play a role in the derivation of argument structure, I take the external argument (Ext) to be a true argument of the affixal head (x), sister-containing the arguments (Ext, Int) of the root (y) (see (1)).

(1)

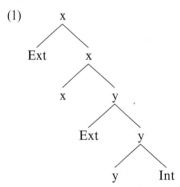

In Lexical syntax (Hale and Keyser 2002), argument structure is defined as the syntactic configuration projected by a lexical item. Hale and Keyser (2002) argue that the fundamental relations of argument structure are represented in terms of the sisterhood relation (see (2)), and define the following types of argument structure (see (3)).

(2) *The fundamental relations of argument structure*
   a. Head-complement: If X is the *complement* of a head H, then X is the unique sister of H (X and H c-command one another).
   b. Specifier-head: If X is the *specifier* of a head H, and if P_1 is the first projection of H (i.e., H′, necessarily nonvacuous), then X is the unique sister of P_1. (Hale and Keyser 2002, 12)

(3) *The structural types of lexical argument structure*

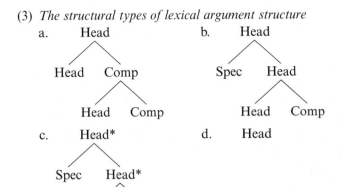

c.   Head*

Spec   Head*

Head*   Comp   (Hale and Keyser 2002, 13)

The configurations in (3) are neutral to the morphosyntactic category (V, N, and so on); however, their heads do have predominant categorial realizations. For example, in English, the predominant realization of (3a) is V; it is P for (3b), A for (3c), and N for (3d). Moreover, languages vary with respect to the categorial realization of the structural types of argument structure.

Chomsky (2000b, 2001) provides a syntactic implementation of Hale and Keyser's theory. The object (internal argument) of a verb is merged with the verb in the derivation of the verb-complement structure. The object moves (or remerges—that is, copy + merge) to the specifier of the verb to satisfy the EPP features of V. With transitive verbs, a small v is merged with the derived structure (VP), and the subject (external argument) is merged with the resulting construct (see (4)).

(4)   vP

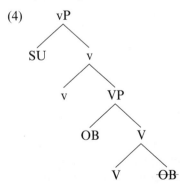

If the EPP feature is purely syntactic and the morphological operations apply to minimal trees, as in Asymmetry Theory, unergatives (i.e., verbs with an external argument only, such as *sleep*, *snore*) and unaccusatives (i.e., verbs with an internal argument only, such as *arrive, fall, depart*) must be distinguished on the basis of the position of their unique argument in their minimal tree.

Derivational affixes affect the argument structure of lexical heads, as shown in Di Sciullo and Williams 1987. However, there is a crucial difference between syntactic and morphological argument structure. All things being equal, in D_S, arguments and nonarguments (DPs and expletive pronouns) may be legible at the PF interface. This is not the case in D_M, where heads are generally legible, but not argument features. Derivational morphology manipulates argument features, and not syntactic XP arguments legible at the PF interface.[4] This is expected, since in Asymmetry Theory, words and phrases are different sorts of objects derived in parallel planes of the computational space.

I take the minimal argument structure of a morphological head to be reducible to the three configurations in (5), where the [+A] features occupy canonical positions. Thus, a root may have one of the three projections in (5).[5] An affixal head may have either the projection in (5a) or the projection in (5c), but not the projection in (5b) since an affix necessarily takes a complement, which is a minimal tree.

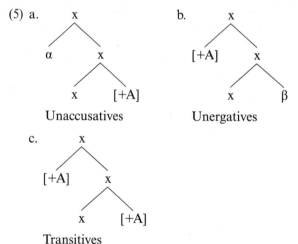

(5) a.
Unaccusatives

b.
Unergatives

c.
Transitives

Now, I would like to suggest that argument structure should be construed as "flexible." By flexible I mean that arguments may occupy noncanonical positions within the argument-structure domain. Because this domain is limited, the flexibility is restricted as well. By definition, a predicate must have one argument and, given the VP Shell (Larson 1988), limitations are imposed on argument-structure recursion; in effect, there are ditransitive verbs but no tritransitive verbs (except perhaps for *buy* and *sell*; see Jackendoff 1990, 191). Flexible argument structure may give rise to argument-structure shift.[6]

Argument structure shift is observed with all sorts of predicates, and is brought about by additional functional structure. Most ditransitive verbs can be used transitively with a different aspect structure (e.g., *John transformed his room* (*into a ballroom*)). Even the most aggressively ditransitive verb can be used transitively with a particle (e.g., *Mary put her gloves on*). Similarly, obligatory transitive verbs can be used intransitively in coordination (e.g., *At her party, Lucy greeted and greeted and greeted*). Furthermore, most transitive verbs can be used without an object (e.g., *John eats* (*an apple*)) and unaccusative-transitive alternations are observed in several languages (e.g., *the boat sank* (*by itself*), *the enemy sank the boat*), also with a difference in aspect structure (see, among other works, Burzio 1986; Perlmutter 1987; Levin and Rappaport Hovav 1995; Hale and Keyser 2002). Moreover, some unergative verbs have a cognate object (e.g., *to sleep a good night's sleep*, *to laugh a hearty laugh*), and they may also occur in constructions such as *to dance one's way out of the ballroom*).[7]

If argument-structure shift is available in the grammar, it comes with a cost. When it takes place, the interpretation of the expression is generally altered (e.g., change in aspect, in genericity, in compositionality, in register), and in some cases it may be nonoptimal without overt additional functional structure, while in other cases it is altogether uninterpretable. This is expected in Asymmetry Theory, since using argument-structure shift amounts to changing canonical asymmetric relations, and a change in the asymmetric relations gives rise to either a difference of interpretation or to gibberish (see chapter 1). Syntax and morphology both have access to argument-structure flexibility, and this explains why morphological objects sometimes have a nonoptimal flavor while still being interpretable (e.g., (#)*this boat is a sinker*, and (#)*this kid is a real out-goer*). Affixation in D_M, like modification in D_S, may provide the supplementary functional structure to bring about argument-structure shift.

In the following section, I define the A-Shell Hypothesis, along with the A-feature Distinctiveness, and I show that in conjunction with the notion of flexible argument structure, predictions can be made with respect to optimal versus nonoptimal D_M and thus with respect to differences in the acceptability of morphological objects. Finally, I provide evidence from languages other than English in support of the A-feature Distinctiveness.

4.1   The A-Shell Hypothesis

In this section, I focus on the articulation of A-features in morphological domains and posit the following.

(6) *The A-Shell Hypothesis*
     A-features are part of the asymmetric relations of the M-Shell.

Morphological compositionality requires that a predicate affix take a root as its morphological argument. The A-Shell expresses this compositionality and articulates the morphological predicate-argument features, as depicted in (7), where the features of a predicate affix sister-contain the features of its root argument.

(7)   pred

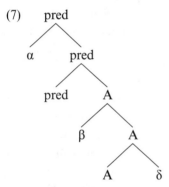

The A-Shell is derived by the application of M-Shift to two trees by substituting one tree for the complement of the other (see (8)). M-Link applies subsequently to the features in nonhead positions.

(8)   a.   pred   b.   A

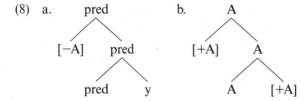

c.

M-Shift ⟨pred, A⟩
→

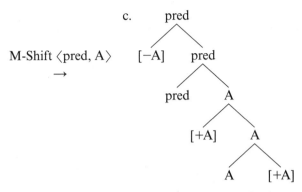

The A-Shell satisfies Strict Asymmetry—each element is part of an asymmetric relation with another element of the same sort. The upper head sister-contains the lower head; the specifier of the upper layer of the shell sister-contains the specifier and the complement of the lower layer. The A-Shell is a morphological domain: it includes a head-complement structure, it is strongly impenetrable, and it is isolable at the interfaces. Moreover, it is a unit with respect to phonological rules, including the stress-assignment rules. It is also a unit with respect to the semantic rules, including functional application (see chapter 3).

M-Shift applies under asymmetric head-head selection. Thus, an affix asymmetrically selects a root of a certain sort. Asymmetric selection imposed by affixes on roots can be expressed in terms of the binary features as follows. Affixes and roots can be defined in terms of the binary features [±A], which together with the predicative features [±pred] are part of the typology of morphological elements (see (9)). The interpretable features of the heads of an M-Shell are [+A] and [+pred], and the uninterpretable features are [−A] and [−pred]. The latter are checked and deleted by M-Shift applying under Agree. The resulting construct has predicate features, and may undergo further morphological composition brought about by affixal trees with predicate or aspectual features.

(9) a. arguments: [+A, −pred]
    b. primary predicates: [−A, +pred]
    c. secondary predicates: [+A, +pred]
    d. operators: [−A, −pred]

An affix asymmetrically selects a root also on the basis of the argument structure of that root, as discussed below.[8] M-Link applying under Agree also ensures that the [−A] features in nonhead positions are checked (see (10)).[9]

(10)

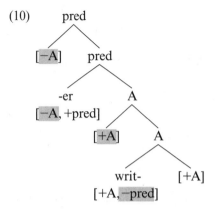

In (10) the [−A] feature in the specifier of the affixal head is checked by the [+A] feature of the specifier of the root, and the latter may be carried along as a free rider. Thus, the external argument of the root becomes the external argument of the derived morphological object used predicatively (e.g., *Max wrote the poem, Max is the writer of the poem*). In addition, the specific affixal head in (10) controls the external argument of the root; consequently the latter cannot be licensed as an adjunct in D_S (e.g., *the writer of the poem (*by Max)*).

The A-Shell differs from other representations of predicate-argument relation. For example, it differs from morphological structures where arguments are represented as a list of variables associated with a predicate (see Booij 1989; Lieber 1981, 1992; Levin and Rappaport Hovav 1995).[10] It also differs from representations of argument structure including thematic roles and semantic primitives (see Gruber 1965; Williams 1981a; Di Sciullo and Williams 1987; Jackendoff 1997).[11] It is compatible with a configurational representation of argument structure (see Hale and Keyser 1993, 2002; Gruber 1997; Roeper 1999).

4.2   A-Feature Distinctiveness

Derivational affixes differ with respect to whether they host a [+A] feature in their specifier. Roots are also specified for [+A] features; some roots host a [+A] feature in their specifier (i.e., transitives and unergatives), while other roots do not (i.e., unaccusatives). As discussed in chapter 2, an uninterpretable/unvalued [−A] feature is checked/valued by an interpretable [+A] feature. Because linked positions may not be covalued, the A-feature Distinctiveness (see (11)) holds in the domain of the A-Shell.

(11) *A-feature Distinctiveness*
   In an A-Shell, Linked positions must be A-distinct.

A-feature Distinctiveness is an effect of M-Link applying under Agree, and it contributes to the optimal legibility of morphological domains at the LF interface.

4.3 Predictions

M-Link applying under Agree relates contravalued A-features. According to the A-feature Distinctiveness, linked covalued features are expected not to give rise to optimal morphological legibility at LF. Thus, in the A-Shell in (12), pairs of linked A-features, including the A-feature of the affix and one of the A-features of the root (i.e., $\langle \alpha, \beta \rangle$, $\langle \alpha, \gamma \rangle$) may not be identical (i.e., $\langle +A, +A \rangle$, $\langle -A, -A \rangle$) without giving rise to morphological gibberish.

(12)

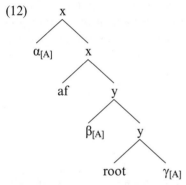

Notwithstanding the differences between specific affixes, linking regularities emerge when considered from the perspective of A-feature Distinctiveness. Predictions can be made with respect to the optimal legibility of morphological objects at LF in terms of the properties of chains: A-feature chains with contravalued members are optimal; A-feature chains with covalued elements are not. The following A-Shells, where x stands for a predicate affix and y stands for a root, represent the optimal and the nonoptimal (#) Agree relations.

(13) a.   [[−A] x [[+A] y [+A]]]

   b. #[[−A] x [[−A] y [+A]]]

   c.   [[−A] x [[+A] y [+A]]]

   d. #[[−A] x [[+A] y [−A]]]

For example, with *-er* affixation, the [−A] feature in the highest specifier position of the A-Shell is checked by the [+A] feature of the specifier
of the root; the latter is no longer available in D_S. As predicted, with
transitive and unergative roots, *-er* affixation is possible (see (14a) and
(14b)); with unaccusative roots, it is nonoptimal (see (14c)).

(14) a. [[−A] x [[+A] y [+A]]]

      Mary is the adviser of Jane.

    b. [[−A] x [[+A] y [−A]]]

      Jane is the sleeper.

    c. #[[−A] x [[−A] y [+A]]]

      #John is the departer.

In the case of the *-ee* affix, the [−A] feature in the highest specifier position is checked by the [+A] feature in the complement of the root; the
latter is no longer available in D_S. As predicted, *-er* affixation is possible
with transitive roots, but not optimal with unaccusatives (see (15)).

(15) a. [[−A] x [[+A] y [+A]]]

      Jane is the advisee of Mary.

    b. #[[−A] x [[+A] y [−A]]]

      #Paul is the sleepee.

Similar linking relations hold for *-ive* and *-able* affixation with the difference that an unlinked [+A] feature may license an adjunct in D_S. In the
case of *-ive*, the [−A] feature in the highest specifier position is checked by
the [+A] feature in the specifier of the root, nonoptimal *-ive* derivations
result with unaccusative roots (see (16)).

(16) a. [[−A] x [[+A] y [+A]]]

      Tigers are impressive.

    b. #[[−A] x [[−A] y [+A]]]

      #Trains are arrivative.

In the case of *-able*, the [−A] feature in the highest specifier position is
checked by the [+A] feature in the complement of the root; optimal cases
of *-able* affixation are based on transitive roots, nonoptimal affixations
result with unergative roots (see (17)).

(17) a.   [[−A] x [[+A] y [+A]]]

   This book is readable.

  b. #[[−A] x [[+A] y [−A]]]

   #This bed is sleepable.

The [+A] feature in the specifier of causative affixes does not enter into a checking relation, and becomes the external argument of the derived causative. The [−A] feature of the inchoative affix does enter into a checking relation with the [+A] complement of the root. As predicted, causative derivations are optimal with unaccusative roots, but not with an unergative root (see (18)), including only the inchoative head x and its complement.

(18) a.   [[−A] x [[−A] y [+A]]]

   They certified the passport.

  b. #[[−A] x [[+A] y [−A]]]

   #They shinified the car.

Linking relations are not optimal if they apply to [+A] features only, or to [−A] features only, contravening the A-feature Distinctiveness—that is, the effect of the operation of the grammar applying under Agree. Further empirical predictions, taking into consideration argument-structure shift, are provided in the next section.

4.4 Flexibility

In several works in generative morphology, affixes categorically select their complement. This takes the form of categorial-selection features for affixes (e.g., *-er*: [V_], *-ize*: [A_], *-able*: [V_]), which are parallel to categorial-selection for lexical items (see, among other works, Borer 1991; Grimshaw 1990; Lieber 1992; Anderson 1992). If an affix c-selects V, the fact that not all Vs may combine with that affix is generally viewed as an idiosyncratic property of derivational morphology. In the theory developed here, an affix asymmetrically selects the head of its complement. Argument-structure shift, which may be brought about by the functional structure of affixes, accounts for the acceptability of otherwise nonoptimal derivations. The following illustrates this point.

   The nominal suffix *-er* combines optimally with transitive roots (e.g., *killer, producer, writer*) and unergative roots (e.g., *dreamer, snorer,* *sleeper*), but not optimally with bare unaccusative roots (e.g., ≠*arriver*, ≠*departer*, ≠*bloomer*), according to my informants. However, *-er* nominalization is possible when there is a transitive (causative) variant for an unaccusative root (see (19)), but not when no transitive variant is available (see (20)).

(19) a. This vase is broken.   (transitive/unaccusative)
     b. Bond broke several vases.
     c. This vase is a breaker.

(20) a.   This train arrives at noon.   (*transitive/unaccusative)
     b. * The conductor arrives the train.
     c. #This rain is an arriver.

The examples in (19) show that *-er* affixation is possible with verbs that allow unaccusative/transitive alternations. The examples in (20) show that when there is no alternation, as with the verb *arrive*, *-er* nominalization is possible in compounds including a modifier, a point to which I come back in section 4.5. Thus, *-er* nominalization is acceptable with unaccusative roots type-shifted to transitive roots (see (21)).

(21) a.

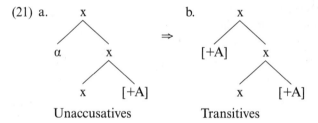

Unaccusatives   Transitives

Thus, *-er* affixation is optimal with a root that has or acquires a [+A] feature in its specifier. Given that the A-Shell is limited to two layers of asymmetric relations, *-er* affixation is correctly expected to be possible with optionally ditransitive roots such as *transform, transmit, sell,* but not with aggressively ditransitive roots, such as *put.*

The restrictions on *-er* affixation are expected given the properties of the A-Shell and the A-feature Distinctiveness, which is the effect of M-Link applying under Agree (see (22)).

(22) a.   [[−A] -er [[+A] y [+A]]]

     b.   [[−A] -er [[+A] y [−A]]]

     c. (#)[[−A] -er [[−A] y [+A]]]

While -er affix requires a root to have or to be able to acquire a [+A] specifier, the -ee affix requires in addition that the complement of the root also host a [+A] feature. This requirement does not come as a surprise, because an affixal head has access to the properties of the root tree it shifts with, including the properties of the specifier and the complement of that tree. Thus, -er affixation is optimal with certain transitive roots, whereas with unaccusative or unergative roots it is not. -Ee affixation is more restricted than -er affixation. It is optimal with a proper subset of transitive roots (e.g., *advisee, employee, nominee*), but not with unergative roots (e.g., *#swimmee, #boxee, #workee*) or unaccusative roots (e.g., *#fallee, #departee, #bloomee*). The linking relations with -ee affixation are summarized in (23).

(23) a.   [[−A] -ee [[+A] y [+A]]]

b. #[[−A] -ee [[+A] y [[−A]]]]

c. #[[−A] -ee [[−A] y [+A]]]

The acceptability of otherwise impossible morphological phenomena due to argument-structure shifting can also be observed with -able and -ive affixations, as well as with -ify and -ize affixations.

Thus, -able affixation is optimal with most transitive roots, whether or not the root has an agent as its external argument (e.g., *hearable, lovable, killable*).[12] This is not the case with bare unergative roots (e.g., *#shinable, #glowable, #snoreable*) or unaccusative roots (e.g., *#arrivable, #fallable, #departable*). If there is a possible transitive variant to an unergative root, -able affixation is expected to be acceptable. The examples in (24) and (25) show that -able affixation improves with a transitive variant of an unergative root. The examples in (26) and (27) show that this is also the case with unaccusative roots. The linking relations are summarized in (28).

(24) a.   John danced well.   (unergative)
b.   #John is danceable.
c.   Julie dances tango with high heels.   (transitive)
d.   Tango is danceable with high heels.
e.   Paul danced a strange dance at midnight.   (cognate)
f.   Strange dances are danceable at midnight.

(25) a.   Paul run.   (unergative)
b.   #Paul is runnable.

   c.   Paul runs a mile in five minutes. (transitive)

   d.   A mile is runnable in five minutes.

   e.   Jackie ran the race with no sweat. (cognate)

   f.   The race is runnable with no sweat.

(26) a.   John climbed. (unaccusative)

     b. #John is climbable.

     c.   Mary climbed Mount Everest. (transitive)

     d.   Mount Everest is climbable.

(27) a.   Lucy left. (unaccusative)

     b. #Lucy is leaveable.

     c.   Lucy left Yellow Knife. (transitive)

     d.   Yellow Knife is leaveable with no tears.

(28) a.   [[$-$A] -*able* [[+A] y [+A]]]

     b. (#)[[$-$A] -*able* [[+A] y [$-$A]]]

     c. (#)[[$-$A] -*able* [[$-$A] y [+A]]]

  -*Ive* affixation is more restricted than -*able* affixation. It is optimal with certain transitive roots, but not with unaccusative and unergative roots, whether or not they can be used transitively (see (29)). It differs from -*able* affixation with respect to its M-Link properties, as discussed below. The linking relations are summarized in (30).

(29) a.   His attitude is progressive. /   This movie is impressive.

     b. #Clowns are laughive.   / #This distance is runnive.

     c. #This car is shinive.   / #Bikers are standives.

     d. #This situation is arrivative. / #Young children are fallive.

(30) a.   [[$-$A] -*ive* [[+A] y [+A]]]

     b. #[[$-$A] -*ive* [[+A] y [$-$A]]]

     c. #[[$-$A] -*ive* [[$-$A] y [+A]]]

  Finally, with -*ize*/-*ify* causative-inchoative affixation, the external [+A] argument of the causative affix is not checked. The external [$-$A] feature of the inchoative affix -*i*- must be checked. Thus, inchoative affixation is possible with an unaccusative root, but not with a transitive root, because the derived A-feature chain would include two covalued features, contravening the A-feature Distinctiveness. The causatives in (31) are based on unaccusative roots, while the ones in (32) are based on transitive roots. The restrictions are summarized in (33).

(31) a. He simplified the problem. (It is simple to ...)
   b. They certified the passport. (It is certain that ...)
   c. They equalized the results. (It is equal that ...)

(32) a.   This operation differs from that one. (x is different from y)
   b.   #These operations differize the results.
   c.   John is a friend of Mohammed. (x is a friend of y)
   d.   #It is hard to friendize with anybody.

(33) a.   [[−A] -i- [[−A] y [+A]]]

   b. ≠[[−A] -i- [[+A] y [−A]]]

   c. ≠[[−A] -i- [[+A] y [+A]]]

Thus, affixes differ with respect to asymmetric selection; however, the linking relations are systematically subject to A-feature Distinctiveness, since M-Link applies under Agree. Summarizing:

(34) a.   [[−A] x [[+A] y [+A]]], where x can be spelled out by -*er*, -*ive*

   b.   [[−A] x [[−A] y [+A]]], where x can be spelled out by

   -i-(*ze*), -i-(*fy*)
   c.   [[−A] x [[+A] y [+A]]], where x can be spelled out by -*able*, -*ee*

Argument-structure shift, brought about by the functional structure of predicate affixes, extends the class of legible morphological objects within the limits imposed by the asymmetric relation of the A-Shell, and helps explain why derivational morphology seems idiosyncratic. In fact, the asymmetry-preserving operations of the grammar apply systematically in D_M. The extended legibility/acceptability of A-Shells can be understood in terms of the independently needed notion of argument-structure shift.

4.5 Extensions

The notion of argument-structure shift covers unexpected cases of derivation that may occur compound-internally. In a compound, a modifier may license a noncanonical argument structure, given argument-structure flexibility. As seen previously, *-er* affixation is not optimal with unaccusative roots, and consequently the legibility of forms such as *departer* is not either (see (35)). The elements of the chain resulting from the application of M-Link would include covalued features, in violation of A-feature Distinctiveness (see (36)). However, nonoptimal objects such as *departer* are possible in compounds including a modifier (see (35)).

(35) a. #Luc is a departer.
     b. #John is an arriver.
     c. #Paul is a faller.

(36)

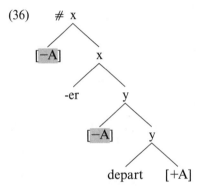

(37) a. Luc is an early-departer.
     b. John is a late-arriver.
     c. Paul is an easy-faller.

One way to account for this fact is to assume that the modifier turns the unaccusative root into an unergative root, a possibility that is available in light of argument structure flexibility. The modifier induces the argument-structure type shifting of the root, and crucially, an [+A] feature is substituted for the [−A] feature in the specifier of the root, which in turn satisfies the configurational requirement imposed by the nominal affix *-er* on the argument structure of its complement. Assuming that the adjectival modifier occupies the specifier position of a projection headed by a functional F head, argument-structure type shifting can be seen as the effect of the linking of the F head of the modifier projection to the root, which in turn changes the value of the A-features of that root (see (38)).

(38)

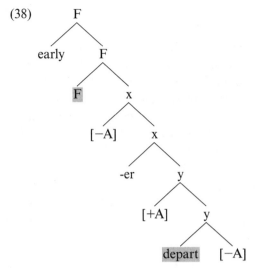

The role of the adjectival modifier in (38) is the following. The modifier applies to the full argument structure and not to a specific argument feature since it sister-contains the other elements of the construct including the external and the internal A-features of the root. The modifier brings about the conditions for the exercise of argument-structure type shifting, providing enough additional information to make clear how it is that the argument structure should be changed. The presence of a modifier in the structure signals that argument structure has been altered in some way. Argument-structure type shifting is mainly observed with nominal deverbal compounds in English, because most productive compounding is nominal.

The role of the modifier in these compounds is also connected to what causes adverbs to improve middles. In English middles, an adverb is generally obligatory, whereas the external argument is no longer part of the argument structure (e.g., *this pasta cooks, this pasta cooks well*). The adverb brings about the conditions for the exercise of argument-structure type shifting. In this case it shifts a transitive to an unaccusative, substituting a [−A] feature for the [+A] feature in the specifier of a transitive root.[13] As expected in the theory developed here, while a modifier may rescue an otherwise nonoptimal morphological derivation, a modifier cannot rescue an otherwise nonoptimal syntactic derivation (e.g., *the train arrives* versus *the conductor arrives the train* and *the conductor arrives the train well*).

4.6 Crosslinguistic Evidence

It is often assumed that languages vary with respect to selection and A-feature Distinctiveness—for example, causative heads select different sorts of complement crosslinguistically, as discussed in Di Sciullo and Williams 1987 and Pylkkänen 2002. A-feature Distinctiveness is observed in a variety of languages. This is the case for French, as evidenced in Di Sciullo 1996a. The following data from Russian (Ru) and Hungarian (Hu) indicate that A-feature Distinctiveness is observed in rich nominal-case languages as well.

(39) a. John mechta-tel'. (Ru) (unergative)
       John dream-er
     b. József álmodoz-ó. (Hu)
       Joe   dream-er
       'Joe is a dreamer.'

(40) a. Robert pisa-tel'. (Ru) (transitive)
       Robert writ-er
     b. Mari ír-ó. (Hu)
       Mary writ-er
       'Mary is a writer.'

(41) a. #Pavel pazbiva-tel'. (Ru) (unaccusative)
       Paul   break-er
     b. #Pali virágz-ó. (Hu)
       Paul bloom-er
       'Paul is a bloomer.'

(42) a. Pavel serdets razbivatel'. (Ru)
       Paul heart   break-er
     b. ?Pali későn virágz-ó. (Hu)
       Paul late   bloom-er
       'Paul is a late bloomer.'

The examples above illustrate the fact that -tel' (Ru) and -ó (Hu) affixations are possible with unergative (see (39)) and transitive roots (see (40)), but not with unaccusative roots (see (41)). Furthermore, in compounds, a modifier may increase the acceptability of the otherwise non-optimal affixations with unaccusative roots (see (42)), as expected given argument-structure flexibility. The examples in (43)–(45) bring further support to A-feature Distinctiveness with im/aem(a) (Ru) and -ható (Hu) affixations.

(43) a. Èta kniga legko chit-aema. (Ru)
this book easily read-*able*

b. Ez a könyv könnyen olvas-ható. (Hu)
this the book easily read-able
'This book is very readable.'

(44) a. #Ètot stul legko sizh-aem. (Ru)
this chair easily sit-able

b. #Ez a szék könnyen ül-hető. (Hu)
this the chair easily sit-able
'This chair is very sittable.'

(45) a. #Poezda prieszh-aemye iz Bostona. (Ru)
trains arrivable from Boston
'Trains are arrivable from Boston.'

b. #A vonatok érkez-hető-k Boszton-ból. (Hu)
the trains arrivable-Pl Boston-from
'Trains are arrivable from Boston.'

Interestingly, strong prefixing languages, such as the African languages, pattern like the other languages with respect to A-feature Distinctiveness. The following data from Yekhee, an SVO strong prefixing north-central Edoid language from the Niger-Congo family (Bendor-Samuel 1988), show that asymmetric selection obtains notwithstanding the linear order of the affixes with respect to the root, which I discuss in chapter 8. The following examples illustrate the fact that in Yekhee, ó-/ọ- affixation is possible with a transitive root (see (46)) and an unergative root (see (47)), but not with an unaccusative root (see (48)).

(46) Mary ó- kèkè ébè lí ó kìà. (Ye)
Mary er- write (of) book that she is
'Mary is a writer.'

(47) John ọ-no vhona Li ọ kia. (Ye)
John er- dream that he is
'John is a dreamer.'

(48) a. #Paul ọnọ de Li ọ kia. (Ye)
Paul er- fall that he is
'Paul is a faller.'

b. #Paul ọnọ vai Li ọ kia.
Paul er- arrive that he is
'Paul is an arriver.'

Thus, evidence from Russian, Hungarian, and Yekhee corroborates the results obtained here on the basis of English. See Di Sciullo (1996b, 1999b) for evidence from Italian and French.

4.7 Summary

The operations of M derive A-Shells, which constitute independent morphological domains, in which uninterpretable [−A] features must be checked and valued by [+A] features. M-Link applies under Agree; thus A-feature Distinctiveness is expected to hold in A-Shells, ensuring optimal legibility at the LF interface. The operations of the grammar in conjunction with argument-structure shift brought about by functional structure help explain why derivational morphology is in fact not "idiosyncratic." The A-Shell and the A-feature Distinctiveness are instances of the asymmetry of morphological relations.

Chapter 5

Aspect-Feature Asymmetry

In this chapter, I consider aspectual modification in morphological objects and provide further evidence for the M-Shell Hypothesis.[1] I focus on the spatial and sequential features that contribute to the aspectual properties of predicates. My proposal is that the M-Shell has an incarnation in the functional layer of the morphological projection and that aspectual features are in asymmetric relation therein. As expected, the relation between the features is parallel but not identical to the aspectual relations in syntactic objects. I start by presenting some facts from Italian as well as previous accounts of aspectual modification.

It is well established that, along with definite DPs, definite PPs may delimit an event or add an end point to a situation (Tenny 1988, 1994; Binnick 1998; Hale 1986; Krifka 1990; Pustejovsky 1988, 1991; Higginbotham 1999). Preposition-like affixes also have this property.[2] Thus, in English, it is possible to delimit an event denoting an activity (e.g., *John ran (for hours)*) by adding a definite PP (e.g., *John ran to the store* (≠ *for hours*)) or a directional affix (e.g., *John outran Paul* (≠ *for hours*)). Interestingly, Italian presents additional cases of aspectual modification brought about by affixes. The examples in (1) show that preposition-like affixes, including *a-* 'at' and *per-* 'though', contribute to the aspectual makeup of the situation or event described by the sentence.

(1) a. Alessio corre (≠ immediatamente). (It)
        'Alessio runs (immediately).'
    b. Alessio a̲ccorse (immediatamente).
        Alessio AT-ran immediately
        'Alessio ran up (immediately).'
    c. Alessio p̲er̲corse   il giornale   (immediatamente).
        Alessio THROUGH ran the newspaper (immediately)
        'Alessio quickly glanced through the newspaper (immediately).'

It is also possible to modify an event by viewing it with respect to a sequence of events. Thus, adverbial phrases may iterate an event, without, however, altering its telicity (whether or not it has an end point). Events without a terminus can be modified by durative adverbs, whereas events with a terminus may be modified by punctual adverbs (e.g., *John ran again (for hours)*, *John ran to the store again (≠for hours)*, *John outran Paul again (≠for hours)*). Situations and events can also be iterated with affixation. Here again, Italian presents more possibilities than English. In some cases, adverbial phrases are the only option in English; in Italian similar semantics can be expressed by means of affixes. Witness the following:

(2) a. Nassimo ha <u>ri</u>corso nel pomeriggio.   (It)
       Massimo has rerun   in afternoon
       'Massimo ran again in the afternoon.'
    b. Massimo ha <u>ri</u>dormito nel pomeriggio.
       Massimo has reslept   in afternoon
       'Massimo slept again in the afternoon.'

In both languages, however, there are regularities pertaining to the linear order of sequential and spatial affixes, namely, the first must precede the second. In some cases a spatial affix must be legible at PF if the sequential affix is. Moreover, in both languages spatial affixes may affect the *Aktionsart* and the argument structure of the verbal predicate it modifies, whereas this is not possible for the iterative affix.

In Asymmetry Theory aspectual features are part of the inventory of features available in M and S. Given the architecture of the grammar, their contribution to morphological structure should be parallel to their contribution to syntactic structure. However, differences are expected depending on the choices of M and S with respect to the specific properties of the primitives, operations, and conditions. By considering the properties of derivational affixes contributing to the aspectual modification of a predicate, I bring further evidence to show that morphological relations are asymmetric. The structural symmetry is coupled with featural asymmetry. I concentrate on the terminus and the iterative features, and argue that they are part of what I call the *Asp-Shell*, the properties of which are not isomorphic to those of the phrasal projection of Asp-features. The four aspectual classes—that is, states, activities, accomplishments, and achievements (Vendler 1967; Comrie 1976; Dowty 1979)—can be defined on the basis of two elementary Asp-features: [±T], which indicates whether a verbal predicate has a natural end point or terminus, and [±S], which indicates whether it has subintervals, as proposed in Di Sciullo 1996c. The combination of these features yields the four eventuality types:

(3) [−S, −T]   states   ex: *to love, to know, to resemble*
    [+S, −T]   activities   ex: *to write, to walk, to run*
    [+S, +T]   accomplishments ex: *to construct, to build*
    [−S, +T]   achievements   ex: *to die, to find, to explode*

One consequence of this typology is that it is possible to identify natural classes of aspectual predicates with respect to the operations of the grammar. For example, [+T] predicates (accomplishments and achievements) do not undergo telic shift—that is, the shifting of predicates denoting activities, [+S, −T] predicates, onto predicates denoting accomplishments, [+S, +T] predicates, as discussed in Di Sciullo 1997. The iterative feature [It] is also part of the aspectual features, and it can be defined in terms of the features [±It] and [±N] for predicate negation, as proposed in Di Sciullo 1996a. The combination of these features yields the following:

(4) [+It, −N]   iterative   ex: *to rebuild, to rephrase*
    [+It, +N]   inverse   ex: *to untangle, to untie*
    [−It, −N]   reinforceative ex: *to remark, to reassure*
    [−It, +N]   privative   ex: *unkind, unpopular*

Considering adverb-like affixes, *re-* may spell out the iterative features, [+It, −N] (e.g., *to refold, to retie*), and it may also spell out the reinforceative features, [−It, −N] (e.g., *to remark*); *un-* may spell out the inverse features, [+It, +N] (e.g., *to unfold, to untie*), and it may also spell out the privative features, [−It, +N], in adjectival predicates (e.g., *untold, uninhabited*). The aspectual features of the adverbial affixes are determined configurationally. Thus, the affix *un-* spells out the privative features when it is an adjunct to a predicate denoting a state, and it spells out the inverse features when it is an adjunct to a predicate denoting an action. Likewise for the iterative and reinforceative features, which can be spelled out by *re-*.

Asp-feature affixes generally precede the root in languages such as English and Italian. In Di Sciullo 1994, prefixes are adjuncts to the verbal projection. This view is also taken in Kayne 1994. Following Williams (1980) and Di Sciullo and Williams (1987), Kayne assumes that heads are the rightmost elements in word structure. Given the Universal Base

Hypothesis, the assumption that specifiers are adjuncts and the fact that prefixes precede heads, he concludes that prefixes must be adjuncts.

The adjunct structure is further articulated into substructures, as shown in Di Sciullo and Klipple's (1994) analysis, according to which prefixes (P) are adjoined either to VP or to V, as in (5).

(5) a. VP   b.   V

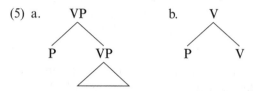

Moreover, as shown in Di Sciullo 1997, there is empirical evidence justifying a structural asymmetry between the external prefixes (temporal: iterative and inverse) and the internal prefixes (spatial: directional and locational). I refer to this asymmetry in terms of the Internal/External Prefix Hypothesis (see (6)), according to which prefixes (P) are external or internal adjuncts to a verbal projection and sister-adjoined at different points within verb structure.[3]

(6) *Internal/External Prefix Hypothesis*
Internal prefixes are adjoined to a projection within the VP.
External prefixes are adjoined to the VP.

The Internal/External Prefix Hypothesis accounts for the linear-order difference between the two sorts of prefixes: external prefixes precede internal prefixes. It also provides a configurational explanation of their different effects on the *Aktionsart* and the argument structure of the verbal predicate. Internal prefixes may modify argument structure and aspect, whereas external prefixes cannot.

I reformulate the Internal/External Prefix Hypothesis in the framework of Asymmetry Theory. In this theory, the notions of prefix and suffix are not primitives; instead the position of affixes follows from the operations of M and independent morphological properties of the languages. Another motive for reformulating the Internal/External Prefix Hypothesis is that elements other than prefixes contribute to the aspectual properties of verbal predicates. For example, tense morphemes, which are suffixes in languages such as French and English, contribute to the boundedness of the event.[4] Furthermore, given the Hierarchy of Homogeneous Projections (see chapter 2), functional elements are generated within the F-layer, which is superior to lexical elements generated in the L-layer. Consequently, internal (spatial) affixes, which are functional elements, should not be generated within the L-layer. According to the Internal/External Prefix Hypothesis, functional (preposition-like (P)) affixes are generated as sisters to V.[5] Thus, in (7), the lower P is the locus of spatial affixes and is part of the argument-structure projection of V (i.e., the L-layer), whereas the higher P is the locus of sequential affixes and is outside of the argument-structure projection of V.

(7)

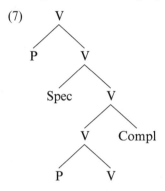

As a consequence of the Hierarchy of Homogeneous Projections, spatial affixes are generated in the F-layer of the morphological projection (along with the sequential affixes) and not in the L-layer. The generation of affixes within the canonical morphological layers ensures that asymmetric relations, such as scope relations, are available at an early stage of the derivation. Aspectual heads scope over (sister-contain) lexical heads.

Morphological relations are expressed in terms of the independently motivated M-Shell in Asymmetry Theory. I show that the restrictions on aspectual modification follow from the Asp-Shell Hypothesis and the Asp-feature Distinctiveness. I first define the Asp-Shell, and contrast it with syntactic representations of Aspect structure, and the Asp-feature Distinctiveness. Then, I consider the predictions of the Asp-Shell Hypothesis and show how the restrictions on aspectual modification in morphological objects are accounted for by the theory.

5.1   The Asp-Shell Hypothesis

According to Asymmetry Theory, affixal modifiers are in the specifier position of functional projections. External aspectual modifiers (sequential: iterative and inverse) are located in the specifier of the morphofunctional projection F_E (external aspect), and internal aspectual modifiers (spatial: directional and locational) occupy the specifier of the morphofunctional projection F_I (internal aspect). The relation between F_E and F_I can be expressed in terms of the Asp-Shell, an instance of the M-Shell. The Asp-Shell is a bipartite asymmetric projection where F_E sister-contains F_I (see (8)), and F_I sister-contains the lexical event structure (Ev).

(8)

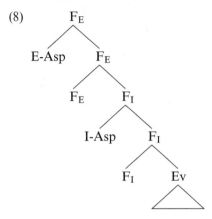

Asp-features, such as the terminus feature [+T] and the iterative feature [+I], are articulated on the basis of the asymmetric relations in morphological domains. I formulate the Asp-Shell Hypothesis as follows.

(9) *The Asp-Shell Hypothesis:*
Asp-features are part of the asymmetric relations of the M-Shell.

In the Asp-Shell, affixes are located in the specifier of their minimal trees, the Asp-features, F_E and F_I, occupy the head positions, F_E sister-contains F_I, and the complement of F_I is a projection of Ev. The Asp-Shell is part of the morphology of all languages, but not all the parts of the shell are legible at PF in each language. For example, in English I-Asp is generally not legible at PF (e.g., *to butter, to powder, to button*), contrary to languages such as Italian (e.g., *imburrare, incipriare, abbottonare*). French differs from Italian in this respect (e.g., *beurrer, poudrer, boutonner*), and an account of this microvariation is provided in chapter 8.

The Asp-Shell is derived by the operations of M. M-Shift takes two minimal Asp-trees—for example, the trees in (10a) and (10b)—and substitutes the second tree into the complement position of the first. This operation yields (10c), where E-Asp sister-contains I-Asp. M-Shift substitutes an event-tree (Ev) for the complement position of F_I.[6]

(10) a.

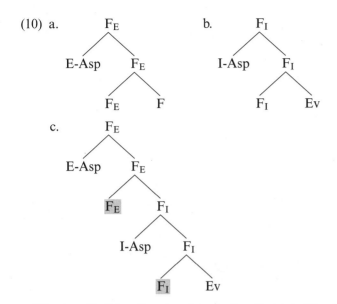

The Asp-Shell is a functional projection that modifies the Ev-projection by extending it. The Asp-Shell is superior to the Ev-projection, given the canonical hierarchy, where functional projections are superior to lexical projections.

M-Shift relates the features of the two Asp-heads, F_E to F_I, given asymmetric selection. It also relates F_I to the E-head, because the Asp-Shell extends the Ev-projection (see (10)). Given that M-Shift applies under Agree, it eliminates uninterpretable morphological features and relates interpretable Asp-features, which may be carried along as free riders. The uninterpretable features are eliminated to satisfy the Interpretability condition, which requires the presence of interpretable features only at the interfaces. I take the relevant uninterpretable feature of F_E to be $[-F_I]$, F_E being $[+F_E, -F_I]$. The $[-F_I]$ feature of F_E is checked by the $[+F_I]$ feature of F_I. I take the relevant uninterpretable feature of F_I to be $[-Ev]$. The $[-Ev]$ feature of F_I is checked by the interpretable $[+Ev]$ feature of Ev (see (11)).

(11)

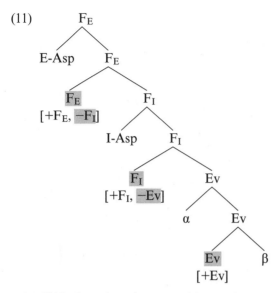

M-Shift also relates interpretable Asp-features, such as the iterative feature $[+I]$, which may be part of the feature structure of F_E, and the terminus feature $[+T]$, which may be part of the feature structure of T_I. The Asp-features must be legible at the LF interface. Moreover, as is the case for A-features, Asp-features are subject to Distinctiveness: while A-feature Distinctiveness applies to specifiers in A-Shells, Asp-feature Distinctiveness applies to heads in Asp-Shells (see (12)).

(12) *Asp-feature Distinctiveness*
     In an Asp-Shell, Linked positions must be F-distinct.

Like the A-feature Distinctiveness, (12) is an effect of the operations of the grammar applying under Agree in the domain of the Asp-Shell. Feature checking applies to the F-features in the head positions of the Asp-Shell, which must be distinct (contravalued).

Given the Asp-Shell Hypothesis, Asp-features may modify a verbal projection in only two ways: either by modifying the event denoted by a predicate as a whole without affecting its internal Asp-features, or by modifying its internal Asp-features.[7] Affixes are unspecified in this respect. For example, in Italian the affix *dis-* is the morphological spell-out of F_E features in verbal constructs such as *disfare* 'to undo', and it is the spell-out of F_I features in configurations such as *discendere* 'to disembark/to descend'. The fact that the same element may be specified for F_E features in some cases and for F_I features in others suggests that the difference between Asp-features is not categorial but configurational. This is expressed in terms of the Asp-Shell, where F_E sister-contains F_I. Thus, the same affix, for example *dis-*, is unspecified for the value of F, hence it can fill the specifier of F_E or the specifier of F_I. In the first case, it has sequential (inverse) features, whereas in the other case, it has spatial (directional) features. The Asp-features of affixes such as *dis-* are determined by their closest sister-contained Asp-head, either F_E or F_I. If the affix modifies an entire event, as in *disfare* 'to undo', *dis-* is an F_E affix, whereas if it modifies part of the event, specifying the direction of the event, as in *discendere* 'to descend', it is an F_I affix.

Summarizing, given the Hierarchy of Homogeneity Projections, Asp-Shells are superior to Ev-Shells. The Asp-Shell is an instance of the M-Shell and is derived by M-Shift and subsequent applications of M-Link. The scope relations among the Asp-affixes and between the Asp-affixes and the Ev projection are set at an early stage of the derivation. The uninterpretable Asp-features are subject to M-Link, which applies under Agree. According to the Asp-feature Distinctiveness, Asp-heads are contravalued because Agree may not apply to covalued features.

5.2 On the Specificity of the Asp-Shell

The Asp-Shell is derived in D_M and not in D_S. In Chomsky 2000b, 102, Asp-features are located on T, as schematized in (13a); in other proposals (Borer 1994, 1998; Cinque 1999), Asp-features head their own syntactic projection, as depicted in (13b). In other works, small v is also the locus of Asp-features.

(13) a.

b.

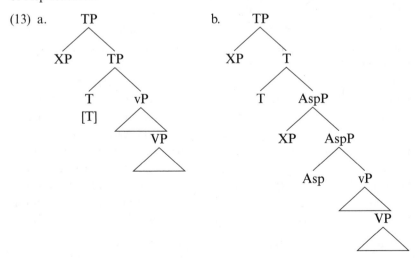

In the Minimalist Program (Chomsky 1995), words enter the computational space fully inflected. The derivation of the word-internal Asp properties has already taken place. Thus, in a syntactic representation such as (13a), the Asp features of a verbal predicate cannot be derived compositionally from the features of its parts.

An entirely syntactic derivation of Asp-features would give rise to a proliferation of syntactic functional projections. Additional AspP projections would be required in (13b) to derive the full range of aspectual differences brought about by verbal affixation and by XP modification. The proliferation of syntactic Asp-projections can be avoided if the contribution of morphology and the contribution of syntax are derived in parallel planes of the computational space, as is the case in Asymmetry Theory. The aspectual role of F_E and F_I affixes to a root is dealt with in M, whereas the contribution of particles and definite DP or PP complements to the telicity of the verbal projection is phrasal and is dealt with in S.[8]

5.3   Predictions

The following predictions emerge from the theory, which now includes the Asp-Shell. First, the linear order of the Asp-affixes—that is, the fact that the sequential F_E affixes precede F_I affixes and the Asp-affixes together precede the root—follows from the geometry of the Asp-Shell in conjunction with the operation of the grammar. M-Flip does not apply to the Asp-Shell when its specifier has PF legible features. Thus, the Asp affixes are not reordered to the right at PF. Moreover, the Asp-Shell is superior to the Ev projection. Consequently, Asp-affixes precede the root they modify. There is no need to stipulate that Asp-affixes are prefixes, because the linear order of the affixes follows from the theory.

Therefore, the theory correctly predicts that sequential affixes precede spatial affixes in the E structure. The strict ordering follows from the application of M-Shift to two minimal Asp-trees, one of which is headed by F_E, and the other by F_I; asymmetric selection and Agree hold from F_E to F_I. Thus, F_E M-Shifts with F_I, whereas the reverse situation gives rise to gibberish (see (14)). Asp relations in M are asymmetric. This prediction is borne out for French (see Di Sciullo 1997) and for Bulgarian (Di Sciullo and Slabakova, forthcoming). The data in (15) from Italian corroborate this linear-order asymmetry between Asp-affixes.

(14) a. $[_{F_E}$ E-Asp F_E $[_{F_I}$ I-Asp $[_{F_I}$ F_I δ]]]   ex: to reencode
       b. *$[_{F_I}$ I-Asp F_I $[_{F_E}$ E-Asp $[_{F_E}$ F_E δ]]]   ex: *to enrecode

(15) a. Carmine ha riaddormentato Maria.   (It)
        Carmine has RE AT sleep   Maria
        'Carmine made Maria sleep.'
     b. *Carmine ha aridormentato Maria.
        Carmine has AT RE sleep   Maria
        'Carmine made Maria sleep again.'

Second, given the geometry of the Asp-Shell, F_E takes the F_I-tree as its complement, and F_I takes the Ev-tree as its complement, given that the Asp-Shell is an extension of Ev-projection. The Asp-Shell Hypothesis predicts that F_E asymmetrically selects F_I and that F_I asymmetrically selects the head of the Ev-projection. Selection failure results in morphological gibberish. This prediction is also borne out.

Considering first F_E modification, E-Asp affixes (iterative and inverse) provide Ev-modification of the entire event denoted by a verbal predicate. Basically, while *re-* iterates a dynamic event, *un-* inverts it. Wechsler (1990) observes that the iterative affix in English generally modifies accomplishments. In Italian, the iterative affix may modify accomplishments (see (16a)) and achievements (see (16b)).

(16) a. Ha ricomposto la struttura.   (It)
        'He rebuilt the structure.'
     b. Ha ritrovato la chiave.
        'He found the key.'

E-Asp modification may only affect events that have an end point or terminus [+T]—that is, accomplishments (see (16a)) and achievements (see (16b)). It cannot modify [−T] predicates, such as states (see (17a)) or activities (see (17b)). The examples in (18) are cases where both E-Asp and I-Asp are spelled out, and where I-Asp contributes a [+T] feature to the verbal predicate. In the examples in (19), the I-Asp [+T] is not morphologically spelled out.

(17) a. *Rosa risa l'italiano.   (It)
        'Rosa reknows Italian.'
     b. *Ha ricondotto la macchina.
        'He redrove/undrove a car.'

(18) a. Sergio è riaccorso   a casa.   (It)
        Sergio is RE AT ran at home
        'Sergio ran up at home again.'
     b. Maria si   è riaddormentata.
        Maria SELF is RE AT sleep
        'Maria fell asleep again.'

(19) a. Sergio ha ricorso nel   pomeriggio.   (It)
        Sergio has RE run during afternoon
        'Sergio ran again in the afternoon.'
     b. Maria ha ridormito nel   pomeriggio.
        Maria has RE slept during afternoon
        'Maria slept again in the afternoon.'

Thus, aspectual selection holds from F_E to F_I. F_E asymmetrically selects F_I. A [+It] F_E asymmetrically selects a [+T] F_I. Furthermore, the [−F_I] feature of F_E Agrees with the [+F_I] feature of F_I. Moreover, the [−T] interpretable feature of [+E], becomes [+T], as discussed below (see (20)).

(20)

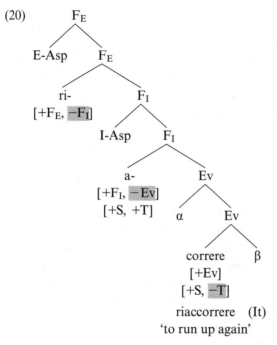

riaccorrere   (It)
'to run up again'

F_I must be [+T], because the modification brought about by F_E [+I] requires that the event denoted by the bare predicate (even if an activity) come to an end at a previous point in time. The examples in (21) further illustrate this point. The verb *write* describes an activity, and may be used without a complement, whereas the verb *to rewrite* requires the presence of a complement—that is, an end point or terminus.

(21) a. Antonio ha scritto (la lettera).   (It)
        'Antonio wrote (the letter).'

    b. Antonio ha riscritto *(la lettera).
      'Antonio rewrote *(the letter).'

The fact that a complement is necessary when a predicate describing an activity is iterated shows that the iterative prefix modifies a predicate describing an achievement or an accomplishment, but not a predicate describing an activity. As mentioned previously, a definite DP or PP complement may add a terminus to the event denoted by a VP (Tenny 1988, 1994, among other works). This fact further illustrates the relation between F_E and F_I. This relation is asymmetric. F_E asymmetrically selects and Agrees with F_I.

Considering the modification brought about by F_I, I-Asp affixes, such as *a-* 'at' and *in-* 'in' in Italian, modify the spatial dimension of Aspect. As is the case for E-Asp affixes, the adjunction of an I-Asp affix to an Ev-projection does not necessarily give rise to an interpretable structure. Typically, [+T] affixes may M-Shift with motion predicates that are [−T]; they may not M-Shift with predicates that are [+T]. More specifically, there are aspectual restrictions on the M-Shifting of I-Asp affixes with an Ev-projection. I-Asp affixes may generally M-Shift with predicates describing activities, but not with states, achievements, and accomplishments (see (22)).

(22) a. *Vera acconosce Lucia.   (It)   (state)
      Vera AT knows Lucia
      'Vera knows Lucia.'
    b. *Pino ha introvato la chiave.   (achievement)
      Pino has IN found the key
      'Pino has found the key.'
    c. Carmine incorre molte difficoltà.   (activity)
      Carmine IN ran many problems
      'Carmine runs into many problems.'
    d. *Maria ha inconstruito la casa.   (accomplishment)
      Maria has IN built   the house
      'Maria built up the house.'

This restriction on I-Asp affixation is a consequence of aspectual selection. This is illustrated in (23), where F_I, asymmetrically selects the head of Ev. The structure in (23) illustrates asymmetric selection applying under Agree and the uninterpretable Asp-feature checking. F_I, which is [+S, +T], head-head selects Ev, which is [+S, −T]. The [−T] feature of Ev is eliminated along with the uninterpretable [−Ev] feature, and the modified feature structure is [+S, +T]. Thus telic shift is a consequence of asymmetric selection applying under Agree.

(23)

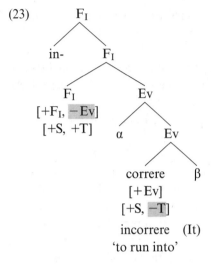

incorrere   (It)
'to run into'

   In effect, an I-Asp affix may modify the *Aktionsart* of the predicate and bring about telic shift—that is, the shifting of a predicate denoting an activity onto a predicate denoting an accomplishment. It may affect the value of the [−T] feature of Ev under certain conditions. It cannot modify unbounded predicates, such as states, nor can it apply to bounded predicates that do not distribute to subintervals, such as achievements. It may only modify activities—that is, events with an initial point and homogeneous subintervals but no end point. This is evidenced by the fact that [+T] I-Asp affixes may not adjoin to [+T] predicates, such as *be born*, *explode*, *find*, and *win* (see (24), (25)).

(24) a.   Gianni vuole vincere la corsa.   (It)
           Gianni wants win   the race
           'Gianni wants to win the race.'
     b. *Gianni vuole avincere la corsa.
           Gianni wants AT win the race
           'Gianni wants to win the race.'

(25) a.   Maria vuole trovare la chiave.   (It)
           Maria wants find   the key
           'Maria wants to find the key.'
     b. *Maria vuole atrovare la chiave.
           Maria wants AT find the key
           'Maria wants to find the key.'

Third, since selection holds from F_E to F_I, and from F_I to E_V, an explanation is available for the restriction on the PF legibility of I-Asp features in denominal and deadjectival verbs, such as *reempower* and *rerenlarge* vs. **repower* and **relarge*. The fact that in these constructs an I-Asp affix must be present when an E-Asp affix is follows from asymmetric selectional holding from F_E to F_I, and from F_I to E_V. Thus, F_E cannot be projected without the projection of F_I (see (26a)). The reverse situation is however possible, (see (26b)), as aspectual selection is asymmetric, it holds from F_E to F_I, but not conversely. Moreover, the aspectual selection relation also holds from F_I to E_V; consequently the absence of such a relation—for example in (26a), where the root *power* has no Ev feature—gives rise to morphological gibberish. Data from Italian also confirm this prediction.

(26) a. $*[_{F_E}$ E-Asp F_E $[_{F_I}$ ~~I-Asp~~ $[_{F_I}$ F_I $\delta]]]$ ex: *to repower
     b. $[_{F_E}$ ~~E-Asp~~ F_E $[_{F_I}$ I-Asp $[_{F_I}$ F_I $\delta]]]$ ex: to empower

(27) Domenico si   è innamorato di Maria.   (It)
     Domenico SELF is IN love   of Maria
     'Domenico fell in love with Maria.'

(28) a. Domenico si   è riinnamorato di Maria.   (It)
       Domenico SELF is RE IN love   of Maria
       'Domenico fell in love with Maria again.'
     b. *Domenico si   e riamorato   di Maria.
       Domenico SELF is RE IN love of Maria
       'Domenico fell in love with Maria again.'

An I-Asp affix is in the specifier of its minimal tree. M-Flip does not apply to that tree, and the affix precedes the root at PF. The fact that denominal and deadjectival verbs may not be modified by an E-Asp affix without an intervening I-Asp affix follows. This fact brings strong empirical support for the asymmetric property of the relations of the Asp-Shell, where F_E immediately sister-contains F_I.

Fourth, given the Asp-Shell, there should be only one I-Asp affix and only one E-Asp affix per Ev projection. More than one Asp-affix of the same sort gives rise to morphological gibberish, as illustrated in (29).

(29) a. $[_{F_I}$ E-Asp F_E $[_{F_I}$ I-Asp $[_{F_I}$ F_I $\delta]]]$ ex: to reenchain
     b. $\#[_{F_I}$ I-Asp F_I $[_{F_I}$ I-Asp $[_F$ F_I $\delta]]]$ ex: *to enenchain

(30) a. Luca è accorso subito.   (It)
         Luca is AT ran immediately
         'Luca ran up immediately.'
     b. *Luca è aaccorso   subito.
         Luca is AT AT ran immediately
         'Luca ran up up immediately.'

Considering F_I, the fact that there can be only one aspect per Ev follows directly from the geometry of the Asp-Shell. It does not have to be stipulated, as in Filip 2001, for example, but follows from the properties of the Asp-Shell, which restrictively allows for only one F_I head.

As for F_E, there is only one possible sort of iteration per event, as further discussed below. Thus in sequences of events, there is only one E-Asp per Ev, and the recursion of E-Asp affixes, as in *reenchain*, is reduced to multiple Ev projections. For example, *to enchain* denotes a single event, *to reenchain* denotes a sequence of two events, and to *rereenchain* denotes a sequence of three events. The recursion of F_E yields sequences of events, and not multiple iterations of the same event. There is only one F_E per Asp-Shell, and the recursion of the iterative affix does not give rise to identical pairs of Asp-features, because the same event cannot be iterated twice. Similar asymmetric relations hold for affixal modification to nominal and adjectival expressions such as *anti-anti-missile* and *post-post-modern*. Thus, a missile is an entity that is not identical to the entity described by *antimissile*, which is not identical to the entity described by *anti-anti-missile*.

Fifth, the fact that only I-Asp may modify an Ev-predicate and bring about argument-structure shift follows from the locality of morphological relations, given argument-structure flexibility (see chapter 3). Unlike F_E, F_I locally sister-contains the A-features in Ev (see (31)). The examples in (32) to (34) illustrate the argument-structure shifts.[9]

(31) a. $[_{F_E}$ E-Asp F_E $[_{F_I}$ I-Asp $\boxed{F_I}$ $[_{Ev}$ α $[_{Ev}$ Ev $[\boxed{+A}]]]]]$
                                                    unaccusatives *fall*
     b. $[_{F_E}$ E-Asp F_E $[_{F_I}$ I-Asp $\boxed{F_I}$ $[_{Ev}$ $[\boxed{+A}]$ $[_{Ev}$ Ev β]]]]$
                                                    unergatives   *sleep*
     c. $[_{F_E}$ E-Asp F_E $[_{F_I}$ I-Asp $\boxed{F_I}$ $[_{Ev}$ $[\boxed{+A}]$ $[_{Ev}$ Ev $[\boxed{+A}]]]]]$
                                                    transitives   *close*

(32) a. Gianni è caduto.   (It)
         Gianni is fell
         'Gianni fell.'

b. È   caduta molta   neve.
(there) is fell   a lot of snow
'There fell a lot of snow.'

c. È accaduto un fatto terribile a Gianni.
(it) occurred a   fact   terrible to Gianni
'Something terrible occurred to Gianni.'

(33) a. Roberto ha dormito.   (It)
'Roberto slept.'

b. Maria ha addormentato Roberto.
Maria has AT sleep   Roberto
'Maria made Roberto sleep.'

(34) a. Paulo ha chiuso l'aula.   (It)
'Paulo locked the classroom.'

b. Paulo ha rinchiuso gli studenti nell'aula.
'Paulo locked the student in the classroom.'

The fact that only F_I but not F_E may affect the *Aktionsart* of an Ev-projection also follows from the locality of morphological relations. I-Asp affixes provide internal aspectual modification to Ev by modifying the direction, the location, or the end point of Ev. Thus, while *correre* 'run' denotes an activity, *accorrere* 'run up' denotes an accomplishment. As expected, *correre* allows durative adverbs such as *for five minutes* but not punctual adverbs such as *in five minutes*. The reverse is true for *accorrere*. In contrast, E-Asp affixes provide external modification to an event by iterating an event or inverting it. E-Asp affixes keep the *Aktionsart* of the Ev-predicate intact (see (35)).[10]

(35) a. Romeo ha (ri)corso ?in due minuti / per due minuti.   (It)
'Romeo ran (again) ?in two minutes / for two minutes.'

b. Romeo è (ri)accorso in due minuti / ?per due minuti.
'Romeo ran up (again) in two minutes / ?for two minutes.'

The difference between F_E and F_I is expected, given the geometry of the Asp-Shell. In an Asp-Shell, F_I locally sister-contains Ev. F_E does not locally sister-contain Ev; only F_I does. Thus only F_I may affect the *Aktionsart* of Ev.

The Asp-Shell Hypothesis in conjunction with the operations of the grammar predicts the ordering of Asp-affixes, the restrictions imposed by asymmetric selection and Agree, the PF legibility of I-Asp affixes in denominal and deadjectival verbs when E-Asp is present, and the effects of I-Asp on the *Aktionsart* and the argument structure of an Ev-predicate, as well as the absence of the effects of E-Asp.

Further empirical evidence for the proposed analysis comes from Hungarian. While the list of E-Asp affixes seems rather limited in Hungarian, the list of I-prefixes is very rich. Hungarian has an iterative affix *újra* and a perfective affix *el*, which also has a preposition-like flavor (Edit Jakab, personal communication). *El-* can be interpreted as a prepositional or a directional element because it means something like 'away' (e.g., *el-megy* 'go away'). The Asp-Shell Hypothesis makes correct predictions for this language as well. First, in Hungarian, E-Asp affixes precede I-Asp affixes, as illustrated in (36).

(36) a.   el-olvas-sa   (Hu)
          PERF-read-3sg
          '(s)he reads it in full'
     b.   újra-el-olvas-sa
          re-PERF-read-3sg
          '(s)he reads it again in full'
     c.   *el-újra-olvas-sa
          PERF-re-read-3sg

Second, E-Asp affixes can attach to [+T] (telic) predicates whereas I-prefixes cannot, as the examples in (37) demonstrate.

(37) a.   újra-győz   (Hu)
          re-win-3sg
          '(s)he wins again'
     b.   *el-győz
          PERF-win-3sg

Third, E-Asp affixes may not attach directly to predicates that have adjectival roots; they can attach to such predicates only through an I-Asp affix that has already been attached to the root, as the sentences in (38) and (39) show.

(38) a.   sápad   (Hu)
          '(s)he turns pale'
     b.   el-sápad
          PERF-turns-pale
          '(s)he turns pale'
     c.   *újra-sápad
          re-turns.pale
          '(s)he turns pale again'

d. újra-el-sápad
    re-PERF-turns.pale
    '(s)he turns pale again'

Finally, there is a difference in the modification brought about by I-Asp and E-Aspect. Consider the examples in (39). In (39b), the perfective affix *meg* affects the *Aktionsart* of the predicate *festette* 'paint', telic shifting it from an activity into an accomplishment. The iterative affix *át* 'again' in (39c) has a different effect.

(39) a. A festő *három óra alatt / három óráig   festette a
         the artist *three hour under / three   hour-long painted the
         képeket. (Hu)
         paintings
         'The artist has been painting the paintings for three hours / *in three hours.'

     b. A festő három óra alatt / *három óráig   meg-festette
         the artist three hour under / *three hour-long VM-painted
         a   képeket.
         the paintings
         'The artist has painted [finished painting] the paintings in three hours / *for three hours.'

     c. A festő három óra alatt / három óráig   festette át
         the artist three   hour under / three   hour-long painted VM
         a   képeket.
         the paintings
         'In three hours / For three hours, the artist has repainted the paintings.'

The postverbal position of the E-Asp affix in (39c) might be due to independent properties of Hungarian, which I will not discuss here (see chapter 8, note 4).

Summarizing, aspectual modification to Ev-predicates takes the form of the Asp-Shell. The Asp-Shell is derived by M-Shift, given asymmetric selection applying under Agree. The Asp-feature distinctiveness ensures that the Asp-heads are Asp-distinct. E-Asp affixes precede I-Asp affixes, and the latter precede the root given the geometry of the M-Shell, its superiority with respect to the Ev-projection, and its impermeability to M-Flip. The fact that I-Asp affixes may affect the *Aktionsart* and the argument structure of Ev is a consequence of the locality of morphological relations, given argument-structure flexibility. Thus, predictions can be made with respect to the contribution of each sort of Asp-feature, F_I or F_E, to the aspectual properties of the Ev-predicate and to its argument structure. Moreover, the Asp-Shell Hypothesis has a large empirical coverage. It accounts for the morphoaspectual modification of Ev-predicates in languages of the same family, such as Italian and French, as well as in languages of different families, such as Bulgarian and Hungarian.

5.4 Some Differences between Aspectual Relations in M and S

Aspectual relations do not have the same properties in M and S. A first difference is the fact that these relations are asymmetric in M, whereas they may not be in S. In a morphological object, E-Asp affix must precede an I-Asp affix, and the inverse order is not found. This indicates that there is no mirror structure with respect to Asp-modification in D_M. However, reversibility of XP aspectual modifiers to the vP is observed in D_S, which suggests that symmetry is also part of the derivation of Asp-modification in D_S (see (40), (41)).

(40) a. Silvio è riaccorso. (It)
          Silvio is re TO run
          'Silvio ran up again.'

     b. #Silvio è ariccorso.
          Silvio is TO re run
          'Silvio ran up again.'

(41) a. Silvio ha corso a casa di nuovo. (It)
          Silvio has run at home once again
          'Silvio ran home again.'

     b. Silvio di nuovo ha corso a casa.
          Silvio once again has run at home
          'Silvio again ran home.'

A second difference between M and S with respect to the properties of Asp-relations is that the Asp-feature Distinctiveness does not hold in S. In (42), the [+It] feature is part of the V and the ADV, and in (43), the [+T] feature is part of the V and the head of the PP.

(42) a. Maria ha ancora riscritto la lettera. (It)
          Maria has again rewritten the letter
          'Maria has rewritten the letter again.'

     b. $[ADV_{F[+IT]}\ V_{F[+IT]}$

(43) a. Maria è accorsa a casa. (It)
Maria is AT run at home
'Maria ran up to her house.'

b. $[V_{F[+T]} \; PP_{F[+T]}$

In (43a), the [+T] feature of F_I is spelled out by the prefix *a-* on the verb, and by the prepositional head of the PP *a casa*, which specifies the location of the terminus of the event. In languages such as Italian, the reduplicated PP is not obligatory for the telic interpretation, but in languages like Hungarian, it is obligatory (Edit Jakab, personal communication).[11] Thus, there can be two occurrences of the same Asp feature in a syntactic domain, so that pairs such as $\langle F_I, F_I \rangle$ are possible.

However, this is not possible in a morphological domain, in which pairs of Asp-features must be distinct. This can be seen in the examples in (44) and (45). The examples in (44) show that both I-Asp affixes *a-* and *in-* may be merged with the verb *correre* 'to run'. The examples in (45) show that pairs such as $\langle F_I, F_I \rangle$ cannot be part of a morphological object. The Asp-feature Distinctiveness holds in M but not in S.

(44) a. Mario è accorso. (It)
Mario is AT ran
'Mario ran up.'

b. Mario ha incorso delle difficoltà.
Mario has IN ran some problems
'Mario ran into problems.'

(45) a. #Mario ainccorre. (It)
Mario AT IN runs
'Mario runs up into.'

b. #Mario inaccorre.
Mario IN AT runs
'Mario runs into up.'

The Asp-feature Distinctiveness seems to fail when considering the properties of the repetitive ADV *ancora* 'again' versus the repetitive affix (see (46), (47)).

(46) Marcello ha ancora riscritto la lettera. (It)
Marcello has again rewritten the letter
'Marcello has rewritten the letter again.'

(47) a. Marcello ha riscritto la lettera. (It)
Marcello has rewritten the letter
'Marcello has written the letter again.'

b. ?Marcello ha ririscritto   la lettera.
Marcello has rerewritten the letter
'Marcello has written the letter again once more.'

In (46), the syntactic object includes a repetitive adverb, *ancora*, and a repetitive affix, *re*. In (47), the presence of a repetitive affix on the verb is generally preferred to a structure with the iteration of the repetitive affix. The Asp-feature Distinctiveness correctly predicts that pairs such as $\langle F_E, F_E \rangle$ are not optimal. Cinque (1999) notes that terms such as *repetitive*, *iterative*, and *frequentative* are sometimes used synonymously but sometimes refer to different kinds of things. He adopts the distinction between repetitive aspect and frequentative aspect. With repetitive aspect, the action is repeated on a single occasion; with frequentative aspect, the action is repeated on different occasions (Bybee, Perkins, and Pagliuca 1994; Comrie 1976). The ADV *again* is a spell-out of the first sort of aspect, while *often* is a spell-out of the second. Because a double position (and scope) is available for ADV expressing repetition, as the example in (48) illustrates, Cinque postulates two positions for the repetitive aspect: $Asp_{repetitiveI}$ and $Asp_{repetitiveII}$.

(48) Gianni ha di nuovo battuto alla porta di nuovo/ancora.   (It)
'Gianni again knocked on the door again.' (Cinque 1999, (44))

According to Cinque, the higher $Asp_{repetitiveI}$ quantifies over the event, while the lower $Asp_{repetitiveII}$ quantifies over the action. The iteration of the iterative prefix also gives rise to the scope difference. Thus in *John rebuilt the house*, the affix scopes over the action described by the verbal predicate *built*, while in *?John rebuilt the house*, with two instances of the repetitive affix, the first affix scopes over the repeated event of *rebuilding the house*. Thus, the recursion of the repetitive prefix does not give rise to anti-symmetry in morphological relations. The ordered pair of features is as in $\langle Asp_{repetitiveI}, Asp_{repetitiveII} \rangle$ and Asp-feature Distinctiveness is satisfied.

Asp-feature Distinctiveness requires that Asp-heads be nonidentical with respect to Asp-features in a morphological domain, thus preventing reflexive relations from arising in optimal derivations.[12] Even in the case of Asp-features, morphology picks out asymmetry only from the set of relations available to the language faculty. Mirror structures with Asp-heads are derived in D_S, but not in D_M.

5.5 Summary

The asymmetry of morphology also manifests itself in the articulation of aspect features. I provided evidence showing that regularity of form and thus regularity of interpretation emerge when the Asp-features are analyzed on the basis of the Asp-Shell. The properties of ordering and legibility of Asp-affixes follow in a regular way, again contradicting the common assumption that derivational morphology is idiosyncratic. Asymmetry Theory allows for the derivation of Asp-relations in morphological objects, while preserving their specificity with respect to syntactic Asp-relations.

Chapter 6
Operator-Variable Feature Asymmetry

In this chapter, I focus on the operator-variable relation in question words, complementizers, and determiners. I propose that they have the same basic morphological form and differ minimally in feature specification.

The properties of the linguistic operator-variable relation have been mainly discussed in syntax (Chomsky 1977, 2001; Lasnik 1999; Ura 1995; Boeckx and Grohmann 2003; Kiss 1991; Aoun and Li 2003) and in semantics (Hamblin 1958; Karttunen 1977; Higginbotham 1996; Heim and Kratzer 1998; Carlson 2002; Hagstrom 2002). The properties of this relation under the word level have been subject to scrutiny only recently (Kayne 1998, 2001; Di Sciullo 2003b; Ambar 2003). Because there are restrictions on the syntactic operator-variable relation, there are also restrictions on the morphological operator-variable relation. These restrictions have been unnoticed, since it is generally assumed that *wh*-words are morphologically simplex (Larson 1987; Aoun and Li 2003). Given the M-Shell Hypothesis, the internal feature structure of functional words can be explored systematically.

According to Asymmetry Theory, functional words have a regular form, and their features are part of asymmetric relations. I argue that the ±wh-feature and ±th-feature are part of the Op(erator)-Shell. The geometry of the Op-Shell leaves little space for variation. Languages use more than one strategy to phrase questions (wh-movement, wh–in situ, question particles) or to denote individuals (DPs, pronouns, clitics, proper names), whereas the shape of question words, complementizers and determiners is severely restricted. The crosslinguistic regularity in the form of functional words indicates that their structure is determined by the characteristic property of morphological relations: asymmetry.

This chapter is organized as follows. I start by describing the properties of *wh*-words and *th*-words. I define the Op-Shell, and show how, in conjunction with the operations and conditions of the grammar, it accounts for the properties of functional words. I identify the differences between the morphological and syntactic Op-variable relations. Each contributes to feature legibility in distinct albeit related planes of the computational space.

6.1   On *wh-* and *th-*Words

Functional words, such as *wh-* and *th-*words, present the characteristic properties of morphological domains. First, they include a head-complement relation, as will become clear immediately. In English, as well as in other languages such as Italian and French, they generally include two components. The first component is a constant morpheme, the *wh-* or *th-*morpheme, and the second component varies through the paradigm (e.g., *wh-o*, *wh-at*, and *th-is*, *th-at*). Their bipartite structure is also evidenced by the fact that there is a *th-*variant for most *wh-*words (e.g., *what*, *that*; *where*, *there*). What is the relation between the two components? Certainly the relation is asymmetric; the reordering of the components gives rise to gibberish (e.g., *#owh* and *#isth*). Furthermore, the first component is obligatory; the second component alone does not qualify as a *wh-* or *th-*word (see (1), (2)). In the case of truncated forms, it is the first component of the construct that survives (see (3), (4)).

(1) Wh*(at) did you do?

(2) Th*(e) cat is on the mat.

(3) Qu'a-t-il lu?   (Fr)
     'What did he read?'

(4) l'étranger   (Fr)
     'the stranger'

The first component includes the head of the functional complex and determines the features of the whole complex. Thus, substituting *th-* for *wh-* affects the feature structure of the whole construct (e.g., *what* is a *wh-*word, whereas *that* is not; it is a demonstrative or a complementizer). The second component of the functional complex is the complement of the functional head. It is generally obligatory and selected by the head as its restrictor. Witness the fact that the restrictor feature (e.g., [+human], [−human], [+location], [+proximate]) differs according to the properties of the head. For example, assuming that the affix *-is* is the morphological spell-out of the +proximate feature, which is a possible restrictor for the head of a *th*-word (e.g., *this* versus *that*), this feature is not a possible restrictor for the head of a *wh*-word, namely, *this* versus **whis*. These facts indicate that functional words, *wh*- and *th*-words, include a head-complement structure. This is their minimal structure, however, because in certain languages preposition-like affixes are adjoined to the basic *wh*-word, as is the case in French *pourquoi* 'for what (reason)', and in Russian *pochemu* 'for what (reason)', which are the counterparts of *why*.

Second, once derived, functional words cannot be altered by further operations without destroying their integrity, for example by attracting/moving a constituent within or by extracting a constituent out of them. Functional words do not include a probe that can attract a goal (see (5)), and the parts of a *wh*-word cannot be attracted by a probe (see (6)).

(5) a.   What did you do?
    b.   *[wh you at] did ~~you~~ do?

(6) a.   What, my friend, did you do?
    b.   *Wh, my friend, ~~what~~ did you do?

Third, *wh*- and *th*-words have an independent interpretation at the interfaces. For example, a *wh*-word behaves as a morphological unit at the phonetic interface, as evidenced by the fact that it bears a unique stress, even in the case of adjunct *wh*-words such as *pourquoi*. At the semantic interface, a *wh*-word is interpreted as a generalized quantifier. It is of the semantic type $\langle\langle et\rangle t\rangle$, which is the type of NPs in general (Barwise and Cooper 1981; Karttunen 1977). Assuming that semantic compositionality (Frege [1891] 1952) extends under the word level for the core morphological relations, the meaning of functional words would then be derived from the meaning of their parts. The fact that *wh*-words are generalized quantifiers would be derived from their internal semantic feature structure. This is not a standard assumption, however, because the semantics of *wh*- and *th*-words is generally considered nonanalytic. Moreover, in type-theoretical semantics, complementizers are often assumed to be semantically vacuous (Heim and Kratzer 1998, 96). They are often syncategorematic—that is, they do not have semantic values of their own, but their presence affects the calculation of the semantic value for the next higher constituent. There are, however, reasons to assume that the morphological components of *wh*- and *th*-words have independent meaning. Complementizers must have semantic features, since their absence may affect interpretability. Consider the following examples.

(7) a. I know ≠ (that) John left.
   b. I know the fact ≠ (that) John left.
   c. Je sais *(que) Jean est parti. (Fr)
   d. Il a reconnu le fait *(que) Jean soit parti.
      'He acknowledged the fact that John left.'

(8) a. The fact (that) John left was expected.
   b. *(That) John left was expected.
   c. Le fait *(que) Jean soit parti était prévu. (Fr)
   d. *(Que) Jean soit parti était prévu.

Without the presence of the complementizer, the interpretation of the expressions in (7a,b) is not optimal. These expressions could be interpreted as consisting of two unrelated propositions. Moreover, in the romance languages, the presence of the complentizer is obligatory (see (7c,d), (8c,d)).

In my view, the role of the complementizer is to relate two different semantic types: the proposition expressed by the embedded clause and the type required to saturate the proposition expressed by the matrix sentence in which it is embedded. The role of the complementizer is similar to the role of the determiner. In several works, including Montague and Kalish 1959, *that* is treated like a nominalizer. It takes a predicate of worlds—that is, a proposition—and returns something the matrix verb can combine with. Under this view, matrix verbs cannot combine directly with propositions, but only through the mediation of a complementizer, in much the same way a verb cannot combine directly with a noun phrase, but only through the mediation of a determiner. Furthermore, the embedding verb can be thought of as taking an individual as an argument rather than a proposition. Supporting this view is the fact that the complement of verbs such as *believe* and *know* is individual-denoting (e.g., *to believe the fact that ...*, *to know the answer*). A complementizer turns a proposition into an individual. It denotes a function from propositions to their individual correlates, an idea also considered by Angelika Kratzer. Thus, the role of the complementizer is to relate two different semantic types: the proposition expressed by the embedded clause, which is of type $\langle st \rangle$, and an individual correlate of that proposition, which is of type e, the type required by the semantics of the matrix clause. My contention is that this property of the semantics of complementizers, and other *th*- and *wh*-words, originates in their morphological structure. The similarity between complementizers and determiners is expressed in

Asymmetry Theory by the fact that they share the same morphological form, the Op-Shell, as defined in the next section.

Summarizing, *wh-* and *th-*words are morphological domains, they have minimally a head-complement structure, they are strictly impenetrable, and they are isolable at the interfaces.

6.2 The Op-Shell Hypothesis

Asymmetry Theory holds that morphological domains are M-Shells. While A-Shells and Asp-Shells articulate argument and aspect features, Op-Shells articulate operator-variable features. The Operator (Op), the variable (Fx), and the restrictor of the variable (Re) are organized according to (9).

(9) *The Op-Shell Hypothesis*
     The Op-features are part of the asymmetric relations of the M-Shell.

In the Op-Shell, the features of the operator and the features of the variable are in a specifier-head relation in the upper layer of the Shell. The features of the restrictor and the features of its dependents are in the lower layer. The generic form of the Op-Shell is (10).

(10)

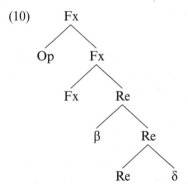

The derivation of the Op-Shell is regular. M-Shift applies to two minimal trees such as the ones in (11a) and (11b), yielding (11c), which satisfies Strict Asymmetry.

(11)

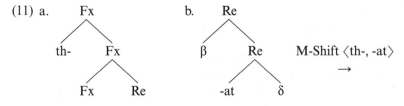

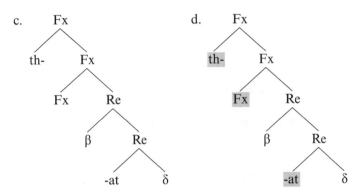

A *wh-* or a *th-*morpheme occupies the specifier of its minimal tree. M-Shift substitutes a Re tree for the complement of an Fx tree. Since M-Flip does not apply to the upper layer of the Op-Shell, whose specifier has PF features, the *wh-* or *th-*morpheme precedes the rest of the functional construct. M-Link applies to the upper layer of the Op-Shell in (11c) and relates the Op features to the variable features. The restricted and bound variable Fx is the head of the Op-Shell and projects its features to the root (see (11d)).

M-Shift and M-Link apply under Agree, resulting in the checking of uninterpretable morphological features, which I take to be [−X] and [−Re], the interpretable features being [+X] and [+Re]. I consider the articulation of these features below.

The morphological elements of the Op-Shell are the operator, the variable, the restrictor, and the dependents of the restrictor. They can be defined by the features [±X] and [±Re] as follows. Let the feature [+X] be part of the interpretable feature structure of a variable and let the feature [+Re] be part of the interpretable features of a Restrictor. The uninterpretable feature of a variable is [−Re] and the uninterpretable feature of a restrictor is [−X]. Thus, a variable is a pure unrestricted placeholder, [+X, −Re], considered independently from the restrictor, which is not a placeholder and has the features to restrict the variable, [−X, +Re]. An operator has neither variable nor restrictor feature before linking takes place, [−X, −Re]. The dependents of the restrictor are restricted variables as discussed below. Let their feature be [+X, +Re]. Summarizing:

(12) Operator (Op)   :   [−X, −Re]
     Variable (Fx)   :   [+X, −Re]
     Restrictor (Re)   :   [−X, +Re]
     Dependents (β, δ)   :   [+X, +Re]

Given M-Shift, the uninterpretable [−Re] feature of the variable is checked under Agree by the [+Re] feature of the restrictor, and the uninterpretable [−X] feature of the restrictor is checked by the [+X] feature of the variable and values it. Given M-Link, the uninterpretable [−X] feature of the operator is checked by the [+X] feature of the variable, and the uninterpretable [−Re] feature of the operator is checked by the previously valued [+Re] feature of the variable (see (13)).

(13)

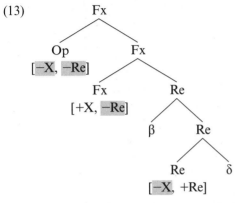

A linking failure gives rise to morphological gibberish. The Op must Agree with Fx, which itself must Agree with Re. For example, a Determiner Op, spelled out by the *th*-affix, does not have the quantificational force to bind a +wh variable, whereas this is possible for the Question Op, spelled out by the *wh*-affix. Consequently, *there* is not a possible question word, whereas *where* is (e.g., *Where to go?* versus **There to go?*).

As seen previously, active pairs of elements in M-Shells are subject to the Distinctiveness Condition. When applying to Op-Shells, this condition is the following:

(14) *Op-feature Distinctiveness*
    In an Op-Shell, Linked positions must be X-distinct.

The uninterpretable features of the operator and the variable are M-Linked and checked in a specifier-head relation. Because checking applies under Agree, the features of the operator and the features of the variable must be distinct—that is, they are contravalued. The Op-feature Distinctiveness for these pairs of elements follows from the operations of the grammar applying under Agree. This is also the case for the checking of the uninterpretable features of the restrictor and the variable, because the variable linked to the operator asymmetrically selects a restrictor of a certain sort. For example, a [+human] restrictor cannot be selected by a

variable bound by a Determiner operator, which is morphologically
spelled out by *th-* in English, and conversely a [+proximate] restrictor
cannot be selected by a Question operator, which is spelled out by *wh-* in
English, as evidenced in section 6.4.2. Thus, the Op-feature Distinctiveness is also a consequence of the application of M-Link to the variable
features heading the upper layer of the Op-Shell and its asymmetrically
selected Re head in the lower layer of the Op-Shell. Finally, there are reasons to take the features of the dependents of Re as distinct, independently of feature checking, as will become clear immediately.

It is generally assumed that the restrictor of a variable bound by an
operator contributes substantive semantic features, such as [+human]
and [−human], to the functional word of which it is part (Chomsky 1977
and related works, including Ambar 1983, 1988, and Ambar and Veloso
2001). I would like to suggest that the dependents of Re, β and δ, host
morphological features enabling functional words to relate semantic
types, as is the case for *wh*-words, which relate sets of individuals $\langle et \rangle$
and worlds, a type I will represent as s. Thus the semantic type of functional words would be derived from the semantic types of their parts. I
will not argue for any specific semantic types, the identification of which
is tangential to the topic of this book. Instead I will refer to them with the
variable τ, which can be replaced by whatever semantic type that turns
out to be appropriate. However, I will take the semantic types of the
Operator-Shell to be distinct, since pairs of elements in M-Shells are dis-
tinct. Thus I will distinguish small (ordinary) τ from big (boldface) $\boldsymbol{\tau}$. The
Op-feature Distinctiveness requires the nonidentity of the features of
dependents of Re; let these features be $[+\tau]$ and $[+\boldsymbol{\tau}]$ (see (15)). For example, if $[+\tau]$ is of type $\langle et \rangle$, the type of sets of individuals, $[+\boldsymbol{\tau}]$, cannot be
of type $\langle et \rangle$. Supposing that $[+\tau]$ is $\langle et \rangle$ and that $[+\boldsymbol{\tau}]$ is different from
$[+\tau]$, $[+\boldsymbol{\tau}]$ can be of any type other than $\langle et \rangle$. It can be of the basic types,
which is the type denoting worlds. As for the semantic features of the
head of the restrictor layer, they are interpretable; they are not checked
and deleted. Thus, in the Op-Shell, Re contributes to the semantic features of the variable linked to the operator and enables the functional
construct to relate different semantic types.[1]

(15)

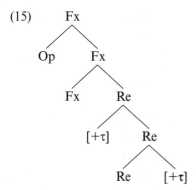

Op-feature Distinctiveness failure gives rise to lack of interpretability in cases where the Re relates identical semantic types. For example, the expression *I know that John arrived* is interpretable; the Re layer of the complementizer *that* relates two distinct semantic types, which can be ⟨st⟩ and e. However, the expression ≠*I know that I wish* is not optimally interpretable, because a complementizer cannot relate identical semantic types.

Thus, the morphological features of *wh*- and *th*-words are part of the asymmetric relations of the Op-Shell, which is an independent morphological domain. The Op-Shell Hypothesis together with the operations of M determine the morphological relations of *wh*- and *th*-words at LF.

6.3   On the Specificity of the Op-Shell

The Op-Shell Hypothesis differs from Tsai's (1994) proposal, which also provides a configurational analysis for the internal structure of *wh*-words. According to his analysis, made in a syntactic and not in a morphological context, an interrogative *wh*-word has a Q(uestion)-operator as a binder for the variable (x) (see (16)).

(16)

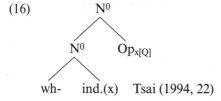

In the configuration in (16), the Q-operator is an adjunct to N^0. However, Tsai makes no commitment as to why and how the Q-operator should adjoin to the *wh*-word. Furthermore, the structure in (16) leaves unmotivated the structural relation between the adjoined Q operator and the variable (x). Moreover, it is unclear whether the variable is an adjunct or a complement of the *wh*-head, and how the features of the restrictor of the variable fit in the structure. According to the Op-Shell Hypothesis, *wh*- and *th*-words have the same morphological structure. The operator is generated in the specifier of the upper layer of the Op-Shell and it locally sister-contains the variable, which sister-contains its restrictor in the lower layer. The Op precedes the variable, which itself precedes the restrictor.

The Op-Shell is not the syntactic Op-variable relation. In syntax, a *wh*-word is an operator that binds a variable introduced in its TP complement, as in (17a,b). The syntactic Op-variable relation is obtained derivationally by overt (Attract/Agree) or covert (QR) movement (among other works, see Chomsky 1995, 2001; Lasnik 1999). The Op-feature is in C and acts as the attractor for the movement of the *wh*-XP in the specifier of CP, as in (17c), and the uninterpretable *wh*-feature of the moved *wh*-phrase is checked and deleted.

(17) a. $[_{CP} [_{XP} \text{wh-R}]_i [_C [_{TP} \ldots t_i \ldots]]]$
     b. $[_{CP} [_{XP} \text{who}]_i [_C [_{TP} \text{did Mary see } t_i]]]$
     c. $[_{CP} +\text{wh} [_C \text{Op} [_{TP} x]]]$

In contrast, the derivation of the Op-Shell takes place without movement, because movement does not occur in D_M. Assuming the copy theory of movement, according to which movement is Copy + Merge, the variable bound by an operator is no longer available in terms of a trace. It can, however, be derived by lambda abstraction, along the lines of Fox 2002, in which case the derived representation is still formally distinct from the Op-Shell. In the Op-Shell, the variable in the head position is adjacent to the operator in the specifier position, whereas the variable is not necessarily adjacent to the operator in the D_S.[2] A further difference lies in that the Op features are in the specifier of the Op-Shell, whereas they are in the head of CP in D_S (see (17c)).[3] Thus, the Op-Shell differs from syntactic representations of the Op-variable relation, as expected in Asymmetry Theory.

6.4 Linear Order, Agreement, and Interpretability

Empirical evidence that *wh*- and *th*-words have internal structure comes from the regularity of form and interpretation. The presence of two designated morphemes indicates that their internal structure is bipartite. The strict linear ordering of the morphemes indicates that they are in asymmetric relations. The restriction on the combination of the morphemes indicates that Agree is at play. Finally, their closely related meanings suggest that their interpretability is based on the same regular form. In what follows, I offer further empirical support for these claims.

6.4.1 Linear Order and Legibility

Crosslinguistic data provide evidence that *wh-* and *th-*words are generally bipartite asymmetric structures, where the Op-variable relation precedes the restrictor relation. The strict ordering of the morphemes spelling out these relations is observed in languages from the same family, such as French and Italian, as well as in languages from different families, including Slavic, Turkic, Finno-Ugric, and Niger-Congo.

The internal structure of *wh-*words in French and Italian exhibits a regular pattern. Regarding the first part of the construct, the *qu-* morpheme is present in the majority of French *wh-*words, as is true of the Italian *ch-* morpheme in Italian *wh-*words (see (18)). As for the form of the second part of the construct, the restrictor layer varies through the paradigm. For example, in French and in Italian, *-i* spells out the [+human] feature, while *-e* spells out the [−human] feature.

(18)
qui (Fr)	**ch**i (It)	'who'
que	**ch**e	'what'
quoi	**ch**e	'what'
quand	**qu**ando	'when'
où	dove	'where'
pour**qu**oi	per**ch**è	'why'
comment	come	'how'

As noted above, the purpose/reason *wh-*word in Romance—for example, *pourquoi* (Fr), *perchè* (It) 'why'—includes a prepositional adjunct, a point to which I come back.

The *th-*paradigms in French and Italian also present regularities. The morpheme *l-* is typically part of the definite determiner along with another constituent, as in *l-a*, and *l-e* (see (19)). Likewise for pronominal clitics, such as *le*, *la*, and *les* in French (e.g., *Jean la regarde* John her looks 'John looks at her') and *lo*, *la*, *le* in Italian (e.g., *Gianni lo vede* Gianno him/it sees 'Gianni sees him/it'). In Italian the morpheme *qu-* is typically part of a demonstrative, along with another constituent, as in *qu-esto*, *qu-esta*, *qu-esti*, *qu-ello*, *qu-ella*, *qu-elli*. French is similar to Italian in this respect (see (20)). The obligatory presence of these morphemes suggests that they head the construct of which they are part.

(19) a. l-a ragazza   l uva   l-e regazze   (It)
     b. l-a fille   l-e raisin   l-es filles   (Fr)
        'the girl'   'the grape'   'the girls'

(20) a. qu-esto   qu-ello   qu-elli   (It)
     b. ce-ci   ce-la   ceux-ci/ceux-là   (Fr)
        'this'   'that'   'those'

Thus, *th*-words and to a large extent *wh*-words in French and Italian present the typical asymmetric property of the relations of the Op-Shell, where the morpheme spelling out the Op-variable relation precedes the morpheme spelling out the Re relation.

Similar facts can be observed in other languages. For example, in Russian, and more generally in the Slavic languages, *wh*- and *th*-words are case marked; this is also true of other languages, including Hungarian. Nevertheless the same regular pattern emerges, as can be seen in the following examples.[4]

(21) a. k-uda   (Ru)
        'where'
     b. k-ogda
        'when'

(22) a. t-uda   (Ru)
        'there'
     b. t-ogda
        'then'

Languages with agglutinative morphology, such as Turkish (see Kornfilt 2004; Lewis 1967; Sebüktekin 1971), also illustrate the same pattern in the formation of *wh*- and *th*-expressions as languages with concatenative morphology, such as English. In Turkish, *wh*-words are formed of a constant initial morpheme followed by a second morpheme whose form varies through the paradigm (see (23)).[5] Furthermore, Turkish exhibits the same properties as English in the derivation of *where-there* with respect to *here* (see (24)).

(23) a. ne-rede   (Tu)
        'where'
     b. ne-vakit
        'when'

(24) a. bu-rada   (Tu)
        'here'
     b. şu-rada, o-rada
        'there'

The bipartite articulation of the Op-Shell can also be observed in African languages. In Yekhee, all words start with a vowel; this is also the case for functional words (see (25)).

The initial vowel of the *wh*-word in (25) bears a tone and spells out the third-person feature; it is probably a remnant for the noun class system (Grace Masagbor, personal communication). The same initial vowel is used in more than one *wh*-word, and it is not the morphological spell-out of the restrictor.[6]

(25) a. ó-vhá   (Ye)
      'who'
     b. é-mè
      'what'

In Yekhee, a *wh*-word starts with a vowel and is generally followed by two parts: a consonant spelling out the *wh*- part and a vowel spelling out the restrictor. In *óvhá* 'who' the vowel *ó* spells out pronominal third-person features, *vh*- spells out the Op, and *à* spells out the restrictor, which is [+human] in this case. In *é-mè* 'what', the initial *é* spells out the pronominal features, *m*- spells out the *wh*-constituent, and the final *è* spells out the [−human] restrictor.

The form of *wh*-words resembles the form of demonstratives (see (26)).

(26) a. ò-nà   è-nà   (Ye)
      'this'   'these'
     b. ò-lì   è-lì
      'that'   'those'

The definite determiners and demonstratives in Yekhee are also bipartite constructions. The definite determiner is formed on the basis of a vowel, which spells out the number, and another constituent. The first morpheme *n*- spells out the *th*-constituent, and the second morpheme *à* spells out the rest of the *th*-word (see (27)). In Yekhee the inflexional affixes are word initial, as shown in chapter 8; consequently they also precede the *th*-word.

(27) a. ọ̀-nà   ówà   (Ye)   b. è-nà   éwà
      SG-th house   PL-th houses
      'the house'   'the houses'

The demonstratives are also bipartite: the initial syllable *ò* is the morphological spell-out of the φ features, *n*- spells out the *th*-constituent, and the following vowel spells out the [±proximate] feature of the restrictor; −*a* is [+proxi] and −*i* is [−proxi] (see (28)).[7]

(28) a. ọ̀-nà   è-nà   (Ye)
         SG+proxi   PL+proxi
         'this'   'these'
     b. ọ́-lì   é-lì
         SG−proxi   PL−proxi
         'that'   'those'

The morphological structure of *wh*- and *th*-words is independent of typological differences. The data indicate that *wh*-words are formed of two asymmetrically related constituents. Notwithstanding the variation between the languages, with respect to the presence of morphological case at the right periphery of the functional word, as in Russian, or the presence of an initial vowel bearing a tone feature, as in Yekhee, the morphological spell-out of the Op-variable relation precedes the morphological spell-out of the restrictor relation. The crosslinguistic evidence provides strong empirical support for the analysis of these constructs in terms of the asymmetric relations of the Op-Shell.

The Op-Shell can be taken to be part of the derivation of *wh*- and *th*-words notwithstanding the observed variation in the legibility of their parts at PF. As mentioned in the previous section, in French, *wh*-words can be spelled out only in part (e.g., in open (information) questions), or not at all (e.g., in closed (yes/no) questions). As with *th*-words, the determiner can also be spelled out in part (e.g., truncated *th*-words), or not at all with proper nouns. In Italian, a *wh*-word may be covert in information questions. For example, in Italian, the bare noun *cosa* 'thing', may be used as an information question, provided the expression bears a question intonation (see (29)). *Cosa* must be the nominal constituent in the *wh*-phrase (*che cosa*), since (29a) and (29b) are equivalents. The *wh*-word is covert in (29b), and the nominal constituent *cosa* is the syntactic spell-out of the restrictor of the covert *wh*-word.[8]

(29) a. Che cosa c'è?   (It)
         what thing there is
         'What is it?'
     b. Cosa c'è?
         thing there is
         'What is it?'

Linguistic variation is also observed with respect to the morphological spell-out of the restrictor as an independent constituent in PP adjunct *wh*-expressions. Hungarian and Turkish differ from English and the Romance languages in this respect (see (30)). In the latter, the *wh*-words are available (e.g., *quando* (It), *quand* (Fr), *when*), independently of the phrasal PP variants.

(30) a. Mi-kor? (Hu)
  what time
  'When?'
 b. Ne-vakit? (Tu)
  what time
  'When?'

Languages also differ with respect to the legibility of the reason/purpose adjunct as a separate constituent. For example, in Russian and in French (as well as the other Romance languages), a preposition precedes the *wh*-words (see (31)). This is not the case in languages such as English, #*for what* versus *pourquoi* (Fr) (e.g., *pourquoi partir?* (Fr) versus **for what to leave?*).

(31) a. Po-che-mu? (Ru)
  for what (reason)
  'Why?'
 b. Pourquoi? (Fr)
  for what
  'Why?'

Russian patterns like French with respect to the morphological spell-out of the preposition-like adjunct in reason/purpose *wh*-words. In English the prepositional element is part of XP-*wh* (e.g., *for what reason did you do it?*). The preposition can be stranded (e.g., *what reason did you do it for?*), which indicates that it is a phrasal constituent. In French *quoi* is the strong form of *que*, both forms deriving from Latin *quid?* (Grevisse [1936] 1986, 491). *Quoi* can be preceded by a preposition in an information question, as in *à quoi penses-tu?* 'What are you thinking about?' *Pourquoi* is analyzed by Grevisse as an adverbial *wh*-expression, because it can modify adverbs as well as verbs (e.g., *pourquoi pas* 'why not', *pourquoi faire* 'why'). Note that in the last example, a difference in bracketing gives rise to a difference in interpretation (i.e., *[[pourquoi] faire]* (reason), and *[pour [quoi faire]]* (purpose)). French may have two derivations for *pourquoi*. In the morphological derivation, the F$_{RA(TIONALE)}$ tree with the preposition (P) in its specifier M-Shifts with the Fx tree of the *wh*-word. This is depicted in (32), where the Ra feature is outside the domain of the Op-Shell of *quoi*. Given M-Link the RA feature is also part of the features of the variable Fx and the features of Re.

(32)

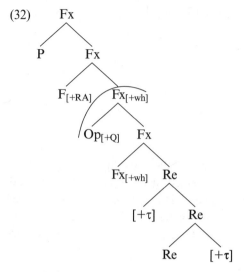

In the syntactic derivation of *pour quoi, à quoi, de quoi, vers quoi,* and so on, the preposition heads the *wh*-phrase. Once derived, the wh-XP is an independent domain and is transferred to D_M. English *why* is derived in D_M and *wh*-XPs, such as *for what, with what,* and the like, are derived in D_S. They are not transferred to D_M, because preposition stranding is possible in that language (e.g., *What did you do that for?, What did you paint this with?, Who did you talk to?*).

I thus take the properties of the Op-Shell to hold crosslinguistically, notwithstanding the differences between languages with respect to the PF legibility of their parts, whether or not parts of the Op-Shell can be PF legible, and whether or not *wh*-words can be derived in D_M as adjuncts to the minimal M-Shell or whether they are derived in D_S and transferred to D_S.

6.4.2 Op-Variable Linking

In the derivation of the Op-Shell, uninterpretable features are checked and interpretable features are carried along as free riders, as described previously. I focus here on the interpretable features of the operator and the variable, limiting the discussion to the operator features [±Q], [±D] and the variable features [±wh], [±th]. Q stands for the question operator and D stands for the determiner operator; wh stands for the features of the wh-variable and th stands for the features of the th-variable.

Considering first the relation between the [±Q] and the [±wh] features, the examples in (33) from Italian illustrate the fact that the same morpheme, *ch-*, is part of a question word (see (33a)), a complementizer (see (33b)), and a *wh*-exclamative (see (33c)).

(33) a. Che fare?   (It)
       what do
       'What to do?'
    b. Penso che Gianni sia intelligente.
       think that Gianni is intelligent
       'I think that John is intelligent.'
    c. Che grande denti hai!
       what big   teeth have
       'What big teeth you have!'

It might be the case that functional morphemes are lexically unspecified for the value of their interpretable features. For example, in Italian *che* is [+Q] in the derivation of a question, and it is [−Q] in the derivation of a complementizer or an exclamative word. However, independently of the given feature specification, the derivation of functional words requires that the operator and the variable be in a specifier-head agreement relation, otherwise feature mismatch would arise. Op-variable agreement is an effect of M-Link applying under Agree.

I will use the [+Q] feature to indicate question operator, the [+Q] feature being part of the feature structure of null or overt (open or information) questions, and the [+wh] feature to indicate the +*wh*-variable.[9] I will use the feature [+D] to mean determiner operator, the [+D] feature being part of the feature structure of null or overt determiners, and the feature [+th] to mean +th-variable. Thus, Op is [+Q] or [−Q], depending on whether it is a question operator or not, and it is [+D] or [−D] depending on whether it is a determiner operator or not. The variable can either be [+wh] or [−wh], [+th] or [−th], according to its agreement relation with the Op, the Op spelling out the *wh*- or *th*-morphology. Thus, the [+wh] feature is part of functional morphemes with *wh*-morphology; the [+th] feature is part of functional morphemes with *th*-morphology.

Question words and complementizers can be defined on the basis of the combination of the [±Q] and [±wh] features (see (34)). The typology in (34) is very close to Chomksy's (1977) original idea that the wh-feature is a unifying feature for a set of movements he referred to as wh-movement.[10] A question word is [+Q, +wh]. The interrogative complementizers (null or overt, in open or information questions) are uniformly [+Q, −wh]. A *wh*-exclamative word is [−Q, +wh]. The noninterrogative complementizer is uniformly [−Q, −wh].[11]

(34) [+Q, +wh]   *wh*-words   ex: What to do?
     [+Q, −wh]   interrogative comp   ex: I wonder if John will
                                           come.

[−Q, +wh]   *wh*-exclamatives   ex: What a big cat!
[−Q, −wh]   noninterrogative comp   ex: I know that John is
                                      intelligent.

Similarly for *th*-words, the same morpheme can be used as a definite determiner, as in expressions such as *they scared the cat*, or as an expletive determiner, as in *the hell* constructions discussed in Obenhauer 1994 and more recently analyzed in Den Dikken and Giannakidou 2002— for example, *they scared the hell out of him*. The definite determiner *the* is [+D] and the variable feature is [+th], while the expletive *the* is [−D] and its variable feature is [−th]. Moreover, indefinite determiners, such as *someone* and *somebody*, are [+D, −th],[12] and relative pronouns are [−D, +wh].[13] The following typology is obtained, defining the feature composition of definite and indefinite determiners, expletives, and relative pronouns.

(35) [+D, +th]   definite Det   ex: The cat is on the mat.
     [+D, −th]   indefinite Det   ex: A cat is on the mat.
     [−D, +th]   expletive Det   ex: They scared the hell out of him.
     [−D, +wh]   relative pron   ex: the person who came in

Thus, the features [±Q], [±wh], differentiate *wh*-words (question word, relative pronoun, exclamative pronoun, and complementizer), as the features [±D], [±th] do for *th*-words (definite determiner, indefinite determiner, expletive and exclamative determiners).

The minimal trees of *wh*- and *th*-words differ only in feature specification in the Op-Shells, where the specifier of the upper layer of the Op-Shell is the locus of the operator feature, and the head is the locus of the variable feature (see (36)).

(36)

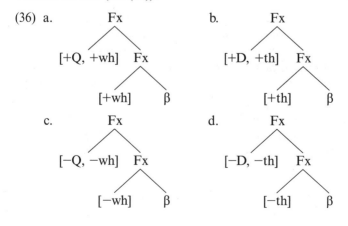

In an Op-Shell, the variable must be linked by the operator and the Op-variable linking applies under Agree, the definition of which is repeated in (37).

(37) Agree (φ_1, φ_2)
   Given two sets of features φ_1 and φ_2, Agree holds between φ_1 and φ_2, iff φ_1 properly includes φ_2, and the node dominating φ_1 sister-contains the node dominating φ_2.

Agree holds in the Op-Shell from the set of features of the operator to the set of features of the variable in the upper layer of the Shell. The features of the operator properly include the features of the variable. The derivation of functional words is consequently restricted. Thus, in an Op-Shell, a [+wh] variable cannot be in a specifier-head agreement relation with a [+Q, −wh] operator. Likewise, a [−wh] variable cannot be in a specifier-head agreement with a [+Q, +wh] operator. Consequently, a *th*-word does not have the quantificational force of a question operator (see (38b)), and a *wh*-word does not have the quantificational force of a demonstrative (see (39b)).

(38) a. What is it?
     b. *That is it?

(39) a. I know that.
     b. *I know what.

Furthermore, the linking of the variable to the operator may also fail if there is no matching restrictor for the variable linked to the operator. Considering the paradigms in (40), *-o* is the morphological spell-out for the [+human] restrictor. The *th*-paradigm is not specified for this feature; consequently **tho* is not a possible *th*-word by linking failure. As pointed out in section 5.1, the [+proxi] feature is not part of the restrictors for a *wh*-variable, whereas it is for a *th*-variable. Consequently, **whis* is excluded by linking failure, while *this* is not (see (40)). Likewise in French, the restrictor feature of the *th*-paradigm includes the gender and number features, whereas this is not the case for the *wh*-paradigm. Op-variable linking failure also accounts for the presence of the gaps in the paradigms (see (41)).

(40) **wh-**   **th-**
      *whe   the
      who   *tho
      what   that

*whis	this
where	there
when	then
which	*thich

(41) **wh-**   **th-**
    que 'what'   le   'the masc.'   (Fr)
    *qua   la   'the fem.'
    *ques   les   'the plur.'
    qui 'who'   *li
    quoi 'what'   *loi

Thus, Op-variable linking has empirical consequences for the morphological form of *wh*- and *th*-words, which further confirms the asymmetry of the relations of the Op-Shell.

6.4.3 The Re Relation

In the Op-Shell, the lower layer is headed by the restrictor of the variable. The form of the restrictor varies through the *wh*- and *th*-paradigms (see (42), (43)).

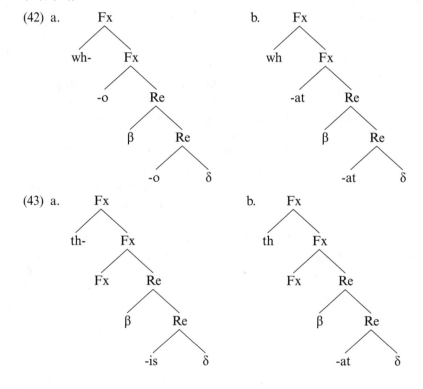

The justification for the lower layer of the Op-Shell is twofold. First, Re restricts the features of the variable in the upper layer of the Shell. Second, Re relates morphological features. I consider these two properties in turn.

The morphological spell-out of *wh*-words differs according to the features of Re.[14] It is generally assumed that semantic features are part of the restrictor of the variable and differentiate the *wh*-words within the *wh*-paradigm. The morphological spell-out of the second constituent of a *wh*-word differs according to the features of Re, which range over a set of semantic features (see (44)).

(44) who: (Fx, Re$_{+HUM}$); what: (Fx, Re$_{-HUM}$); where: (Fx, Re$_{+LOC}$); when: (Fx, Re$_{+TIME}$); how: (Fx, Re$_{+MANNER}$); which: (Fx, Re$_{+PART}$); whose: (Fx, Re$_{+POSS}$); why: (Fx, Re$_{+RA}$)

There is, however, a basic property of Re that is not captured by an analysis where it contributes only singular features to the Op-variable construct. My contention is that this property is the relational property of Re, which participates in word-internal compositional semantics and identifies the semantic objects that can combine with the functional construct. For example, in the case of *wh*-words, Re ensures that *wh*-words relate sets of individuals ⟨et⟩ to worlds s. Thus, in world 1, a possible answer to the question in (45) is *John*, in world 2, it could be *John and Mary*, in world 3, it could be *Lucy, John*, and *Julie*, and so on.

(45) Who came in?
     What x | x a human, x came in

I proposed above that Re relates two semantic types located in its specifier and complement positions, and given the Distinctiveness Condition, these types must be distinct. I represent this asymmetric relation with the type neutral variable τ, taken as an interpretable feature. The difference between small (ordinary) τ and big (boldface) **τ** indicates that the types are distinct (see 46)).

(46)

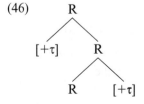

Thus, the restrictor of a *wh*-word such as *who* has a [+human] feature and it relates two distinct semantic types, say, ⟨et⟩ (i.e., sets of individuals) and s (i.e., worlds), which is in fact very close to the meaning of *who*. This relation between two distinct semantic types holds for all the members of the *wh*-paradigm.

Complementizers also relate two semantic types, possibly ⟨st⟩ and e, as mentioned previously.[15] Furthermore, the complementizer *that* occurs with tensed propositions, and the infinitival complementizer *to* occurs with nontensed propositions (see (47), (48)). I take the semantic feature [+time] to be associated to the head of the Re layer of the complementizer *that*, and the semantic feature [−time] to be associated to the head of the Re layer of the complementizer *to*.

(47) a. I think that winter is nice.
     b. I suspect that it will snow.
     c. I know that snow is white.

(48) a. I want to go.
     b. I prefer to leave.
     c. I expect to be on time.

This proposal extends itself naturally to the lower layer of *th*-words. The restrictor of the variable of D operators also relates different semantic types, which could very well be ⟨et⟩ and s—that is, sets of individuals to worlds (see (49)). In fact, a definite determiner singles out an individual as a salient part of a domain of interpretation (see Heim and Kratzer 1998).

(49) The cat is on the mat.
     $\exists x \mid x$ is a cat, x is on the mat

The semantic difference between the definite determiner, the expletive determiner, and the demonstrative rests on the semantic features of the head Re. Consider the following:

(50) a. This cat is on the wrong mat.
     b. What the hell is this?
     c. This cat, that cat, those cats, and these cats have to go.

The definite and the demonstrative determiners single out a set of individuals located in worlds, but this is not the case for the expletive determiner. For example, in (50a, c) *cat* is located in some world, whereas this is not the case for *hell* in (50b). The definite determiner differs from the expletive determiner in other languages, including French, in expressions such as *Jean a levé la main* 'John raised his hand', discussed by Vergnaud and Zubizarreta (1992). I take these determiners to differ with respect to the value of the [±Loc] feature of Re. Determiners exhibit differences regarding the localization of the set of individuals in a world. While the definite determiner singles out a set of individuals located in a world of interpretation, the expletive determiner does not. Thus, these two sorts of determiners differ with respect to the feature [±loc]. Moreover, demonstratives differ from the other determiners with respect to the [±proxi(mate)] feature. Assuming the adverb *here* is [+proxi] whereas the adverb *there* is [−proxi], the difference in acceptability of the DPs in (51) is attributed to the presence of the feature [±proxi] on the head of the Re layer of the demonstratives.

(51) a.   I want this cat here.
     b. #I want that cat here.
     c. #I want this cat there.
     d.   I want that cat there.

I take the head of the Re layer of determiners and demonstratives to be the locus of the [±loc] and the [±proxi] features. As it is the case for the other functional words, Re relates different semantic types—for example, sets of individuals ⟨et⟩ and worlds s. Thus, the differences between the functional words are attributed to the features of the operators in conjunction with the features of the restricted variable it binds.

In my view, D and Q operators have a basic morphological structure and differ only in feature specifications. This structure includes semantic types in terms of interpretable features that participate in the derivation of the meaning of morphological expressions on the basis of the meaning of their parts.

6.5   Derived Op-Shells for *wh*- and *th*-Words

The Op-Shell covers the morphological properties of [±Q] elements, including question words and complementizers, and [±D] elements, including definite, indefinite, and expletive determiners, demonstratives, and pronouns, which have the same asymmetric form.

(52) *wh*-words

$[_{+wh}$ OP$_{+Q}$ X$_{+wh}$ $[_{Re}$ $+\tau$ $[_{Re}$ Re$_{+HUM}$ $+\tau]]]$ (*who*)

$[_{+wh}$ OP$_{+Q}$ X$_{+wh}$ $[_{Re}$ $+\tau$ $[_{Re}$ Re$_{-HUM}$ $+\tau]]]$ (*what*)

$[_{+wh}$ OP$_{+Q}$ X$_{+wh}$ $[_{Re}$ $+\tau$ $[_{Re}$ Re$_{+PLACE}$ $+\tau]]]$ (*where*)

$[_{+wh}$ OP$_{+Q}$ X$_{+wh}$ $[_{Re}$ $+\tau$ $[_{Re}$ Re$_{+TIME}$ $+\tau]]]$ (*when*)

[+wh OP+Q X+wh [Re +τ [Re Re+MAN +τ]]] (*how*)

[+wh OP+Q X+wh [Re +τ [Re Re+RA   +τ]]] (*why*)

(53) Complementizers

[−wh OP−wh X−wh [Re +τ [Re Re+TIME +τ]]] (*that*)

[−wh OP−wh X−wh [Re +τ [Re Re−TIME +τ]]] (*to* infinitive)

(54) Determiners

[+th OP+D X+th [Re +τ [Re Re+LOC   +τ]]] (*the*, definite)

[−th OP−D X−th [Re +τ [Re Re−LOC   +τ]]] (*the*, expletive)

(55) Demonstratives

[+th OP+D X+th [Re +τ [Re Re+PROXI +τ]]] (*this*)

[+th OP+D X+th [Re +τ [Re Re−PROXI +τ]]] (*that*)

The theory provides a unified analysis of the feature structure of ±*wh*-words and ±*th*-words in terms of the asymmetric relations of the Op-Shell.

6.6 Summary

The bipartite structure of a functional word and the irreversibility of its parts is a consequence of the core property of morphological relations, which provides support for Asymmetry Theory. The morphological structure of the Op-Shell parallels the syntactic structure of the Op-variable relation, because they are both based on asymmetric relations; they differ, however, with respect to their derivations. Functional constructs exhibit regularities of form and interpretation. I have proposed that Q and D operators include operator-variable-restrictor relations. Assuming that their parts relate distinct semantic types, it is possible to develop a calculus determining how the meaning of functional words is derived from the meaning of their parts.

Languages vary with respect to the legibility of the parts of the Op-Shell at PF, the choice of the adjunct strategy for the purpose/reason *wh*-words, and the choice of deriving functional words in D$_S$ or in D$_M$. However, the asymmetric relation requiring the operator-variable relation to precede the relation headed by the restrictor in Q and D operators holds crosslinguistically, independently of whether a case morpheme occurs at the right periphery of the constructs, as is the case in Russian and in Hungarian, or whether a vowel occurs in the initial position, as in Yekhee. Notwithstanding the variation, it is thus possible to provide a unified analysis for the functional words based on the morphological asymmetric relations.

Chapter 7
Asymmetry at the Interfaces

The expressions generated by the language faculty must be legible at the interfaces. Hence the central question raised by the Minimalist Program is: What conditions must language satisfy in order to be usable by the external systems? The strongest minimalist thesis is that language is the optimal solution to such conditions. Chomsky (2001) suggests that the Uniformity and the Inclusiveness Conditions are two conditions consistent with the idea that the language faculty is an optimal solution to minimal language design specifications. According to the Uniformity Condition, languages are uniform, variation being restricted to detectable properties of utterances. The Inclusiveness Condition requires that no new elements, such as features, traces, and indices, be introduced in the course of computation. These conditions restrict the properties of the operations and representations of the grammar.

In this chapter, I consider the legibility of scope and linear precedence relations from a minimalist perspective, including the Legibility Condition of Asymmetry Theory, according to which only interpretable elements in asymmetric relations are optimally legible by the external systems (see chapter 2). I assume that scope is uniformly expressed in terms of the sister-containment relation, such that a scope-bearing element sister-contains the constituent it scopes over at LF (May and Higginbotham 1981; Higginbotham 1985; Aoun and Li 1993, 2003; Reinhart 2000). I also adopt Fox's (2000) Economy approach to scope relations, mainly that QR (quantifier raising) applies only when there is scope ambiguity. Hence, I posit the following:

(1) At LF, scope relations must be legible.

(2) At PF, linear precedence relations must be legible.

I take the above to hold in word structure as well as in phrasal syntax and I focus on word-internal scope and linear precedence relations.

Word-internal operators, such as bare quantifiers and negation, scope over (sister-contain) the other elements of the structure of which they are part. Thus, in *no one*, *no* scopes over *one*, and *one* does not scope over *no*. Affixal scope, however, is not always consonant with the linear precedence relations, at least in languages like English. Thus, in constructs such as *readability*, the rightmost affix scopes over the preceding one. I take word-internal linear precedence and scope to be dissociated.

The main issue in this chapter with respect to LF is to derive word-internal scope relations while preserving the minimalist legibility conditions, given Asymmetry Theory. Ideally, there should be uniformity across languages with respect to word-internal scope. The main issue with respect to PF is how to derive a linear order of morphemes given the Universal Base Hypothesis. Because affixes can only be heads or specifiers of their minimal trees and since the affixes sister-contain the elements of the root trees, all affixes precede roots before linearization.

This chapter is organized as follows. First, I consider word-internal scope relations. I show that given the operations of M, the scope relations can be derived straightforwardly. Second, I show how the mirror operation Flip, defined in chapter 2, derives the linear order of the constituents in the domains transferred from D_M to D_Φ. I also consider some cases where this operation applies to the domains transferred from D_S to D_Φ.

7.1   Strict Scope

7.1.1   Word-Internal Scope-Taking Elements

Functional words such as *nobody, everybody, somebody, anybody, no one, everyone, someone, anyone*, and *something* are revealing with respect to word-internal scope. These constructs have the following properties. First, they are composed of two separable constituents (e.g., *no* and *body*, *any* and *one*, *some* and *thing*, and so on). Second, the inverse order of the constituents gives rise to gibberish: **oneany, *oneevery, *onesome*. Third, the first constituent scopes over the second. For example, in *no one*, negation scopes over the indefinite, and not the other way around (see (3)). Because scope is expressed under sister-containment, *no* sister-contains *one*.

(3) a.   No one knows Gödel's theorem.
    b.   ≠Someone does not know Gödel's theorem.

In Asymmetry Theory, functional words are derived by the application of M-Shift to minimal trees. M-Link applies to the derived Op-Shell and, in the case at hand, the variable (Fx) in the upper layer of the Shell is linked to its Re(strictor) in the lower layer, and the Op(erator) is linked to the restricted variable in the upper layer. In an Op-Shell, the Op sister-contains the other constituents, and scopes over them (see (4)).

(4) a. $[_{Fx}$ Op $[_{Fx}$ Fx α]]
    b. $[_{Re}$ β $[_{Re}$ Re δ]]
    c. $[_{Fx}$ Op Fx $[_{Re}$ β Re δ]]   M-Shift ⟨Fx, Re⟩
    d. $[_{Fx}$ Op Fx $[_{Re}$ β Re δ]]   M-Link ⟨Fx, Re⟩
    e. $[_{Fx}$ Op Fx $[_{Re}$ β Re δ]]   M-Link ⟨Op, Fx⟩

Scope relations cannot be altered in functional words. I will refer to this property as *Strict Scope* and define it as follows.

(5) *Strict Scope*
    In an M-Shell including two scope-taking elements, A and B,
    if A sister-contains B, A scopes over B, and
    if A scopes over B, A sister-contains B.

Strict Scope can be seen as a consequence of the fact that an M-Shell constitutes a unit of the morphological computation, parallel to the notion of phase of Chomsky 2001. An M-Shell is strictly impenetrable; uninterpretable feature checking does not lead to movement, as discussed in chapter 3. No rule, including covert movement rules altering scope properties, such as QR, may affect its internal structure.

As expected, Strict Scope holds in D_M but not in D_S. In a sentence containing two quantifiers, scope ambiguity may arise and a given quantifier may have narrow or wide scope. This is illustrated in (6) to (8).

(6) Every student in this room knows one language.

(7) a. Every student knows one language.
    b. There is one language that every student knows.

(8) a. [every student x [one language y [x knows y]]]
    b. [one language y [every student x [x knows y]]]

Scope ambiguity may not arise in morphological objects. Thus, *n*-words, such as *nobody*, are analyzed either as indefinites or as negative polarity items (Ladusaw 1992, 1994; Giannakidou 2000). In some languages, including Italian and Spanish, they can occur with a negative head if they are postverbal, as seen in example (9a, b) from Italian.

In other languages, including Quebec French (QFr), they may occur pre-verbally or postverbally with a negative head, as the examples in (9c, d) illustrate.

(9) a. Gianni *(non) ha   visto *nessuno*.   (It)
       Gianni   NOT have seen nobody
       'Gianni did not see anybody.'

   b. *Nessuno* *non ha   visto Gianni.
      Nobody   NOT have seen Gianni
      'Nobody did not see Gianni.'

   c. Jean n'a (pas)   vu *personne*.   (Fr)
      Jean Neg have not seen *n*-word
      'Jean did not see anybody.'

   d. *(Pas) personne* n'est   (pas) venu.   (QFr)
      Neg   nobody   Neg has (not) come
      'Nobody came.'

An *n*-word itself, however, includes negation and an indefinite, and negation always precedes the indefinite; see (10) and (11).

(10) Nessuno è venuto.   (It)
     'Nobody came.'

(11) *Uno ne(ss) è venuto.   (It)
     'One no came.'

Given Strict Scope, no scope ambiguity is possible in an *n*-word. NEG scopes over the indefinite. Consider (12), where $\approx$ indicates a likely paraphrase and $\neq$ an impossible one.

(12) a. He saw nothing.
     b. $\approx$There is no thing that he saw.
     c. $\neq$There is a thing that he did not see.

Functional words, including a quantifier or negation and a *wh*-word, are not different with respect to Strict Scope. In (13), *everywhere* includes the universal quantifier, *somewhere* in (14) includes the existential quantifier, and *nowhere* in (15) includes negation. The ordering within these constructs is strict; the operator and the *wh*- cannot be reordered (e.g., *wherevery*, *wheresome*, *whereno*). As expected, there is no scope ambiguity in these constructs, as shown in (16), which is parallel to (12).[1]

(13) They are everywhere.

(14) It is somewhere.

(15) You can find it nowhere.

(16) a. It is nowhere.
b. ≈There is no place where it is.
c. ≠There is a place where it is not.

Thus, the negation scopes over the indefinite in (16a), as in (16b), whereas the inverse scope interpretation, where the indefinite has wide scope over the negation, as in (16c), is not a possible paraphrase of (16a).

The scope relations follow from the position of the constituents of the Op-Shell. In (17), the Op in D_2 scopes over the features of the operator in D_1.

(17) $[_{Op+D}$ every w $[_{Opwh}$ wh- x_{wh} $[_{Re}$ β here γ]]]

In the case of *everyone*, *every* precedes *one* and scopes over *one*; likewise in the case of *n*-words, like *no one*, the negation *no* precedes and scopes over the indefinite *one*.[2]

Scope is rigid in D_M, in contrast to D_S where, in some cases, an operator may have narrow or wide scope. Strict Scope follows from the strong impenetrability of morphological domains, which is not observed in syntactic domains. The facts above provide evidence for the strict asymmetry of morphological relations, and the limits it imposes on possible word-internal scope interpretations at LF.

7.1.2 Affixes, Head, and Scope

If an affix is a head, its features determine the properties of the projection of which it is part. This holds for the formal as well as semantic features. Because a morphological object may contain more than one affix, the relative position of an affix may determine whether it is a head, and whether it scopes over the other constituents (see (18)).

(18) a. form -al -ize
b. form -al -ize -able
c. form -al -ize -able -ity

According to Williams's (1981a) Right Hand Rule, the head of a word order is its rightmost constituent. According to Pesetsky (1985), the scope of affixes is derived by word-internal application of QR. The question is whether the notions of head of a word and affixal scope are related. Can affixal scope be derived by the notion of head of a word based on the linear ordering of affixes? One possibility would be to define affixal scope in terms of an inverse head relation. In a morphological object including more than one affix, the scope of an affix with respect to the others would then be determined by its position in the inverse ordering of the affixes (see (19) and (20)).

(19) a. root > af_1 > af_2 > af_3 linear order at PF
     b. af_3 > af_2 > af_1 > root   affixal scope at LF

(20) a. read > -able > -ity   linear order at PF
     b. -ity > -able > read   affixal scope at LF

With *readability*, the rightmost affix *-ity* is the head of the word and scopes over the other affixes to its left (see (20)). However, affixal scope cannot be an inverse head relation, because constituents that are analyzed as nonheads by the RHR may also affect scope relations. Consider the example in (21a), where the negative (NEG) affix *un-* precedes the modal (MOD) affix *-able*. In the likely ($\approx$) paraphrase (21b), the negation precedes the modal (NEG > MOD), whereas this is not the case in the impossible ($\neq$) paraphrase (21c).

(21) a.   This sentence is unreadable.
     b. $\approx$It is not possible to read this sentence.
     c. $\neq$It is possible not to read this sentence.

Thus, affixal scope cannot be defined in terms of the inverse head relation, given the RHR, according to which *-able* is the head of *unreadable*. Moreover, it cannot be defined in terms of an inverse head relation on the basis of Di Sciullo and William's (1987) relativized notion of head of where *un-* would also be a head, since *-able* would still wrongly scope over *un-* at LF (see (22)).

(22) a.   un- > read > -able   linear order at PF
     b.   un- > able- > read   affixal scope at LF
     c. $\neq$MOD > NEG > read

If there is a relation between headedness and scope in word structure, a definition of head based on linear precedence relations is not appropriate.

If affixal scope cannot be equated with a notion of inverse head based on linear precedence relations, and that movement, including LF movement such as QR, is not available in D_M, how can it be derived? In Asymmetry Theory, affixal scope follows from the application of M-Shift. This operation applies to minimal trees under asymmetric selection and derives the scope relation between the affixes. Given the geometry of the M-Shell, an affix scopes over the constituents it sister-contains. For example, *unreadable* in (23), where NEG (spelled out by *un-*) scopes over MOD (spelled out by *-able*), is derived by the recursive application of M-Shift. Likewise in (24), PROPERTY (spelled out by *-ity*) scopes over NEG. The examples in (25) and (26) are similar.

(23) [un- F [[−A] -able [[+A] read [+A]]]]   (unreadable)

(24) [[+R] -ity [un- F [[−A] -able [[+A] read [+A]]]]]   (unreadability)

(25) [re- F [[−A] -able [[+A] produce [+A]]]]   (reproducible)

(26) [[+R] -ity [re- F [[−A] -able [[+A] produce [+A]]]]]
     (reproducibility)

Affixal scope is based on the unalterable sister-contain relation derived in D_M. It can be identified on the basis of the configurational definition of head$_F$, proposed in chapter 3. Affixal scope is strict and is legible at LF on the basis of the asymmetric sister-contain relation. The precedence relations, including the linear order of affixes, are legible only at PF, as discussed below.

7.2   Linear Order

7.2.1   Head Movement

Head movement has been proposed to derive the head adjacency and linear order of inflectional affixes in the course of the syntactic derivation (Chomsky 1981, 1986; Baker 1988; Travis 1984). According to this operation, a head syntactically adjoins to a superior head. Thus V-to-I, for example, ensures the adjacency between V and I (Pollock 1989), as well as the linear order of the morphemes. Head movement is generally assumed to be a leftward movement—that is, a head adjoins to the left of its target (Kayne 1994). Head movement, like XP movement, leaves a trace or a copy of the displaced element and the relation between the trace and the moved head is subject to locality, given the Head Movement Constraint.

(27) *Head Movement Constraint*
     An X^0 may only move into the Y^0 that properly governs it.
     (Travis 1984, 131)

The result of head movement is illustrated in (28), where the head Y is adjoined to the left of the head X, leaving a trace (in the trace theory of movement) or a copy (in the copy theory of movement), of the moved head in its source position.

(28) a.

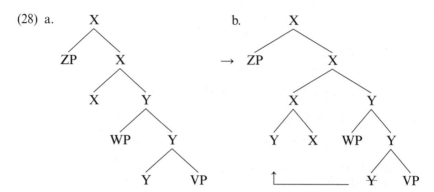

Head movement has been shown to be problematic in more than one way. Di Sciullo and Williams (1987) have pointed out some theoretical and empirical problems with this operation. More recently, the role of this operation in syntax, as well as the locality of the HMC, have been questioned. It has been observed that movement duplicates XP movement for feature checking and patterns with A-movement regarding the locality conditions. Most cases of head movement have been proposed to be re-analyzed as remnant phrasal movement with large-scale pied-piping (see among other works Kayne 2000; Koopman and Szabolcsi 2000; Mahajan 2000).

Another motivation to dispense with head movement in narrow syntax is that iterative head movement increases the computational load and runs counter to the Minimalist Program, where computational complexity counts. Furthermore, head movement, and more generally sister adjunction, do not expand a tree, and thus contravene the Extension Condition. Chomsky (1998, 1999, 2001) suggests that head movement is restricted to morphophonology.[3]

Interestingly in Asymmetry Theory, the linearization of morphological domains cannot be the result of head movement, whether syntactic or morphophonological. Movement is not part of the operations of D_M; thus head movement is not either. Head movement creates points of symmetry, which are not found in D_M (see chapter 1).

Consider the set of ordered pairs in (29a) and (29b), which describes the relations between the terminal categories in the trees in (29a) and (29b) respectively. The relation in (29a) is asymmetric. There are no two pairs with the same members that occur in the reverse order, and there is no pair in which members are identical. However, the relation in (29b), describing the result of the application of head movement to (29a), is symmetric.

(29) a. {⟨ZP, X⟩, ⟨X, WP⟩, ⟨WP, Y⟩, ⟨Y, VP⟩, ⟨ZP, WP⟩,
⟨WP, VP⟩, ⟨X, Y⟩, ⟨X, VP⟩}
   b. {⟨ZP, Y⟩, **⟨Y, X⟩**, ⟨X, WP⟩, ⟨WP, Y̶⟩, ⟨Y̶, VP⟩, ⟨ZP, X⟩,
⟨X, Y̶⟩, ⟨WP, VP⟩, ⟨X, VP⟩, **⟨Y, Y̶⟩**}

Given Asymmetry Theory, head movement is not part of D_Φ either, since it would create points of symmetry in the phonological derivation that would have to be eliminated by further movement in order to satisfy the Legibility Condition, defined in chapter 2, according to which only interpretable features in asymmetric relations are interpreted optimally by the external systems. Head movement increases the computational load of the grammar, whether it applies in narrow syntax or in the phonological derivation.

But if head movement is not available in the syntax or the phonology or the morphology, how then is linearization obtained in a morphological expression? I will explore the hypothesis that the linear order of morphemes in morphological objects is an effect of an operation that applies in D_Φ and that derives the mirror image of a minimal tree under certain conditions. This operation helps reduce the computational complexity at the PF interface as well as deriving the linear order of the morphological constituents, given language-specific morphophonological properties.

7.2.2 Flip

I propose that the linear order of affixes is derived in D_Φ by an operation that violates neither the Inclusiveness nor the Extension Conditions and that does not introduce symmetry in derivation.

Given Asymmetry Theory, the Universal Base Hypothesis holds in D_M, and the output of D_M does not yield the linear precedence relations between morphological constituents. Morphological domains are transferred from D_M to D_Φ in order to reach the PF interface where linear order must be legible by the sensorimotor system. I propose to derive the linear order of the morphological constituents by deriving the mirror image of the configurations (minimal trees) of which they are part. Thus in (30a), X and Y are part of two configurations; the mirror image of the configuration to which they belong derives a configuration in (30c) where Y precedes X.

(30) a.

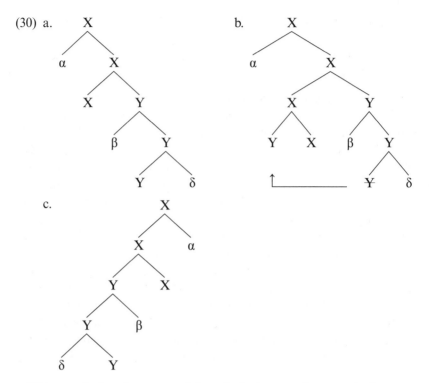

This reordering does not violate Inclusiveness, because it does not introduce supplementary elements in the derivation, such as traces contrary to a head-movement derivation. Thus, from a minimalist viewpoint, an operation that does not violate the Inclusiveness Condition is preferable to one that does.

The question arises, however, whether a mirror operation violates the Extension Condition. It does not if this condition is a prohibition against downward expansion of a node. In fact, this operation satisfies the essential intuition behind the Extension Condition. Given that it applies to a structure that has not yet had precedence relations interpreted, there is a clear sense in which it adds structure to a tree, since adding information about precedence is essentially just adding structure.[4]

The mirror operation applies to a minimal tree under certain conditions. In languages such as English, affixes heading their minimal tree (e.g., predicate affixes and operator-bound affixes) are located in the right periphery of the word, whereas affixes that sit in the specifier of their minimal tree (e.g., modifier affixes and quantificational affixes) are located in the left periphery of the word. In D_M, the mirror operation applies only when the specifier of a minimal tree has no phonological features. I assume that adjacency is obtained between two heads if there is no intermediate PF visible constituent. Thus, in (30c), Y and X are adjacent. Crucially, the mirror operation does not generate points of symmetry in D_Φ because it applies to a tree that has not yet had precedence relations interpreted. Moreover, given the parallel architecture of Asymmetry Theory, semantic relations are read at LF, and linear precedence is legible at PF. The mirror operation applying in D_Φ does not introduce symmetry in D_M because D_Φ and D_M are two separate planes of the computational space. They are not part of the same derivational path.

   Thus, in expressing the relations between the terminal elements in the structure in (30a) in terms of sets of ordered pairs (see (31a)), it can be observed in (31b) that head movement introduces symmetry in the derivation. This is not the case for the mirror operation (see (31c)). There are no two ordered pairs in (31c) where the members appear in an inverse order. This is the case, however, for the set in (31b).

(31) a. $\{\langle \alpha, X\rangle, \langle X, \beta\rangle, \langle \beta, Y\rangle, \langle Y, \delta\rangle, \langle \alpha, \beta\rangle, \langle \beta, \delta\rangle, \langle X, Y\rangle,$
         $\langle X, \delta\rangle\}$

     b. $\{\langle \alpha, Y\rangle, \mathbf{\langle Y, X\rangle}, \langle X, \beta\rangle, \langle \beta, Y\rangle, \langle Y, \delta\rangle, \langle \alpha, X\rangle, \mathbf{\langle X, Y\rangle},$
         $\langle \beta, \delta\rangle, \langle X, \delta\rangle, \mathbf{\langle Y, \cancel{Y}\rangle}\}$

     c. $\{\langle Y, \alpha\rangle, \langle \delta, \beta\rangle, \langle \beta, X\rangle, \langle X, \delta\rangle, \langle Y, \beta\rangle, \langle Y, \alpha\rangle, \langle Y, X\rangle,$
         $\langle \delta, X\rangle\}$

   If head movement is not an option, remnant movement could be used to derive the linear ordering of morphological elements. In a remnant analysis of *readable*, for example, assuming the Universal Base Hypothesis, requiring *-able* to precede its root complement *read*, a first movement of *-able* to a higher functional projection would be followed by a subsequent head movement of *read* to a superordinate head position. In the resulting structure, which yields the correct linear order, the affix follows the root (see (32)).

(32)

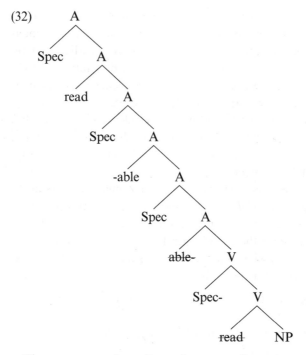

There are a number of questions regarding a remnant-movement derivation of word structure. First, under feature-driven movement, it is not clear what non–ad hoc feature would force remnant movement of *read* in (32). Second, this movement is still head movement. Third, a remnant-movement analysis could be seen as being "cheaper" than a mirror operation, since it does not require an additional operation for linearization, assuming that head movement is available in the grammar. However, remnant movement is more costly than a mirror operation in terms of the number of steps in the derivation. Thus, a mirror operation is preferable to remnant movement on minimalist grounds.[5]

The structural relations derived by the grammar must meet the conditions imposed by the external systems to be optimally legible. I postulate the existence of an operation that applies in D_Φ and derives the mirror image of a minimal tree; I call this operation *Flip*.[6] The generic form of this operation, introduced in chapter 2, is repeated in (33). The morphological and syntactic instantiations of this operation are in (34) and (35). The effects of these operations are illustrated in (36) and (37) respectively.

(33) Flip (*T*)

Given a minimal tree *T*, Flip (*T*) is the tree obtained by creating a mirror image of *T*.

(34) M-Flip (*T*)

Given a minimal tree *T* such that the Spec of *T* has no PF features, M-Flip (*T*) is the tree obtained by creating the mirror image of *T*.

(35) S-Flip (*T*)

Given a minimal tree *T* such that the Spec of *T* has PF features, S-Flip (*T*) is the tree obtained by creating the mirror image of the Spec of *T*.

(36) a.   b.

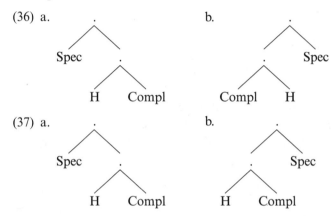

(37) a.   b.

Flip shares with the core operations of Asymmetry Theory the unifying property of subsuming more specific operations, as discussed below. Moreover, it brings additional support to the notion of minimal tree, and more generally to the asymmetry of the relations generated by the grammar.

7.3 Mirror Structures

Given the architecture of the grammar, the generic operations of grammar apply under different conditions in D_S and in D_M. Consequently, it is expected that the application of Flip will differ according to whether it applies to the outcome of D_M or D_S. In section 7.3.1, I illustrate the application of Flip to the outcome of D_M, and in section 7.5.2, I illustrate the application of Flip to the outcome of D_S.

7.3.1 No PF Features in Spec

M-Shift associates two minimal trees, under asymmetric selection, and M-Link ensures feature checking under Agree. The result of M-Shift and M-Link is a configuration where an affix precedes and sister-contains the root. M-Flip must apply to a minimal tree only when its specifier has no

PF features. This operation derives the linear order of the morphological constituents, as illustrated in (38) with *readable*.

(38) a.

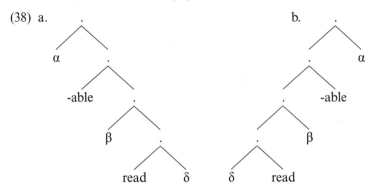

Thus, the PF features of *read* will precede the PF features of *-able* at the PF interface, avoiding the problems associated with a head-movement derivation (see (39)). In particular, M-Flip does not introduce points of symmetry in D_Φ.

(39)

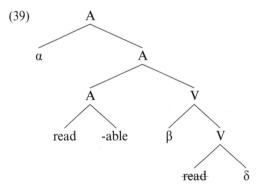

Thus, the linear order of the morphemes in morphological objects is derived by M-Flip, yielding a mirror image of a minimal tree at the PF interface, only when the specifier of that tree has no legible PF features.

7.3.2 PF Features in Spec

M-Flip does not apply to a minimal tree with legible PF features in the specifier position. There are two cases where this situation obtains. The first one is the case of affixal modifiers, which are generated in the specifier of their minimal tree. M-Flip does not apply to the upper layer of (40a), because the specifier of the F-tree has PF features. See also (41).

(40) a.   b.

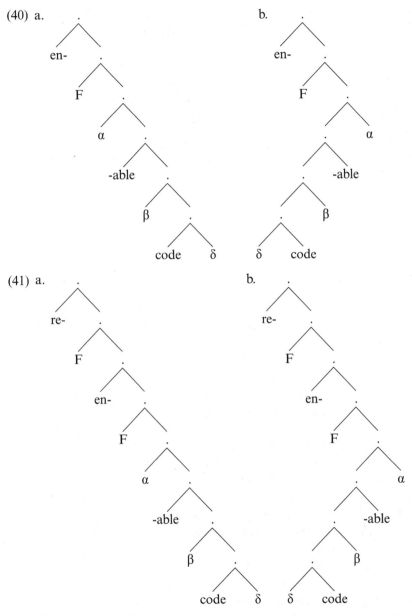

(41) a.   b.

M-Flip derives the linear order of the morphological constituents without additional stipulation. This would not be the case, however, for head
movement. Rightward or leftward head adjunction would have to be
sensitive to descriptive notions such as prefixes or suffixes. Descriptive

notions such as these are not primitives of the grammar, according to Asymmetry Theory. The position of a morphological type of affix is not stipulated but follows from the operations of the grammar.

The second case of nonapplication of M-Flip is the upper layer of the Op-Shell, where the specifier is the locus of Op affixes, such as the *wh*- and the *th*-affixes. Because the specifier of the minimal tree including operator affixes is PF legible, it is not subject to M-Flip (see (42)).

(42) a.   b.

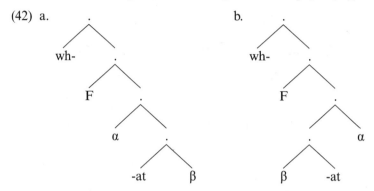

M-Flip does not apply to the upper layer of Op-Shells, including quantifiers (e.g., *someone, everyone*) or quantifier-like morphemes (e.g., *polyedron, omni-patrician, multi-directional, omni-directional*) or numeral-like morphemes (e.g., *bi-cycle, tri-cycle, mid-term, quarter-term, semi-colon; semi-grammatical, quadri-phonic, mono-cyclic*). Because M-Flip applies only when the specifier of a minimal tree has no PF features, it does not apply to constructs including quantifier-like affixes, since these affixes occupy the specifier position of their minimal tree. Assuming that in these constructs, the quantifier sister-contains the other constituent, a derivation with head movement would require that the root be adjoined to the right of the affix, and a derivation with remnant movement would require additional derivational steps to derive the linear order of the constituents. Thus, head movement or remnant movement is not extendable to derivational morphology without further stipulations, and they add complexity to the derivations.

7.4   Apparent Counterevidence

There are cases where the generalization expressed by M-Flip seems to fail. One such case involves the comparative affix *-er* and the superlative affix *-est* (e.g., *smarter, smartest*). In English, these affixes are in the right periphery of the morphological object. This should not be the case because these affixes have operator properties, and according to Asymmetry Theory, they would occupy the specifier position of their minimal tree and thus not be subject to M-Flip.

However, Corver (1997) argues, with some plausibility, that the comparative -er along with words such as *more, less, enough* are Q-heads and that they are not of the same syntactic category as elements such as *so, as, how(ever), too,* which are "degree heads." Adopting Cover's intuition, I point out that even though the comparative and superlative affixes are quantifier-like items, they are also predicate affixes, because they affect the argument structure of a root by adding an argument to its argument structure, given argument-structure flexibility (see (43), (44)).

(43) a. John is tall (*than Paul).
     b. John is taller (than Paul).

(44) a. Mary is tall (*of all).
     b. Mary is the tallest (of all).

The fact that comparative and superlative affixes follow the root is thus only an apparent counterexample to our generalization. Because the comparative suffix does affect the argument structure of the root, we have a reason to generate them in head position. From there, M-Flip applies to the minimal tree headed by a comparative or a superlative, and derives a mirror image of that tree, in which the affix follows the root (see (45)).

(45) a.   b.

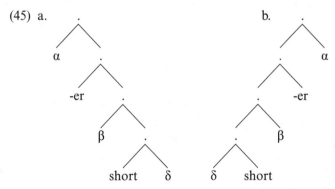

Like the comparative and superlative affixes, the inflectional affixes head their minimal trees. Thus, they are also subject to M-Flip in languages such as English. Consequently, they follow the root at PF. Crosslinguistic variation with respect to the position of inflectional and derivational affixes is discussed in chapter 8.

7.5   Extensions

7.5.1   Compounds

M-Flip also applies in the derivation of compounds in languages in which compounds are derived in D_M (see chapter 2). For example, in English, M-Flip applies in the derivation of deverbal compounds. In the theory developed here, a deverbal compound includes a predicate-argument structure, where the internal argument of the root follows that root and the affixal head precedes the predicate-argument complex (see (46a)). Because there is no specifier with PF legible features in the configuration, M-Flip applies in D_Φ to every minimal tree, deriving its mirror image. Consequently, the linear order of the constituents of the deverbal compounds is obtained at PF (see (46b)).

(46) a.

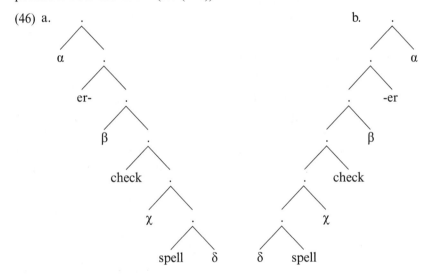

M-Flip is also in play at PF for linearization in compounds, when the conditions for its application are met. Root compounds include modification relations, and M-Flip does not apply to a minimal tree with PF features in the specifier position, as is the case for the F tree in (47).

(47) a.   b.

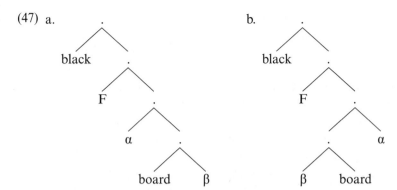

M-Flip applies to the derivation of deverbal compounds in the grammar of the languages in which compounds are derived in D_M, as is the
case for modern Greek, the Slavic languages, and English. This operation
does not apply in the derivation of deverbal compounds in Romance languages and in African languages such as Yekhee, where compounds are
derived in D_S (see Di Sciullo 2004).

7.5.2   XP Modifiers

S-Flip applies to a minimal tree that has been transferred from D_S to D_Φ
only when the specifier of the minimal tree has PF features. This is the
case for modification structures such as sentential adverbs. The examples
in (48) illustrate the fact that the adverbs may occur at either periphery of
a proposition.

(48) a. Eventually, John will arrive.
      b. John will arrive eventually.
      c. Perspicuously, Mary smiled.
      d. Mary smiled perspicuously.

Assuming that modifiers are generated in the specifier of functional
categories (see Cinque 1999), S-Flip derives the order of the adverbial to
the right (see (49)).

(49) a.   FP   b.   FP

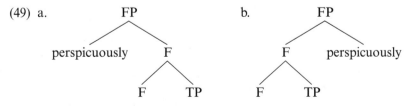

S-Flip is more restricted than the Transportability Convention proposed by Keyser (1968), which allowed for a [+transportable] constituent,

for example an adverb, to occupy any position in a derived tree, preserving the sister relationships with all the other nodes in the tree. The Transportability Convention was formulated in a framework allowing *n*-ary branching, and it required that adverbs maintain their sisterhood relations. Flip applies to functional projections à la Cinque. The projections are restricted to binary branching structures, and each functional head has distinct F features. S-Flip is more restricted that the Transportability Convention because it only sanctions the transportability of an adverb to its mirror-image position.

Thus, assuming that adverbs are generated in the specifier of functional projections—that is, to the left of the verbal projection—their ordering at the right periphery of a sentence is derived by S-Flip. The examples in (50) present a similar situation with time and place PP modifiers.

(50) a. John reads in the morning.
b. Mary swims at noon.
c. John sleeps in his office.
d. Paul walked to the store.

Given that, in English, V does not raise to T and that PP modifiers are generated in the specifier of a functional projection, and thus precede the vP (see (51a)), their position to the right of the vP is derived in D$_\Phi$ by the application of S-Flip to that functional projection (see (51b))

(51) a.

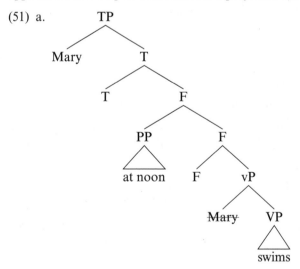

b.

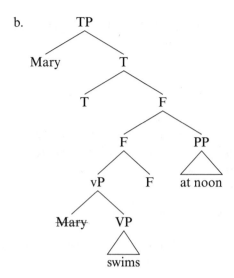

Interestingly, in structures such as (52) S-Flip is obligatory, whereas in structure such as (53) S-Flip is optional.

(52) a. *Mary at noon swims. / Mary swims at noon.
     b. *Jane in the park walks. / Jane walks in the park.

(53) a. Mary often swims. / Mary swims often.
     b. Jane rarely runs. / Jane runs rarely.

(54) a. *Mary more often swims. / Mary swims more often.
     b. *Jane very rarely runs. / Jane runs very rarely.

S-Flip must apply to a minimal tree when the constituent in the specifier position is "heavy." This can be seen by comparing (53) and (54). In (53) the bare adverb may precede or follow the VP, whereas in (54) a complex adverbial structure must follow the VP. Similar facts obtain in French with adjectival modification (see (55)–(58)).

(55) a. un homme [fier] / un [fier] homme   (Fr)
        a man proud / a proud man
     b. un homme [fier de ses enfants] / *un [fier de ses enfants] homme
        a man proud of his children / a proud of his children man

(56) a. une nouvelle [importante] / une [importante] nouvelle   (Fp)
        a news important / an important news
     b. une [très importante] nouvelle / une nouvelle [très importante]
        a very important news / a news very important

c. une nouvelle [très importante pour les étudiants] / *une [très
   importante pour les étudiants] nouvelle
   a news very important for the students / a very important for the
   students news

(57) a. une lecture très riche / une très riche lecture   (Fr)
        a reading very rich / a very rich reading
     b. une lecture très riche en idées / une très riche en idées lecture
        a reading very rich in ideas / a very rich in ideas reading
     c. une journée d'hiver très froide
        a winter day very cold

(58) a. un homme [grand] / un [grand] homme   (Fr)
        a man tall / a tall man
     b. un homme grand comme ça / *un grand comme ça homme
        a man tall like this / a tall like this man

The examples above show that S-Flip applies in D$_\Phi$ under certain conditions. It must apply when the constituent occupying the specifier position is heavy, otherwise its application is not obligatory and may depend
on Focus. M-Flip has different properties. It applies when the specifier
position has no PF features, and it is obligatory.[7] These differences
are expected in the fully parallel model of Asymmetry Theory, where the
generic operations apply differently in the derivation of morphological
and syntactic objects (see (59)).

(59)   PF legibility of Spec   Heaviness of Spec
     a. M-Flip   −   N/A
     b. S-Flip   +   +

Flip contributes to linearization at PF, where linear order is legible by
the sensorimotor system and where computational complexity must be
reduced given tractability considerations, as discussed in the next section.

7.6   Tractability

Tractability considerations require morphology to have asymmetry as its
essential property. Asymmetry minimizes the computational complexity
of grammar, thus contributing to the use of grammar by the external systems. The reduction of computational complexity is part of the legibility
conditions in the Minimalist Program. It has mainly been discussed with
respect to the application or nonapplication of the syntactic operations of
the grammar (Chomsky 2000a, 2000b, 2001). I would like to suggest that

the operations in D_Φ also contribute to the reduction of the computational complexity.

M-Flip applies in the derivation of morphological expressions for linearization. Evidence from computational analyses suggests that this interface operation is forced by bare output conditions for tractability considerations.

Given Asymmetry Theory, morphological features can be part of M-Shells in the specifier and complement positions without being associated with PF legible features, as in (60), where α, β, δ and γ have no PF legible features.

(60)

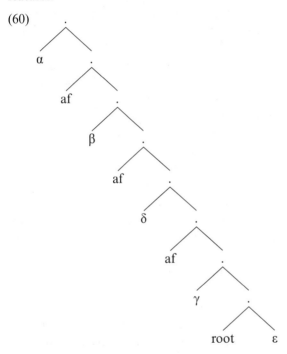

M-Shells are transferred to D_Φ; M-Flip applies to the layers of the M-Shells and helps reduce the computational complexity derived by the grammar. The computational implementations of morphosyntactic parsing reported in Di Sciullo and Fong 2001a, 2001b, show that exponential complexity arises if [Spec [Head Compl]] configurations for morphological expressions are presented at the interface with the sensorimotor system with no PF legible features in Spec. There is a substantial difference in parsing efficiency with respect to specifier-head order. In terms of an LR shift-reduce parser, placing the specifier on the right is considerably more efficient than placing it on the left.

On the basis of the results of Di Sciullo and Fong, it is possible to take linearization by specifier-head-complement reordering to be forced by tractability considerations. Computational complexity grows exponentially if specifiers without PF legible features sit to the right of their head.

Di Sciullo and Fong considered the computational consequences of varying the specifier-head-complement linear order for the LR shift-reduce parsing framework. The results show that there is a considerable difference, both in terms of the number of LR actions performed and the stack depth required to process a word like *formalize*, analyzed as *form-al-i(z)-e*. While ninety-six LR actions are required to parse *formalize* with specifiers to the left, only twenty-one LR actions are necessary to parse *formalize* with specifiers to the right. The simple explanation is that the LR machine has to be able to predict an arbitrary number of empty positions before it can shift or "read" the first item, namely, *form*. In contrast, in a situation where specifiers are generated on the right side only, the LR machine only needs to generate a single empty argument position before a shift can take place. Hence only twenty-one actions and a stack depth of two are required in this case, compared to ninety-six and a stack depth of five in *formalize*. For detailed discussion, see Di Sciullo and Fong 2001a, 2001b.

The results of the experiment also suggest that separating prefixation from suffixation gives optimal efficiency. This also bring external evidence to different affix structures in the derivation and parsing of morphological objects. This suggests that there is a difference in the tractability of affixes depending on whether they are in a head position or in the specifier position. In Asymmetry Theory, M-Flip applies to minimal trees in the first case and not in the second case.

The Legibility Condition, according to which asymmetric relations are necessary for optimal interpretation, along with the requirement that computational complexity be minimized, provides a rationale for the existence of the Flip operation. Flip is a PF operation minimizing computational complexity. Thus, asymmetry, as a property of the relations and of the operations of the grammar, helps make grammars usable by the performance systems, ensures linearization, and contributes to the reduction of the complexity of the grammar.

7.7 Summary

In this chapter, I have provided evidence to the effect that asymmetry is a property of morphological relations at the interfaces. This is expected, given the Legibility Condition.

I have shown that strict scope holds in morphological domains at the LF interface, whereas it does not hold in syntactic domains. Given the architecture of Asymmetry Theory, word-internal LF relations are dissociated from PF linear precedence relations. Word-internal scope relations are legible at LF and linear precedence relations are legible at PF. I have proposed that a mirror operation applies in the derivations to PF. Flip derives the effects of head movement and remnant movement in morphology. It also derives the effects of mechanisms proposed to account for the position of modifiers in syntax. This operation applies under different conditions in D_M and D_S, and derives linear precedence relations without increasing computational complexity. Results from computational experiments indicate that positing nonlegible PF specifiers to the right of the head significantly reduces the number of actions performed by the LR parser, as well as the stack depth required to parse complex morphological expressions.

Chapter 8

The Persistence of Asymmetry in Variation

In this chapter, I consider morphological variation and argue that it is a particular case of a more general property of grammar. I assume that variation in morphological objects is subject to the Uniformity Principle (Chomsky 2000a), as is the case for syntactic variation. I posit that asymmetry is preserved in morphological variation in the sense that asymmetric relations are required for variation and moreover that variation does not destroy asymmetry.[1] Morphological variation in the linear order of affixes and their legibility at the PF interface can then be reduced to a difference in the properties of functional features in the languages under consideration.[2] Variation under the word level shares common properties with syntactic variation, but differs in certain respects, because D_M and D_S take place in parallel planes of the computational space.

I consider two cases of variation in morphological objects. The first is the difference in the position of affixes with respect to the root. The second is the variation in the legibility of affixes at PF. I contrast Yekhee and English, in the first case, and compare the properties of spatial affixes in the verb structure of Italian and French, in the second case. I focus on the following questions: (1) Why are most affixes located to the left of the root in Yekhee while most affixes are located to the right of the root in English? (2) Why is there a difference between Italian and French in the PF legibility of affixes preceding the root in parasynthetic constructions?

The proposed analyses rely on the operations of the grammar and independent properties of the languages under consideration. They do not require additional mechanisms, or appeal to descriptive notions such as prefixes and suffixes. The differences in the position of the affixes and their legibility at the PF interface follow straightforwardly.

8.1   The Preservation Hypothesis

Linguistic data ranging from microvariations to historical changes indicate that variation is a pervasive phenomenon in grammars. However, linguistic variation is not sporadic and random, but falls within the limits imposed by the language faculty.

Chomsky (2001) suggests that the uniformity principle is a Legibility condition that contributes to make the language faculty an optimal solution to the language design. According to the uniformity principle, languages are uniform and variation is restricted to detectable properties of utterances.[3] This means that functional properties are universal, although phonetically they are manifested in various ways. Variation in the position of affixes with respect to roots and their legibility at the PF interface can also be reduced to differences in the properties of the functional features in singular grammars. I explore the view, argued for independently in Di Sciullo (forthcoming), that variation is possible because of uninterpretable feature checking.

According to Asymmetry Theory, morphological uninterpretable features are checked by M-Link applying under Agree. Furthermore, the PF legibility of the specifier of a minimal tree determines whether a mirror image of that tree is derived in D_Φ or not. Moreover, the outcome of M-Flip does not destroy the asymmetry of the structure to which it applies, because it does not apply in D_M. It applies in a different plane of the computational space, i.e., in D_Φ, to a structure that has not yet had precedence relations interpreted. In this theory, linguistic variation is possible and is limited by asymmetric relations. I posit the following:

(1)   *The Preservation Hypothesis*
      Asymmetry is preserved under variation.

I provide evidence to show that the interaction of the operations of the grammar with independent properties of individual languages enables variation to occur in morphological objects. The variation affects the linear order of affixes, as well as their legibility at PF. First, I present an analysis of word-internal variation with respect to the position of affixes in morphological objects contrasting Yekhee and English. I show that the variation naturally follows from the theory. Second, I consider the difference in the PF legibility of affixes preceding the root in Italian and French verbs, and show that the facts also follow from the theory.

8.2 PF Orderings

I proposed in chapter 7 that the linearization of morphological structures is obtained by the operation M-Flip only when the specifier of the minimal tree to which the operation applies has no PF features. This operation interacts with language-specific properties and determines variation in the linear ordering of morphological constituents. I consider variation in the position of affixes in Yekhee and in English in this perspective.

English and Yekhee differ in the position of derivational and inflectional affixes. In English, most affixes follow the root. In Yekhee, however, affixes typically precede the root. The question arises why the two languages have such diametrically opposed orderings.

Yekhee is a Edoid language strong prefixing north-central from the Niger-Congo family (Bendor-Samuel 1988, Greenberg 1963). Syntactically, Yekhee is a strict SVO verb serializing language. This is schematized in (2), with typical linear ordering of SVO constituents, and with typical verb internal inflectional affixes.

(2) [Subject [[agreement Tense Verb stem] Object]]]

However, the order of affixes in the word structure differs from that of English: Edoid languages are often referred to as rich-prefixing languages (Elugbe 1989), because affixes precede the root. The variation between English and Yekhee in the ordering of affixes cannot be attributed to a broad typological difference, since both languages are SVO. Morphological variation should follow from differences other than the order of syntactic constituents. Since D_M and D_S are parallel planes of the computational space, the variation in one system can parallel the other, but cannot be dependent on the other. I relate the variation between English and Yekhee in the position of the affixes to a basic difference between these languages, namely, the fact that Yekhee is a tone language and English is not. Tone bears a central importance in Yekhee, as it does more generally for the Kwa languages. The language manifests two tone levels, high tone (') and low tone (`). A syllable is a tone-bearing unit in Yekhee. Tone performs both lexical and grammatical functions in the language, but its function at the level of grammar is more complex. Nouns are lexically marked whereas verbs are not. It is the verbal inflection that brings about the tonal properties of verbs.

Tone is associated with inflectional affixes, including tense, temporal aspect, and mood, to the left of the verb. Past tense is signified by a floating high tone, which is borne by the pronominal subject marker and the verb, as the example in (3) illustrates.

(3) Mary ọ   H   dé   àkpà.   [Mary ọ dâkpà]   (Ye)
    Mary 3sg. Past buy cup
    'Mary bought a cup.'

In (3) the tone of the verb affects the initial tone of the noun object, while the pronominal prefix bears a rising tone. In the present progressive (PRP), the tonal alternation is the initial tone of the noun object. The low tone becomes high. The PRP morpheme is a floating low tone.

(4) Mary ọ   dé   àkpà.   [Mary ọ dákpà]   (Ye)
    Mary 3sg. PRP buy cup
    'Mary is buying a cup.'

In the case of the future tense, the FUT morpheme /rhâ/ bears a falling tone. The low-tone portion of the future-tense morpheme influences the verb phrase. This is demonstrated in the tonal change on the first tone of the noun object, which is realized as a down-stepped high tone.

(5) Mary ọ   rhâ   dé   àkpà.   [Mary ọ rhádákpá]   (Ye)
    Mary 3sg. FUT buy cup
    'Mary will buy a cup.'

Tone is also associated with derivational affixes.

(6) a. émà wò   (Ye)
       -able drink
       'drinkable'
    b. ò   gwà ókò
       er- drive car
       'driver'
    c. é   bì
       -ness dark
       'darkness'

The examples in (6) show that, unlike in English, in Yekhee the equivalents of -able, -er and -ness, are expressed by tone-bearing affixes preceding the root. Yekhee is a tone language; every lexical item is marked with tone. Typically, tonal differences are associated with semantic differences. In nouns, minimal pairs contrasting high and low tones are attested, as shown in the examples in (7). Only lexical tones are considered in these examples.

(7) a. èbè   -   ébè   (Ye)
       'enemy'   'leaf'
    b. ákpá   -   àkpá
       'lamp'   'kite'
    c. ìvhìà   -   ívhìà
       'mat'   'children'
    d. òpè   -   ópè
       'fear'   'rat'
    e. ígbà   -   ìgbà   -   ìgbâ
       'thorns'   'chins'   'gathering(s)'

Yekhee does not have any recursive derivational suffixation of the kind attested in English and in the Romance languages, such as *read-able-ity*. In Yekhee only one derivational affix may be merged with a root. Derivational affixes occur in the left periphery of the word. For example, derived nouns begin with one of the following vowels: *i-, e-, ẹ-, o-, ọ-, u-, a-* (see (8)). Verbs can also be formed on the basis of nouns by the adjunction of an affix to the left of the noun (see (9)).

(8) a. nà rhẹ zẹ   →   ọ̀- zébè   (Ye)
       for to read   er- read
       'to read'   'reader'
    b. nà rhẹ gbè   àkànìa   →   énè- gbàkànìa
       for to work$_V$ work$_N$ ee- work
       'to work'   'employee'
    c. bì   →   é-   bì
       'be dark'   ness- dark
                                  'darkness'
    d. rùẹ   →   ó-   rùẹ
       'greet'   ing- greet
                                  'greetings'

(9) a. àkànìa   →   gbè   àkànìa   (Ye)
       'work'   work$_V$ work$_N$ 'to work'
    b. ìgùà   →   dè   ìgùà
       'knee'   fall$_V$ knee$_N$ 'to kneel'

On a par with verbal inflection, nominal inflection also precedes the root. Plural formation is characterized by the alternation of the initial vowel (see (10)).

(10) a. ákpá   íkpá   (Ye)
        'cup'   'cups'
     b. úkpò   íkpò
        'cloth'   'cloths'
     c. ini   ini
        'elephant' 'elephants'
     d. ope   epe
        'rat'   'rats'

Nouns that have initial [a], [u], [i] in the singular take [i] in the plural (see (10a–c)), whereas those with initial [o], [ọ], [e], and [ẹ] in the singular take initial [e] in the plural (see (10d)). The phonetic form of the plural is therefore phonologically conditioned.

The data above illustrate the fact that affixes, derivational and inflectional, precede the root in Yekhee. These data constitute the opposite of what is observed in English. How is it possible to account for this variation without stipulating that Yekhee is a "rich-prefixing" language (Bendor-Samuel and Hartell 1989; Elugbe 1989)? The following analysis, based on Asymmetry Theory, takes into consideration a major difference between Yekhee and English. Yekhee has a characteristic property that English lacks—namely, it is a tone language. In what follows I show that the variation observed follows from the theory in conjunction with this morphophonological difference between the languages under consideration.

I propose that in a tone language such as Yekhee, the specifier of an affix is filled by a formative that Agrees in some features with the head. This formative is devoid of segmental content, but not of suprasegmental content (i.e., tones). This might be the case, for instance, if the tone is linked to an empty segmental slot. Since tone must be realized on overt segments—that is, in the affix itself—the posited formative might be the locus of so-called floating tones documented in the works on suprasegmental phonology.

Thus an unvalued tone feature [−To] is part of the features of D_M in Yekhee. The [−To] feature must not only be legible at PF, but also at LF, because a difference in tone may give rise to a difference in semantic interpretation (see (7)). In Yekhee, the [−To] feature occupies the specifier position of an F-tree, and an inflectional head is [+To] (see (11)). The latter is valued by the former as an effect of M-Link applying under Agree. The specifier position thus becomes PF legible, M-Flip does not apply to the F-tree, and the tense affix remains in situ, preceding the root (see

(12)). M-Flip must apply in English, however, because the specifier of an F-tree headed by an inflectional affix such as the past tense affix *-ed* is not PF legible.

(11)

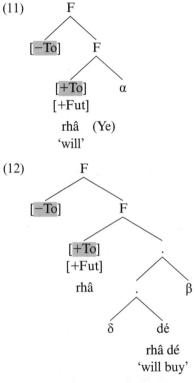

(12)

rhâ dé
'will buy'

Similarly, the [−To] feature in the specifier of the minimal tree headed by a predicate affix is valued by the [+To] feature in the head position of that tree. The uninterpretable [−To] feature is thus valued, and the specifier position is then PF-legible. Consequently, M-Flip does not apply to that minimal tree, and the affix stays in situ, preceding the root (see (13)).

M-Flip does apply, however, in the equivalent structure in English, since in this language affixes do not have a [−To] feature to be valued by a [+To] feature in the head of their minimal tree. The specifier of the minimal tree headed by a predicate affix is not legible at PF, which in turn triggers the application of M-Flip (see (14)). Therefore, a predicate affix follows the root in English.[4]

(13) a.   b.

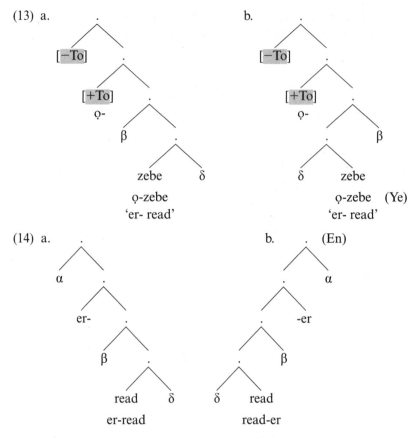

(14) a.   b.   (En)

The fact that inflectional affixes and predicate affixes precede the root in Yekhee and follow the root English is derived, given independent properties of the languages under consideration.

The proposed analysis also provides an account of the variation between these languages in deverbal compounds. As predicted, the affix precedes the verbal complex in Yekhee deverbal compounds, whereas it follows it in English (see (15)).

(15) a. ò- gwà ókò   (Ye)
        er- drive car
        'car-driver'
     b. ò- dò áki
        er- sell market (wares)
        seller-market (wares)
        'trader'

c. ò- gbè èlàmì
   er- kill meat
   killer-meat
   'butcher'

This variation also follows from the fact that the [+To] feature of the affix values the uninterpretable [−To] feature in the specifier of the affix tree, which becomes PF legible. Thus, the minimal tree headed by the predicate affix does not undergo M-Flip, and the affix stays in situ. In English, however, since the specifier of the minimal tree headed by the predicate affix is not PF legible, M-Flip applies, and the predicate affix is in the right periphery of the morphological object at PF.

In Yekhee, a complement follows the head in deverbal compounds, and this is also the case for a modifier (see (16)). This is also the case in French (e.g., *conducteur du dimanche* driver of Sunday 'Sunday driver', *système nerveux* system nervous 'nervous system', *lève tôt* rise early 'early bird'). Parts of deverbal compounds are derived in D_S in both languages, as discussed in chapter 2, whereas compounds are derived in D_M in languages such as English and modern Greek. Notwithstanding the variation, the affix precedes the root in Yekhee compounds, including a modification relation.

(16) a. ò- gwà ókò èlè úkà (Ye)
        er- drive car day Sunday
        driver-Sunday
        'Sunday driver'
     b. ò- kìà kèsì kèsì
        er- walk small small
        walker-slow
        'slow walker'

The proposed analysis accounts straightforwardly for word-internal variation with respect to the position of the affixes. In contrast, a head-movement or a remnant-movement analysis could not account for the difference between Yekhee and English without increasing the computational load of the grammar. Given independent properties of the languages, M-Flip derives the difference in the linear order of the affixes. Moreover, the asymmetry is maintained in all relations derived by the grammar, whether in D_M or in D_Φ, without increasing the global computational load of the grammar, and thus satisfying minimalist requirements.

8.3   PF Legibility

In the previous section, I proposed that the variation in the position of an affix to the right or to the left of a root can be reduced to the PF legibility of the specifier position of its minimal tree, given the operations of the grammar. In this section, I consider another case of morphological variation: the PF legibility of I-Asp affixes in the verb structure of two languages of the same family, Italian and French. The variation does not target E-Asp affixes (iterative and inverse), as evidenced in (17), but it targets I-Asp affixes, as evidenced in (18) and (19).

(17) a. attaccare, distaccare, riattaccare, ridistaccare   (It)
     b. attacher, détacher, rattacher, redétacher   (Fr)
         'to attach', 'to detach', 'to reattach', 'to detach again'

(18) a. a-botton-are   (It)
         at-button-Vinf
     b. boutonn-er   (Fr)
         button-Vinf
         'to button'
     c. in-cipri-are   (It)
         on-powder-Vinf
     d. poudr-er   (Fr)
         powder-Vinf
         'to powder'

(19) a. a-(n)ner(o)-ire   (It)
         in-black-Vinf
     b. noir(c)-ir   (Fr)
         black-Vinf
         'to darken'
     c. in-bianch-are   (It)
         on-white-Vinf
     d. blanch-ir   (Fr)
         white-Vinf
         'to whiten'

How is this microvariation accounted for? According to Asymmetry Theory, Asp affixes are located in the specifier of their minimal tree, and thus they are not subject to M-Flip. The fact that languages vary according to the legibility of these affixes in some cases cannot be expressed in terms of a broad parametric difference. For example, the Romance languages are assumed to differ from English with respect to lexicalization patterns (Talmy 1985, 1991, 2000).[5] Differences between satellite and nonsatellite languages would not be relevant here, because fine-grained variation is observed between the languages of the same family. The variation could not be attributed to a difference between rich I-Asp versus non rich I-Asp languages either. If this were the case, it would be impossible to account for the fact that I-Asp affixes are not equally subject to this variation. Thus, in both Italian and French, locational affixes are PF legible, whereas variation is observed with directional affixes (see (18), (19)). Compare the examples in (18) and (19) with the ones in (20).

(20) a. a-(c)cost-are   (It)
        a-(c)cos-ter   (Fr)
        'to coast'
     b. im-bottigli-are   (It)
        em-bouteill-er   (Fr)
        'to bottle'
     c. a-(l)larg-are   (It)
        é-(l)arg-ir   (Fr)
        'to enlarge'
     d. im-pover-ire   (It)
        a-(p)pauvr-ir   (Fr)
        'to empoverish'

Moreover, the variation does not affect derived verbs whose root is the instrument of the event.[6]

(21) a. martellare   (It)
        marteler   (Fr)
        'to hammer'
     b. segare   (It)
        scier   (Fr)
        'to saw'
     c. gommare   (It)
        gommer   (Fr)
        'to erase'
     d. rastrellare   (It)
        ratisser   (Fr)
        'to rattle'

One difference emerges by comparing the examples in (18) and (19), where variation is observed, with the examples in (20), where there is no variation between the languages under consideration. In the first case, the affixes that bring about the aspectual modification to the event are directional; they introduce an entity undergoing a change. Those in (20) are locational; they introduce an entity that occupies a specific position in the structure of the event. The nominal constituents in (17) and (18) undergo a change of place or state, whereas the ones in (19) denote a location, the end point of the event, either a physical point or a point in abstract space (see Di Sciullo 1999b). An analysis of this microvariation taking into account this fine-grained difference and independent properties of the languages under consideration can be formulated along the following lines.

According to Asymmetry Theory, there is only one minimal tree for I-Asp in the Asp-Shell, where F_E sister-contains F_I, and F_I sister-contains Ev the lexical event head (see (22)).

(22)

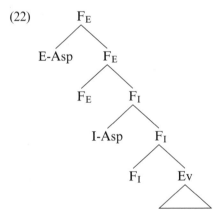

Given (22), there is only one F_I head, and only one I-Asp affix may occupy the specifier of F_I. The F_I head can be the locus of directional or locational features, both contributing to the aspectual properties of the projection of which they are part, as seen in chapter 5.[7] Preposition-like affixes, such as *a* and *in* in Italian and French, may occupy the specifier of F_I (see chapter 5). I will take these affixes to be unvalued for specific interpretable I-Asp features. Di Sciullo and Klipple (1994) observed that the interpretation of preposition-like affixes, as well as prepositions, varies according to the conceptual pseudospace (see Gruber 1965; Jackendoff 1972, 1983; Hale 1984) of the verbal projection which they are part of. Assuming that the conceptual pseudospaces include directional (D), locational (L), abstract state (A), and scalar (S), preposition-like affixes may be unspecified for certain pseudospaces, their interpretation being determined in the verbal projection. Thus, the affix *in-* is interpreted in the directional conceptual field with *imburrare* 'to butter', in the locational field in *imbottigliare* 'to bottle', in the abstract-state field with *innamorare* 'to fall in love', and in the scalar field with *impoverire* 'to empoverish'. The affixes occupy the specifier of their minimal tree with an unvalued [$-F_I$] feature. This feature is valued by being checked with the [$+F_I$] feature of the head of the F_I tree. The latter is specified for the spatial feature [+dir] or for the feature [+loc] of I-Asp. Given M-Link applying under Agree, the uninterpretable features of the affixes are checked by the interpretable (directional, locational, abstract state, scalar) feature of the head of the F_I tree.

(23)

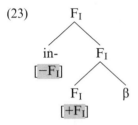

The derivations of verb structures including the spatial [+dir] and [+loc] features of F_I are depicted below with pairs of M-trees including only the projections relevant to our point.

(24) a.   b.

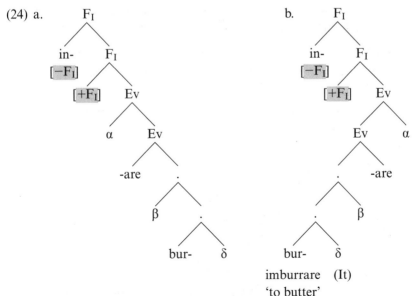

imburrare   (It)
'to butter'

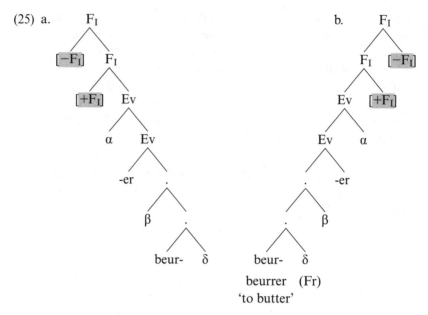

beurrer   (Fr)
'to butter'

In (24), the Italian case, Spec-F_I has PF features and the minimal tree headed by F_I does not undergo M-Flip. This operation applies in (25), the French case, where Spec-F_I has no PF features.

While French and Italian differ with respect to the PF legibility of the directional [+F_I], these languages do not differ with respect to the locational [+F_I]. Compare the pairs of M-trees in (26) and (27), which include only the relevant projections for this discussion.

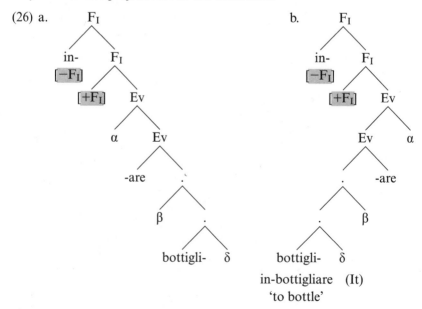

in-bottigliare   (It)
'to bottle'

(27) a.   b.

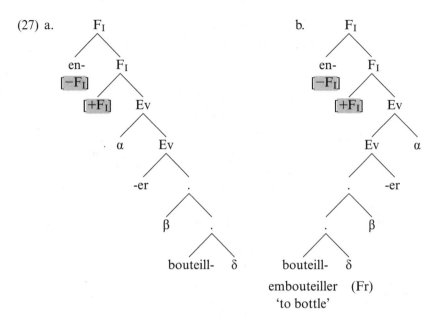

embouteiller   (Fr)
'to bottle'

I propose that the variation in the legibility of the I-Asp affixes at PF can be reduced to whether the directional feature of I-Asp is spelled out by a functional element or not. Evidence to this effect comes from the fact that Italian, contrary to French, spells out direction ([+dir]) as separate functional elements in D_S, such as particles and bare prepositions.

Indeed, Italian, but not French, has directional particles, such as *via* 'away', *su* 'up', and *giù* 'down'. The examples in (28) illustrate the differences between the two languages.

(28) a. Maria ha portato giù/sù il piano.   (It)
        Marie a descendu/monté le piano.   (Fr)
        'Mary brought down/up the piano.'
     b. Maria ha portato il piano giù/sù.   (It)
        'Mary brought the piano down/up.'
     c. Maria ha buttato via i documenti.   (It)
        Marie a jeté les documents.   (Fr)
        'Mary threw away the documents.'
     d. Maria ha buttato i documenti via.   (It)
        'Mary threw the documents away.'

The expression *giù*, *sù*, and *via* in Italian are particles and not PPs. Unlike to PPs, the particles cannot be clefted (see (29)).

(29) a. Gianni ha portato il piano su/giù/via.   (It)
         'Gianni brought the piano up/down/away.'

b. *È su/giù/via che Gianni ha portato il piano.
'It is up/down/away that Gianni brought the piano.'
c. Gianni ha portato il piano nel sofitto.
'Gianni brought the piano in the attic.'
d. È nel sofitto che Gianni ha portato il piano.
'It is in the attic that Gianni brought the piano.'

The syntactic status of particles is subject to debate (see Den Dikken 1995; Svenonius 1996; Hale and Keyser 2002). However, in Den Dikken 1995, as well as in other works, particles are heads. The fact that only directional particles are found in Italian, and not pure telic particles as in English (see (30)), supports the analysis that the directional feature of I-Asp is spelled out as an independent functional element in Italian.

(30) a. Mary finished up the book.
b. John closed off the light.
c. Carla closed down the bar.

(31) a. Maria a finito completamente il libbro.   (It)
b. *Maria a finito su il libbro.
c. John ha chiuso la luce.
d. *John ha chiuso giù la luce.
e. Carla ha chiuso il bar.
f. *Carla ha chiuso giù il bar.

Further evidence in favor of the proposed analysis comes from the fact that Italian also differs from French with respect to directional resulta- tives. The examples in (32) show that in Italian the directional feature of I-Aspect is part of the head of the PP complement of the verb (see (32a,c)), whereas in French an additional prepositional projection is required (see (32b,d)).

(32) a. Il fiume serpeggia al mare.   (It)
'The river snakes to the sea.'
b. Le fleuve serpente *(jusqu')à la mer.   (Fr)
'The river snakes *(until) to the sea.'
c. Questa scalinata sale al castello.   (It)
'This stairway climbs to the castle.'
d. Cet escalier monte *(jusqu') au château.   (Fr)
'This stairway climbs *(until) to the castle.'

This provides evidence that prepositions in Italian, including the prep- osition *a*, can be the morphological spell-out of the directional feature of I-Asp, as well as it can be the prepositional head of the syntactic constituent describing the end point of the event. The affix *a-* has a similar role in morphological objects, since it may give rise to telic shift, as discussed in chapter 5, and further evidenced here in (33).

(33) a. Ha corso (per cinque minuti).   (It)
       'She/He ran (for five minutes).'
     b. È accorso (in cinque minuti).
       'She/He ran up (in five minutes).'
     c. Ha percorso il giornale (in cinque minuti).
       'She/He glanced through the newspaper (in five minutes).'

(34) a. Elle a couru (pendant cinq minutes).   (Fr)
       'She ran (for five minutes).' .
     b. Elle est accourue (en cinq minutes).
       'She ran up (in five minutes).'
     c. Elle a parcouru le journal (en cinq minutes).
       'She glanced through the newspaper (in five minutes).'

There is, however, a configurational difference between the syntactic and the morphological structures with respect to the position of the directional I-Asp element. In D_S, it occupies the head position, whereas in D_M it is located in the specifier position of its minimal tree.

Thus, the variation in the legibility of the directional affix that precedes the root in parasynthetic constructions falls out from the interaction of the operations of the grammar and independent properties of the languages under consideration. For example, in Italian, contrary to French, the directional feature of I-Asp is spelled out as a separate functional element.

8.4 Variation in M and S

The proposed analysis offers an explanation for the variation observed between Italian and French with respect to the spell-out of the directional feature of I-Asp as an independent functional element (either as a specifier in D_M or as a head in D_S). The analysis also covers the variation in the legibility of directional affixes in parasynthetic constructs and the variation as to the presence or the absence of an independent functional head in verb particle and in PP resultative constructions.

Moreover, the proposed analysis equally accounts for the fact that in Italian and in French the locational feature of I-Asp is also spelled out as an independent functional element. Consequently, both languages have PF legible Locational affixes in parasynthetic constructs (e.g., *imbottigliare* (It) *embouteiller* (Fr) 'to bottle') (see (26)). The syntactic correlate of this similarity between Italian and French is that the dative alternation is not observed in these languages (see (35), (36)), the Locational feature of I-Asp being spelled out as the head of the dative PP.

(35) a. Gianni ha dato un libbro a Maria.   (It)
         'Gianni gave a book to Mary.'
     b. *Gianni ha dato Maria un libbro.
         'Gianni gave Mary a book.'

(36) a. Jean a donné un livre à Marie.   (Fr)
         'Jean gave a book to Mary.'
     b. *Jean a donné Marie un livre.
         'Jean gave Mary a book.'

The proposed analysis is truly Minimalist in spirit, since it does not use the notion of second order features such as strength, and it provides a single explanation for variation in word structure and in phrasal structure in terms of a difference in the spell-out of the directional feature of I-Asp as an independent functional element.

This proposal contrasts with the standard analysis of the broad variation observed between Romance and Germanic languages with respect to verb particles, resultatives, and dative constructions, which have been considered to be related constructions in various works, including Larson 1988, Hoekstra 1988, and Snyder 1995. According to these works, verb particles, resultatives, and dative constructions are available in Germanic languages but not in Romance languages. A closer scrutiny of the variation observed between Italian and French suggests that these constructions do not form a natural class, and that finer-grained differences must be taken into consideration. The variation between Italian and French follows from an independent difference between the languages under consideration—that is, a difference in the spell-out of the directional feature of I-Asp as an independent functional element, in conjunction with the operations of the grammar.

8.5 Summary

The Asymmetry Hypothesis, according to which asymmetry is a core relation of the language faculty, and the Preservation Hypothesis, according to which asymmetry is preserved under variation, are closely related. Moreover, the dynamic modularity of the grammar allows for a single difference in the properties of functional elements to have parallel effects in morphological and in syntactic variation.

The operations of the grammar, in conjunction with independent properties of the languages, allow for fine-grained analyses to be made with respect to word-internal variation, including variation in the linear order of affixes as well as variation with respect to their legibility at PF. I have discussed two cases of variation in word structure: the variation in the position of affixes and the variation in the legibility of directional affixes at PF. The data demonstrate that asymmetry is preserved under variation in word structure: morphological variation targets the properties of functional elements in specifier-head relations. This is also the case in phrasal syntax. For example, Di Sciullo, Paul, and Somesfalean (2003) showed that, in Romanian, the absence of complement-noncomplement asymmetry in extraction from weak islands and its presence in strong islands boil down to different ways of checking the EPP feature of v and V; thus a difference in locality is obtained giving rise to the observed variation between the languages under consideration. Moreover, Di Sciullo (forthcoming) shows that intrasentential codeswitching (Italian/French/English) is restricted to feature checking sites. These results point in the same direction: variation can be limited to differences in the properties of functional features in asymmetric relations.

Concluding Remarks

The Arguments in a Nutshell

Given the *Asymmetry Hypothesis*, according to which asymmetry is a core property of the relations of the language faculty, the properties of morphological relations are expected to be asymmetric. The *Strict Asymmetry of Morphology* is a hypothesis that is validated crosslinguistically, as evidenced on the basis of a large variety of languages, including languages from the Romance, Slavic, Finno-Ugric, Turkic, Niger-Congo, and Germanic families. According to Asymmetry Theory, M and S differ with respect to the properties of their primitives: whereas D_M accesses asymmetry from the start, D_S does not have access to the asymmetry of morphology and must generate its own asymmetry. The early asymmetric property of the relations in D_M contrasts with the properties of relations in D_S, which are strictly asymmetric only at a later stage. D_M and D_S differ also with respect to the operations implementing the generic operations of the grammar. Moreover, given the fully parallel architecture of the grammar, morphological domains are derived on a par with syntactic domains and transferred to D_Φ and D_Σ. Interactions between D_M and D_S, as well as between the latter and D_Φ and D_Σ are restricted to isolable domains of computation. The fully parallel model provides a rationale for the existence of shared properties of form and interpretation as well as formal and semantic differences between morphological and syntactic objects.

It is, of course, tempting to treat the parallelism as an isomorphism, and thus identify morphology with syntax (see Embick and Noyer 2001). One problem with this view is the increase of the computational load of the grammar. A single syntactic derivation for both words and phrases requires additional rules to derive word-internal properties in addition to the rules deriving phrasal properties, because syntactic and morphological properties are not coextensive. In some cases, these rules violate the core properties of the operations of the grammar, such as Locality and Strong

binding. If, as I argue, the similarities between morphology and syntax
are the result of parallel derivations, there is no increase in computational
complexity; on the contrary, the parallel derivations contribute to the
efficiency of the language design. The grammar articulates asymmetry in
more than one component, each component being an implementation of
the generic properties of the grammar. The operations of D_M preserve the
asymmetry of the morphological primitives, whereas the operations of D_S
build up syntactic asymmetric relations and neutralize points of symmetry
as they arise.

I proposed that the form of a minimal morphological object is the M-
Shell. The M-Shell is derived by the application of M-Shift to two minimal trees, substituting one minimal tree for the complement of the other.

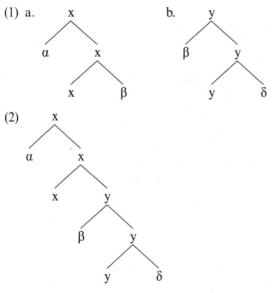

The derivation of the M-Shell is determined by Strict Asymmetry—
that is, the requirement imposed on every element of an object generated
by the grammar to be in an asymmetric relation with another element of
the same sort as early as possible. Strict Asymmetry is met at each step of
the derivation, because a new affixal head or specifier will sister-contain
another element of the same sort generated at an earlier stage. The M-
Shell constitutes a morphological domain, given the properties of its
internal structure, its strong impenetrability, and its isolability at the
interfaces.

The persistence of asymmetry through D_M is ensured by the properties
of the morphological operations, which do not introduce symmetry at
any point of a derivation. Instead, each application of M-Shift builds a

supplementary layer of asymmetric relations. M-Link applies to positions in derived M-Shells and, as is also the case for S-Shift, it applies under Agree, which is an asymmetric relation that holds between active contravalued features. The M-Shell articulates A, Asp, and Op-variable features, and the different instances of the M-Shell differ minimally with respect to the application of the M-Link operation: A positions only or Asp head positions only or Op-variable-Restrictor only (see (3)–(5)). M-Shift and M-Link ensure the checking of the morphological uninterpretable features.

(3) a.

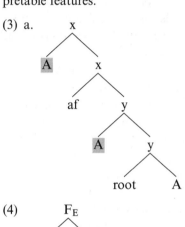

b.

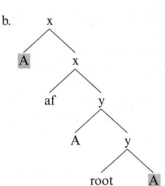

(4)

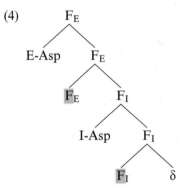

(5)

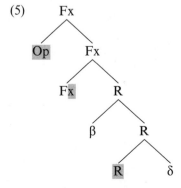

Because morphology manipulates interpretable semantic features (argument, aspect, and operator-variable features), it is tempting to assume that the derivation of morphological expressions is performed exclusively via the syntax and semantics of a logical language (see Hoeksema 1985). However, this avenue fails to express the configurational asymmetry of morphology. I have shown throughout chapters 5 to 7, on the basis of a variety of languages from the Romance, Slavic, Finno-Ugric, Turkic, Niger-Congo, and Germanic families, that the same asymmetric form, the M-Shell, supports different semantic relations: predicate-argument, aspect, and operator-variable. Distinctiveness holds for all the featural relations in D_M and is a consequence of the properties of the operations of the grammar applying under Agree.

Furthermore, the properties of functional words, including scope-taking affixes, indicate that the scope relations are fixed within the Op-Shells. Strict Scope, along with the inalterability of the Asp-Shell and A-Shell, bring compelling support to the strict asymmetry of morphological relations. The Legibility Condition ensures that optimal interpretation is obtained under asymmetric relations at LF. Moreover, in D_Φ, the image of a projection of D_M is derived, without leaving a copy or a trace. Flip is triggered by the sensorimotor system for tractability considerations. This operation reduces the complexity derived by the grammar at PF and contributes to linearization. Flip applies to minimal trees whose specifier presents different sorts of complexity, depending on whether the operation applies at the outcome of D_M or D_S. M-Flip must apply to an M-Shell whose specifier has no PF-legible features and S-Flip must apply to an Asp-Shell or an Op-Shell only when the specifier is "heavy" (i.e., includes a complement). The complexity seems to be reduced to the property of the initial position, the specifier, of having insufficient or excessive PF structure.

(6)

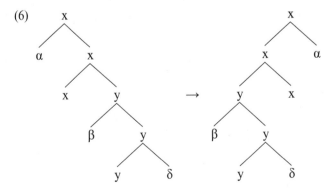

(7)

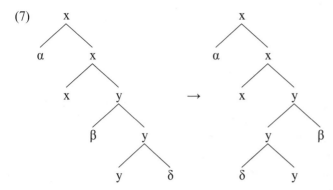

In (6), the top layer of the M-Shell undergoes M-Flip; in (7), the lower layer undergoes the operation. Thus, the ordering of the affixes is derived at PF, and there is no need to stipulate whether an affix is a prefix or a suffix.

The operations of Asymmetry Theory participate in an explanatory account of crosslinguistic variation regarding the linear order of affixes and roots, in derivation and in compound formation, given independent properties of the languages, such as the availability of a tonal system in African languages. Other facts from the Romance languages regarding the position and the legibility of affixes at PF indicate that M-Link plays a role in variation, given independent properties of the languages such as the spell-out of the directional feature of aspect as an independent functional element. In both cases, the asymmetry of morphological relations is preserved in variation. Moreover, in light of the full parallelism of the architecture of the grammar, morphological variation can also be located in the choice of a sort of derivation, D_S or D_M, for a given linguistic object, as is the case for the derivation of compounds in languages such as English and modern Greek, on the one hand, and the Romance languages and the African languages, on the other. English and modern Greek pick out D_M; French and Yekhee pick out D_S.

The asymmetry of morphology, as part of the Global Economy of grammar, helps explain why language is an optimal solution to the interface legibility conditions.

Asymmetry in a Broader Perspective

According to Asymmetry Theory, the primitives of M include elementary asymmetric relations, and morphological expressions are derived by asymmetry-preserving operations: M manipulates asymmetric relations only. Why should asymmetry be the characteristic property of relations in

D_M as well as of relations in D_S? In these concluding remarks, I would like to provide a possible answer to this question by relating the role of asymmetry in grammar to Economy.

Economy is part of grammar in terms of principles of optimization. These principles enable the grammar to take the optimal decision at a given choice point. It has been shown that principles of economy or optimality, often identified with "least effort," play a crucial role in determining the properties of linguistic expressions at both PF and LF. Chomsky (1995) suggests that movement is available as a "last resort" operation, applicable only when necessary. The derivations must be as economical as possible and should contain no superfluous steps.

Economy conditions have been proposed to relate the properties of representations and derivations to interface legibility. For a representation or a derivation to be identified as the optimal solution to the interface legibility conditions, it must qualify as the most economical solution for legibility by the external systems. Economy of derivations ensures that an operation will apply in a derivation only if its output is legible at the interfaces. Fox (2000) argues that QR applies only when there is a scope ambiguity. No sentence with ambiguous scope relations is interpretable at LF. The Inclusiveness Condition (Chomsky 1995) ensures that no new element (e.g., traces, index, and so on) may be introduced in the derivation if not already in the numeration. "Inclusiveness holds of narrow syntax, and each feature is interpreted at the level of LF or associated with phonetic features by the phonological component" (Chomsky 2000b, 118). The Inclusiveness Condition is associated with a division of labor between syntax and phonology. Inclusiveness ensures both Economy of derivations and representations.

The principle of Full Interpretation (Chomsky 1995, 2000b) states that there should be no superfluous symbols in representations. This principle plays an important role at the PF interface because it excludes representations where a symbol has no phonetic interpretation. Full interpretation also applies at the LF interface, imposing the requirement that every symbol of that representation have a language-independent interpretation. Principles of Economy of representation are formulated in a number of works, including Grimshaw 1994, Speas 1994, Bošković 1997, and Williams 2003.

I would like to suggest that economy is a global property of the language design, and that the fully parallel architecture of Asymmetry Theory is a consequence of the Global Economy of grammar. Parallel derivations contribute to the optimality of the language design, because the core properties of the grammar are used in more than one dimension of the computational space.

In Asymmetry Theory, a small set of primitives are used in the different components, and the operations have specific instantiations in the parallel derivations. This property of the architecture of the grammar is a consequence of the Economy of the grammatical system, making an optimal use of its basic properties. The parallel model reduces the computational complexity of the overall grammatical system. Fewer choice points arise in a parallel model than would arise in a model where the different sorts of grammatical objects, morphological, syntactic, and phonological, would be the outcome of a unique derivational path. Efficiency of derivation and interpretation can be ensured if the morphological and syntactic properties of linguistic expressions are processed in separate planes of the computational space, scope and other semantic relations being interpreted by the conceptual-intentional system, and linear precedence relations being interpreted by the sensorimotor system.

The fact that asymmetric relations are part of the derivations of the grammar irrespective of the nature of the derived objects, be they morphological, syntactic, phonological, or semantic, signals that economy is part of the architecture of the language design. Global Economy does not bear directly on the properties of the derivations or the representations, such as the Inclusiveness Condition and the Full Interpretation Condition; it provides a rationale for their existence.

One effect of the Global Economy is the pervasiveness of one property of relations—that is, asymmetry—through the building blocks of grammar. Asymmetry is part of the definition of the primitives, the operations, and the conditions of the grammar. It is used directly or derived as soon as possible in the derivations. Given the Global Economy of the grammar, it does not come as a surprise that asymmetric relations are determinant in more than one plane of the computational space. Asymmetry is also part of the interface conditions. As proposed in chapter 2, the Legibility Condition states that optimal legibility may only be obtained under asymmetric relations. Whereas Full Interpretation requires no superfluous symbol at the interfaces, the Legibility Condition requires the symbols to be part of asymmetric relations at the interfaces. Asymmetry must play a key role at the interfaces, because the expressions derived by the grammar, $\langle$PF, LF$\rangle$, must be easily tractable by the external systems, which can be viewed as asymmetry-recovering systems. From this perspective, asymmetric relations would provide the perfect property of relations enabling different systems to interface. This too would not be so surprising, because to be transferred from one derivation to another a grammatical object must constitute an isolable domain of interpretation where strict asymmetry must hold. If asymmetric relations enable the units of the computation to transfer through the different planes of the computational space, this property of relations would also be the perfect property enabling the contact between the expressions derived by the grammar and the external systems.

In fact, if the language faculty did not consist of a restricted set of primitives, operations, and conditions, it would be impossible to explain why language acquisition follows the same stages independently of language or ethnic group—for example, the production of substantive categories precedes the production of functional categories; the production of constituents including minimal asymmetries is followed by the production of constituents including extended asymmetries. The asymmetry of morphology, as an instance of the basic asymmetry of relations, opens a path in the understanding of the properties of the language design.

Notes

Chapter 1

1. The notion of asymmetry is often used to refer to a difference between two elements with respect to a given property of grammar. This is the case, for example, in the discussion on the subject-object or the complement-noncomplement extraction asymmetries.

The discussion goes back to Ross's (1967) constraints banning extraction of a constituent from different sorts of islands (opaque embedded contexts), including relative clauses, and coordinate structures. It has been observed that subjects differ from objects with respect to extractions from islands and that, moreover, complements and adjuncts also differ in this respect (see (i), (ii)).

Subject/object asymmetry
(i) a. ?What do you recall whether Bill bought?
   b. *Who do you recall whether bought a book?
   c. What do you think that Mary left on the table?
   d. ?Who do you think that left the book on the table?

Object/adjunct asymmetry
(ii) a. Which car did John say that Bill fixed?
   b. *Which mechanic did John say that fixed the car?
   c. Which car did John wonder how to fix?
   d. *How did John wonder which car to fix?

Subject-object and complement-noncomplement asymmetries have been accounted for by different principles pertaining to the distribution of empty categories, to the properties of the domain from which extraction takes place, and to the locality restriction on movement.

These principles include the Empty Category Principle in Chomsky 1981, the Constraint of Extraction Domains in Huang 1982, the notion of blocking category in Chomsky 1986, the principle of Relativized Minimality in Rizzi 1990, and the Minimal Link in Chomsky 1995. Questions still remain unresolved in this area—for example, regarding the role of the referential versus nonreferential status of the extracted constituent, as well as the ban of extractions out of specifiers and more generally out of a displaced constituent, which I will not discuss further here. But see Di Sciullo, Paul, and Somesfalean 2003b and Di Sciullo and Isac 2004.

2. See the appendix to chapter 1 for the definitions of set theoretical notions as well as for the definitions of the structural relations of precedence, dominance, and sister-containment.

3. If asymmetry is central to the language faculty, it does not mean that other properties of relations, such as symmetry and reflexivity, are not among those available to the cognitive system. The hypothesis being put forward here is that asymmetry is a central property of the relations available to the language faculty.

4. May (1977, 1985) has a principle determining the relative scope of operators that m-command each other. Thus, in his system, interpretation is also possible in the absence of asymmetric c-command. However, problems arise with May's principle, which I will not discuss here.

5. It is possible to say (i) and (ii) without giving contrasting focus to the second occurrence of *John* and interpret both occurrences of *John* as the same person.

(i) John is John.

(ii) Only John can be John.

However, the second occurrence of *John* in (i) and (ii) is not referential but predicative. It denotes the property of being the individual *John* and not the individual *John*. The predicative position is not a referential position.

6. Kayne's approach to scope ambiguities is problematic if asymmetric c-command maps onto precedence in linearization. The question arises then as to how inverse scope is possible in (5) given that *someone* follows *everyone* by virtue of being c-commanded. However, it might be the case that inverse scope is derived in a parallel derivation, given the full parallel model of grammar defined in chapter 2. Under this view, all covert movements including QR for scope ambiguity and reconstruction would be derived in parallel.

7. The fact that the nucleus and the following C form a constituent is demonstrated by a variety of phonological phenomena such as closed-rime shortening and rimal weight. The fact that branching rimes can be recognized as units can be illustrated with stress contrast in English. In the following words, stress falls on the penultimate syllable: *consénsus, asbéstos, agénda, amálgam, uténsil*. However, in the following set stress falls on the antepenult: *aspáragus, jávelin, metrópolis, vénison, América*. Stress falls on the penult if it is heavy (i.e., if the nucleus and the following consonant form a constituent), otherwise it falls on the antepenult. Thus, the nucleus together with a consonant following it that is not itself followed by a vowel must form a constituent. There are a wide variety of phonological phenomena supporting the structure in (7) where [VC] is a constituent. What is not attested, however, are phenomena that would refer uniquely to the sequence CV, where V is within the nucleus but not within the rime. A hypothetical example would be some phenomenon that would depend crucially on the unit [ve] in say [vendor]. Clearly, given the structure in (7), there is no way of referring to [ve] in [vendor]. I thank Mohamed Guerssel (personal communication) for the above.

8. Roeper (1998) suggests that particles occurring to the left of a verbal structure (e.g., *the cat turned the chair over, the cat overturned the chair*) are derived by leftward head movement, along the lines of Kayne (1994). However, there are cases

where this is not possible (e.g., *to turn down an offer*, **to downturn an offer*; *to blow up*, **to up blow*). The fact that particles may in some cases precede the verb in English is not typical of other languages. In Italian, there is a small set of directional particles, including *via*, *giu*, and *su*. Only *via* may both follow and precede the verb (e.g., *vai via* 'go away', *il viavai di gente* 'the flow of people'). Directional particles are not directional affixes. The former typically follow the verb, while the latter precede it (see Di Sciullo 1997). The status of particles is controversial. Den Dikken (1997) takes particles to be part of small clauses, Svenonius (1996) analyzes them as being underlying transitive elements, and according to Hale and Keyser (2002) they are part of L-syntax. I will assume that particles are not derived in the morphology. If particles are derived in the syntax, the fact that they may in some cases be dislocated is expected. The fact that the interpretation of the verbal complex differs whether the particle follows or precedes the verb suggests that movement may not be at play (e.g., *to look something over*, *to overlook something*).

9. Among the differences, the following are observed in Di Sciullo 1996c: the absence of subject-verb agreement within compounds (e.g., **John is a writes-er* versus *John writes novels*), the lack of a syntactically active operator-variable relation able to license a parasitic gap (e.g., **the employee of John without interviewing* versus *the person that John employed without interviewing*), the lack of syntactically active argument able to license a definite adjunct (e.g., **this is readable by John* versus *this can be read by John*). Di Sciullo and Williams (1987) also note the impossibility of moving a *wh*-constituent within a word (e.g., **[How complete-ness] do you admire*, **the who-killer did the police catch*), and Giorgi and Longobardi (1991) note the impossibility of moving a DP within a word (e.g., *a [person's informant] about himself*, **a [person informant] about himself*).

10. Kayne does not make the set theoretical distinction between antisymmetry and asymmetry. While it is true that every asymmetric relation is also antisymmetric, the reverse is not true. Every antisymmetric relation is not also asymmetric. Reflexivity may be part of an antisymmetric relation, whereas this is not the case for an asymmetric relation.

11. In (12), given a phrase marker P, T is a many-to-many mapping from nonterminals to terminals, A is the set of all pairs of nonterminals such that the first asymmetrically c-commands the other, and T is the set of terminals.

12. The definition of asymmetric c-command operative in the LCA does not make reference to the first branching category, as in Reinhart's (1983) definition, here in (i), but only to the first dominating node; see (14). Moreover, Kayne's definition applies to categories and not to segments, a distinction first introduced in May 1977—that is, an adjunct cannot asymmetrically c-command another category because the node that it immediately dominates is not a category but a segment of a category.

(i) α c-commands β iff α does not dominate β and β does not dominate α, and the first branching node dominating α also dominates β.

13. Whether or not the LCA derives the properties of X-bar Theory is a controversial issue. Collins (1997) refutes it on Minimalist grounds, whereas Moro (2000) endorses it and takes the LCA to be violable in the course of a derivation.

In Chomsky 1993, the effects of X-bar Theory are derived from the definition of Merge and the definition of minimal and maximal categories. Minimal and maximal categories are no longer thought of as primitives of syntax in the minimalist framework, but are defined configurationally as follows: a minimal category projects; a maximal category does not project anymore (Chomsky 1993, 2000a). In the Minimalist Program, the grammar has no internal interface, and thus includes no condition on internal interfaces. Chomsky (1995) suggests that the LCA applies only at PF; if this is the case, it does not derive the properties of X-bar Theory, which follow in Minimalist terms from Merge and the definition of minimal and maximal projections.

14. Whether mirror structures are mapped onto symmetric relations is controversial. I will mention two analyses where this does not happen. While maintaining the raising analysis, Guéron (1992, 1994, 2001) proposes that the complement of a specificational copula sentence is an asymmetric structure where the subject of the small clause is in the specifier and the predicate is in the complement position, as in (ia). According to her analysis, predication is an asymmetric relation; the properties of the copula BE are such that the copula takes an NP in its complement as well as an NP in the specifier position.

(i) a. Moby Dick is John's favorite book. (predicational)
    b. John's favorite book is Moby Dick. (specificational)
    c. e T+BE [$_{Sc}$ [$_{NP_1}$ Moby Dick] [$_{NP_2}$ John's favorite book]]
    d. e T [$_{VP}$ [$_{NP_1}$ Moby Dick] BE [$_{NP_2}$ John's favorite book]]

Moreover, mirror structures can also be found in cases where predication is not at stake. This is the case for locative inversion and quotative inversion in English; see (ii) and (iii), the formal properties of which have been discussed in Collins (1997) within the Minimalist framework.

(ii) a. John rolled down the hill.
     b. Down the hill rolled John.

(iii) a. "I am so happy," Mary thought.
      b. "I am so happy," thought Mary.

Locative inversion and quotative inversion are also "mirror structures." Collins (1997) brings evidence to the effect that these structures are asymmetric.

As mentioned by an anonymous reviewer, if asymmetric relations are also characteristic of syntactic relations, this would provide further support for the Asymmetry Hypothesis, according to which asymmetry is a core relation of the language faculty, and thus to Asymmetry Theory. The question of explaining why morphology lacks the so-called mirror structures of syntax would still remain.

The distinctiveness of syntax and morphology could lie in the role of focus. While focus markers are observed in the morphology of several languages, including Tagalog, a language of the Philippines, as evidenced in chapter 2, a difference in the order of the morphological constituents if possible in morphology (see (37), (38)) gives rise to a difference in semantic interpretation, whereas a difference in the order of syntactic constituents (see (39)–(42)) gives rise to a difference in information structure. Syntax may interface inferential and discourse-related systems, whereas this is not a possibility for morphology. This is implemented in Asymmetry theory by the availability of pied-piping in syntax and its nonavailability in morphology. See chapter 2.

15. Questions can be raised about a thesis like Dynamic Antisymmetry. For instance, if syntactic movement is required to destroy symmetric relations, then movement should not leave a copy, because symmetry can always be defined with respect to the copy of the moved constituent. In addition, if constituents move to prevent symmetry then, reconstruction should never be possible because the reconstructed element would lead to symmetry (Calixto Aguero, personal communication). However, if the copy of a moved constituent and the moved constituent itself are not identical (in fact the copy has no phonetic features), movement would not lead to symmetry. Moreover, if QR and Reconstruction are not part of the syntactic derivation, but rather take place in the semantic derivation, Fox (2000, 2002) suggests that QR is triggered only when there is a difference in interpretation, the question of whether covert movement creates symmetry does not arise.

That morphological relations are asymmetric only can be shown independently from the hypothesis that points of symmetry drive movement. The irreversible property of morphological relations indicates that morphological relations are not symmetrical. Movement does not occur in morphological objects, be it overt or covert. The fact that scope ambiguity does not arise in morphological objects, discussed in chapter 7, also signals that morphological relations are asymmetric only.

Chapter 2

1. The Minimalist Program (Chomsky 1995, 2000a, 2000b, 2001) provides a basic framework for the exploration of the properties of the language faculty and its interfaces with the external systems. In Chomsky 2001, the language faculty includes a set of features, interpretable and uninterpretable. It also includes a set of operations—Select, Merge, Agree, Move, Delete, Transfer—and a pair of interface expressions $\langle PF, LF \rangle$. PF is the interface with the external sensorimotor system and LF is the interface with the conceptual-intentional system. Select is a one-time selection of elements of the lexicon (Lex) that will be accessed in the derivation (D). Select applies to Lex and yields a lexical array (LA). Narrow syntax (NS) maps LA to a derivation (D_{NS}). The phonological component (Φ) maps the outcome of D_{NS} to PF. The semantic component (Σ) maps the outcome of D_{NS} to LF. The operation Transfer hands independent domains—that is, phases —from D_{NS} to PF and LF cyclically. Economy conditions, such as the Minimal Link and Full Interpretation, ensure the well-formedness of derivations and representations.

In this framework, the properties of the morphological component, its articulation in the grammar, and its connections with the external systems are open areas of research. Asymmetry Theory presents specific hypotheses on the morphological component in the overall architecture of the grammar.

2. To use language optimally, lexical, morphological, phonological, and syntactic knowledge must be available in parallel. One phenomenon indicating that this

must be the case is across-the-board blocking. For example, phonological knowledge must be available for syntactic blocking (e.g., the phonological knowledge blocks the morphological comparative with -er, as in #intelligente/more intelligent); morphological knowledge must be available for syntactic blocking (e.g., this book is readable, *this book is able to be read); lexical knowledge relative to the impenetrability of idioms must be available for syntactic blocking (e.g., tabs were put on John versus *his way was lost by John).

The hypothesis in (i), proposed in my earlier work, is compatible with modular models of grammar and cognition (e.g., Fodor 1979; Chomsky 1986), as opposed to nonmodular models such as connectionism (e.g., Rumelhart and McClelland 1986; Smolensky, Mozer, and Rumelhart 1996), because it preserves the modular architecture with distinct components and derivations.

(i) *Modularity of Computational Space Hypothesis*
    The computational space includes interacting types of derivations leading to target types of configurations. (Di Sciullo 1996c, 5)

This hypothesis is also compatible with parallel morphology/syntax models proposed in Shibatani and Kageyama 1988, Borer 1998, 1991, and Rohrbacher 1994, according to which the output of morphological processes may be inserted at D-structure, or later, and may interact with syntactic representations. See note 19.

3. For example, an element with phonological features only will be inserted only in D_Φ. This is the case with the vowel -o- or -e-, found crosslinguistically in compounds (e.g., *ital-o-american, lexic-o-semantic*). In languages such as modern Greek, they occur in roots as well as deverbal compounds (e.g., *pag-o-vun-o* ice mountain 'iceberg', *kapn-o-kalierj-i-a* 'tobacco-cultivation') (see Ralli 1992; Ralli and Raftopoulou 1999). The vowel has phonological features and its occurrence is phonologically conditioned. It does not have uninterpretable features to check in D_M or in D_S, and if it has no semantic features that must be legible at LF, it is not inserted in D_M, but only in D_Φ.

4. Syntactic words, such as *prêt-à-porter*, include a phrasal constituent ZP, as in the representation [$_{YP}$ Y [ZP]], while being strongly impenetrable (i.e., nor Y nor ZP may move out of YP). Syntactic words are derived in D_S and transferred in D_M where they are analyzed as M-objects and interpreted as such by Φ and Σ. As shown in Di Sciullo 1992, as well as in Di Sciullo and Williams 1987, these constructs are nominal expressions even though they include a phrasal constituent, VP, AP, PP, and NP (e.g., *boit-sans-soif* (drink without thirst) 'drinker', *dur-à-cuire* (hard to cook) 'tough cookie', *sans-le-sous* (without the penny) 'penniless, have-not', *homme-de-paille* (man of straw) 'straw man'). Their morphological status is derived by a morphological operation that reanalyzes them as M-objects: [$_X$ α X [$_{YP}$ Y [ZP]]], where X has nominal properties, and α has uninterpretable features such as the [−A] feature, as well as interpretable features, including the referential [+R] feature, which is the external argument structure of nouns in Di Sciullo and Williams 1987, Grimshaw 1990, Zwarts 1992, and Spencer 1998, among other works. Syntactic words are derived in D_M by the morphological operation M-Shift, defined in section 2.4.2, which in this case substitutes YP for the complement of X. Syntactic words constitute evidence for the transfer of an

isolable domain of D_S to D_M. It is possible, according to Asymmetry Theory, because of the dynamic modularity of the architecture of the grammar.

5. Discontinuous constituents present evidence that parts of D_M are transferred to D_S. French negation *ne … pas* is an example of discontinuous constituents. Both members of the morphological object may be projected in D_S discontinuously (e.g., *il n'a pas vu que …* 'he did not see that …'), or not (e.g., *ne pas voir que …* 'not to see that …'). Furthermore, one member of the construct may not be transferred from D_M to D_S (e.g., *Il voit pas que …* 'he does not see that …'). A discontinuous constituent is derived in D_M, and a projection F intervenes between the parts of the constituent, X and Y.

(i) D_M :

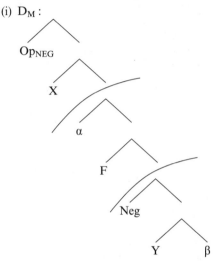

Parts of (i) can be transferred to D_S, and the F projection can be either null or filled by syntactic material. Discontinuous constituents may also relate propositions, as is the case with discontinuous conjunctions such as *if … then* (e.g., *if the earth is in orbit around the sun (then) it is not the center of the universe*; *(if) the earth is in orbit around the sun, consequently it is not the center of the universe*). Another example of discontinuous constituents is the Japanese question marker *ka*, which is part of a discontinuous constituent (e.g., *nani … ka* (Ja) 'what'). *Ka* is optional in *nani … ka* and is a question operator, but not when it is part of an indefinite expression *nanika* 'something' (but see Hagstrom 1998 for another view).

6. According to Kayne (1994, 35), the Universal Base Hypothesis is motivated in syntax by the fact that of the two orders, specifier-head-complement and complement-head-specifier, the former is significantly more plausible than is the latter. While head-complement and complement-head orders are widely attested, the specifier-head order strongly predominates, and there is no constituent for which head-specifier is the crosslinguistically predominant order. There is evidence that the Universal Base Hypothesis extends to morphology. It is generally the case that some affixes precede the root and that others follow. In languages such as English and the Romance languages, the affixes that follow the root are

more closely related to the root than the affixes that precede the root, suggesting that structure (2) is also characteristic of morphological structure. Crosslinguistic evidence indicates that the specifier precedes the head in the internal structure of morphological objects. So-called strong-suffixing languages (e.g., Turkic and Finno-Ugric languages) are not only purely suffixing. For example, Sebüktekin (1971, 20) observes that in Turkish, prefixation is used in loanwords (e.g., *gayri-müslim* 'non-Muslim' and *na-tamam* 'incomplete').

7. For example, in D_M the canonical position of the internal argument of a morphological head is the position β in (2), and the canonical position of the external argument is the position α in (2). These positions may be altered in the course of a derivation, and I will introduce, in chapter 4, the notion of "flexible argument structure", in this perspective. Argument-structure flexibility offers an explanation for otherwise unexpected cases of morphological derivation, as well as tying together the different cases of so-called argument-structure alternations discussed in Levin and Rappaport Hovav 1995, Pustejovsky 1995, and Hale and Keyser 2002, among other works.

8. In type-theoretic semantics (Montague 1970, 1973), there are two primitive semantic types: individual e and truth value t. The semantic type assigned to individuals is e and the semantic type of truth value is t. Derived types for various sorts of functions take the form of ordered pairs, whose members are simpler types. Derived types, such as $\langle et \rangle$ and $\langle\langle et \rangle\ t \rangle\rangle$, define functions of which arguments are of the type of the first coordinate of the ordered pair and whose values are of the type of the second coordinate of the pair.

In Di Sciullo and Williams 1987, the rule of functional composition was proposed for the derivation of the argument structure (theta-grid) of morphological objects including derivational affixes on the basis of the argument structure (theta-grid) of their parts. I am now proposing that compositionally, implemented in terms of functional application, is part of the semantics of morphological objects. The irregular part of the semantics of morphological objects falls into the domain of the lexicon. See section 3.4.3.1 for discussion.

9. Clitics are generated in functional projections with phi (φ) features and case, as well as interpretable features including aspect features. Only argumental clitics are linked to an argument position within the L-projections; adjunct clitics are not. Moreover, clitics have their own morphological structure, which is derived in D_M (see chapter 6). In D_S, they are generated in the F-projection, and A-clitics are linked to A-positions in the L-projection. Their linear order is obtained at PF.

10. The Hierarchy of Homogeneous Projections is compatible with the constraints on affixal scope relations, which are postulated in various works, including Baker 1988, Jackendoff 1972, and Speas 1990, Grimshaw 1994 as well as in the following proposed by Rice (1998) to account for the ordering of morphemes in Salve, a Northern Athapaskan language.

(i) When one morpheme is in the scope of another, the morpheme of greater scope must be higher in the tree than the morpheme within its scope. (Rice 1998, 679)

Functional elements scope over lexical elements, and scope relations are established among functional and lexical elements. Rice (1998) proposes to derive the surface placement of the verb stem by verb raising. The result of the head movement can be obtained without violation of the Extension condition, as discussed in section 2.4 and in chapter 7.

11. In Chomsky 2001, the interpretable features are the categorial features $(+/-N, +/-V, D, T,$ and so on), and the phi-features of N (person, number, gender). Uninterpretable features are the phonological features, the case features of N, the phi-features, the case features of V and T, the [+wh] feature of *wh*-phrases, the EPP feature, and any other features not listed under the set of interpretable features.

12. See Borer 1998 for a discussion of whether the properties of derivational morphemes are to be checked by syntactic feature checking, along the lines of Chomsky 1995. See also Roeper 1999 for feature checking in morphology.

13. The operations of Asymmetry Theory differ from the ones defined in Chomsky 2000b for the syntactic component of the grammar. In particular, Merge (see (i)) is the indispensable operation of recursive systems, and it can apply to structurally unanalyzed objects. Move (see (ii)) implements the displacement property of natural languages and includes pied-piping. Uninterpretable features are checked under Agree (see (iii)), which plays a central role in both Merge and Move. The selectional properties of lexical categories N and V, and functional categories, such as complementizer and small v, can be reduced to Agree.

(i) *Merge*
Target two syntactic objects α and β, form a new object $\Gamma\{\alpha, \beta\}$, the label LB of $\Gamma(LB(\Gamma)) = LB(\alpha)$ or $LB(\beta)$.

(ii) *Move*
Select a target α, select a category β that is moved, β must have uninterpretable features, α must be phi-complete to delete the uninterpretable feature of the pied-piped matching element β, merge β in Spec-LB(α), delete the uninterpretable feature of β.

(iii) *Agree*
$\alpha > \beta$
Agree (α, β), where α is a probe and β is a matching goal, and ">" is a c-command relation. Matching is feature identity. The probe seeks a matching goal within the domain XP, generated by the probe. Matching of probe goal induces Agree. (Chomsky 2000b)

The syntactic operations in (i)–(iii) do not apply in the derivation of morphological objects. If morphological objects were derived by Merge, they could be analyzed as symmetric relations and mirror structures would be derived, contrary to fact. If they were derived by Move, dislocation would be predicted, contrary to the facts.

14. Shift may participate in argument-structure type shifting (see chapter 4). Link applies under sister-containment. Linking relations, contrary to coindexing relations, are asymmetric, a point made in Higginbotham 1985.

15. Agree may occur independently of Move in Chomsky 2000b, since it occurs with Merge: the verb agrees with the uninterpretable case feature of its complement, which is checked and deleted. Agree subsumes specifier-head agreement and is a part of movement. It also may subsume long-distance agreement (see Potsdam and Polinsky 2001). As defined in Chomsky 2000b, asymmetric c-command must hold between the agreeing elements, which must also be active —that is, have uninterpretable features to check. The Defective Intervention Condition and the Phase Impenetrability Condition (Chomsky 2000b) ensure that Agree is bounded. However, in Chomsky 2001, Agree requires a previous Match relation, which is based on feature identity.

16. Given two sets A and B, if all the members of A are also the members of B, A is a subset of B. A is a proper subset of B, or is properly included in B, whenever A is a subset of B but A is not identical to B.

17. Asymmetry Theory differs from Tree Adjoining Grammar (TAG) (Kroch, Aravind, and Joshi 1985; Joshi, Levi, and Takahashi 1975; Joshi 1985). Asymmetry Theory shares with TAG the hypothesis that grammar may combine trees based on the application of a small set of formal operations. M-Shift is similar in some sense to the TAG Substitution operation. However, unlike Substitution, M-Shift does not require categorial identity, because roots have no categorial features; furthermore Shift applies under Agree, which is not the case for Substitution and adjoining is not part of the operations of Asymmetry Theory. Moreover, the central hypothesis of TAG, according to which any operation must apply strictly within an elementary tree, does not hold in Asymmetry Theory, because M-Shift applies to two minimal trees, and M-Link applies to an M-Shell targeting positions across two minimal trees. See Frank 2002 for a comparison between TAG and the Minimalist Program.

18. The parallels between S and M do not follow from models where M and S are totally different (Aronoff 1976 or Jackendoff 1975; Anderson 1992). Furthermore, the differences between morphological and syntactic objects do not follow from an architecture where M and S coincide (Lieber 1992; Julien 1996; Marantz 1997). In Asymmetry Theory, the parallels and differences between the morphological and syntactic objects are a consequence of the architecture of the grammar. Asymmetry Theory shares properties with the models proposed in Shibatani and Kageyama 1988, Borer 1998, 1991, and Rohrbacher 1994, while it differs from these proposals with respect to the component-specific derivation of morphological objects as well as with respect to the properties of the morphological and syntactic components in the overall architecture of the grammar. For example, in Parallel Morphology (Borer 1991), the interaction between morphological and syntactic structures depends on whether morphological structures have a corresponding syntactic structure or not; the output of the word-formation module is inserted at different points of a syntactic derivation, or at a later point, in postlexical phonology. For instance, while result nominals are derived in the morphology and are inserted at D-structure, event nominals are derived in the syntax via head movement, the result of which would enter the morphology. However, the asymmetric property of the relations underlying derived nominals such as *destruction* is constant whether the nominal has result or event properties: no reordering is pos-

sible between the affix and the root. In the fully parallel model of Asymmetry Theory, because morphology and syntax differ with respect to the nature of their primitives and vocabulary items, there is no need to stipulate points of insertion in the course of the syntactic derivation, since only isolatable domains may be transferred from one plane to the other. Moreover, morphological and syntactic operations are different operations in Asymmetry Theory, while being specific instances of the generic operations of the grammar. There is no syntactic operation that applies in the derivation of morphological objects. Thus the Atomicity Thesis (see Di Sciullo and Williams 1987) is preserved.

19. Strict Asymmetry shares with Collins's (1997) Condition of Integration (see (i)) the idea that it is independent from thematic properties or case properties. It is a purely formal requirement.

(i) Every category (except the root) must be contained in another category.
    (Collins 1997, 66)

However, the condition of Integration is satisfied by the first application of Merge, which makes two objects sister and daughter of another category. But Strict Asymmetry is not satisfied by first Merge if Merge applies to unstructured objects in syntactic derivations. Strict Asymmetry is satisfied by first Merge if Merge applies to structured objects—that is, when it applies to morphological derivations.

Chapter 3

1. In the Derivation by Phase model, "the derivation of Exp proceeds by phases, where each phase is determined by a subarray LA_i of LA, placed in 'active memory.' When the computation L exhausts LA_i, forming a syntactic object K, L returns to LA, either extending K to K' or forming an independent structure M to be assimilated later to K or to some extension of K. Derivation is assumed to be strictly cyclic, but with the phase level of the cycle playing a special role" (Chomsky 2001, 12).

2. The notion of "shell" goes back to Larson's (1988) VP Shell. It also has a more recent incarnation in Chomsky's (2000a) small vP structure [$_{vP}$ SU [OB [$_{vP}$ OB]]]. The notion of M-Shell is parallel to the syntactic shell.

3. A nonbranching structure for *wh*-words is proposed by Larson (1987). A bare sisterhood relation is assumed to constitute morphological domains in Marantz 2003.

4. The first sister of a head is selected by that head. Thus, selection is represented in terms of sisterhood in earlier works in generative grammar, going back to Chomsky 1965, where subcategorization features restrict the operation of lexical insertion at the level of deep structure.

5. In Distributed Morphology, the notion of root ($\sqrt{}$) is central. The category of a root is provided by an abstract functional head, such as n, v, or a. Each category is a phase delimiter and triggers the interpretation of its complement. A head adjoined via head movement to another head counts as being in the complement of this higher head, so head movement is not an escape hatch for phonological and semantic interpretation in a phase. See Marantz 2003.

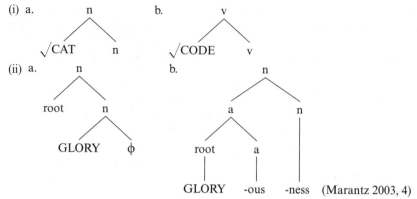

GLORY   -ous   -ness   (Marantz 2003, 4)

A morphological phase is not expressed in terms of the sisterhood relation in the theory developed here (see chapter 1).

6. Di Sciullo and Williams (1987) point out that some affixes do not contribute to the categorial features of the constituent of which they are part. This is true for diminutive affixes, which can combine with adjectives, nouns, and adverbs in Spanish (see (i)). These affixes are taken to be unspecified for categorial features in Di Sciullo and Williams. The head$_F$ is proposed to account for the cases such as the one in (i), which does not fall under the Right Hand Rule. The head$_F$ correctly predicts that the head with respect to a given feature F is the rightmost, as in the example in (ii) with inflectional features. According to the head$_F$, (iii) has two heads, one with respect to categorial features and the other with respect to inflectional features.

(i) poco 'little', poquita; chica 'girl', chicita; ahora 'now', ahorita

(ii) ama bi   tur
      +fut +passive

(iii) arrive s
      +V   +sing

7. The linear order of affixes legible at PF is subject to variation. In some languages, affixes occur at the right periphery of the root; in other languages, they typically occur at the left periphery; in still other languages, affixes occur on both sides of the root. An explanatory theory of morphology should make morphological variation follow from the operations of the grammar in conjunction with language-specific properties. This issue is addressed in chapter 8.

8. In [$_{ZP}$ Z ... [$_{HP}$ α [H YP]]], the complement YP is immune to agreement with something in the next phase up. Only H and its edge (either specifiers or elements adjoined to HP) are accessible to agreement with some element in ZP. H and α belong to ZP for the purposes of Spell-Out. YP is spelled out at the level HP. H and α are spelled out if they remain in situ. Otherwise, their status is determined at the next strong phase ZP.

9. In Chomsky 2001, the phi-features of V and T are uninterpretable in narrow syntax, whereas the phi-features of N (person, number, and gender) are interpretable. I assume that in M, a minimal tree whose head has an agreement paradigm

also has uninterpretable phi (φ) features—that is, [−φ], attached to it when it leaves the morphological LA. Thus, like [−A], [−φ] is part of the uninterpretable morphological features.

10. Agree-concord is subject to different locality restrictions, and it does not lead to the checking of uninterpretable features. Agree-concord is observed in a variety of constructions including multiple ECM (Hiraiwa 2001), multiple NOM (Hiraiwa 2001), negative concord (Przepiorkowski and Kupsc 1997), definite spread (Borer 1998; Hazout 1991, 2000), multiple case and φ agreement, multiple case and clitic doubling (Kalluli 1995), multiple *wh*-questions, and so on. Thus, Japanese allows optional ECM across a CP boundary, as in (i).

(i) a. *#John-ga*   [CP [TP *Mary-wo   me-wo   waru-i*]   *to*] *omoikondei-ta*
       John-Nom   Mary-**Acc** eyes-**Acc** bad-Pres C   believe-past
       'John believed Mary's eye to be bad.'

   b. **John-ga*   [CP [TP *Mary-ga   me-wo   waru-i*]   *to*] *omoikondei-ta*
       John-Nom   Mary-**Nom** eyes-**Acc** bad-Pres C   believe-past
       'John thinks that Mary has bad eyesight.' (Hiraiwa 2001)

The *v* probe has uninterpretable phi-features and the goal DP has uninterpretable structural case. Once the uninterpretable phi-features of the *v* probe are determined, *v* should no longer be able to enter into agreement relations and should be "frozen." However, the second DP in the embedded CP also has uninterpretable case features that need to be valued.

Furthermore, infinitives in Japanese cannot check structural nominative case. The nominative case of the embedded subject in (ii) below is checked via Agree with the matrix T. Multiple nominative DPs can appear within an infinitival embedded clause. The fact that these DPs are lower than the embedded adverbial phrase indicates that there is no overt raising of these DPs out of the embedded clause.

(ii) *John-ga*   [*yosouijouni   nihonjin-ga   eigo-ga   hido-ku*]
     John-Nom   than-expected the-Japanese-**Nom** English **Nom** bad-inf
     kanji-ta.
     think-past.
     'It seemed to John that the Japanese are worse at speaking English than he expected.' (Hiraiwa 2001)

Hiraiwa's (2001) analysis—that is, Multiple Agree (iii) (multiple feature checking) with a single probe as a single simultaneous syntactic operation—increases computational complexity, because features can be [+multiple] or [−multiple]. It runs counter to the Earliness Principle (Chomsky 2001) and PIC. See Di Sciullo and Isac 2003 for discussion.

(iii) Multiple Agree as a single simultaneous operation
      α > β > γ
      └──┴──┘

Agree (α, β, γ), where α is a probe and both β and γ are matching goals for α

11. For the view that Agree and Move are distinct and independent operations, which are not parasitic on each other, see Wurmbrand 2003; Guasti and Rizzi 1999; Chung 1998. For the view that Agree and Move are indeed related, see Chomsky 2000b.

12. The independence of a morphological domain at the PF interface cannot be tested with sentential pronominalization or movement, as is the case for syntactic domains. The independence of a syntactic phase at the PF interface can be shown with tests such as sentential pronominalization (e.g., *Where is John? Mary would know that*), and pseudoclefting (e.g., *What she did was change our way of thinking about language*). These tests show the independence of CP for propositional interpretation. Likewise, it is possible to identify other syntactic domains, including the following: vP, VP, DP, PP. Each domain consists of at least one sister-contain relation. An empirical consequence of the independence of adjunct PPs is that it makes it possible to explain the cases of apparent violation of condition B of the Binding Theory, which is assumed to apply at the LF interface (Aguero 2003; Reinhart 2000; Fox 2000). According to condition B, a pronominal is free in the binding domain of which it is part. If the binding domain is the domain of asymmetry with independent interpretation and PP constitutes such a domain, it follows that the pronoun *him* in [John saw a snake [near him]] is indeed free in its domain. The interpretation of the binding relations must apply to the prepositional component (PP) before applying to the whole propositional component (CP).

13. Morphemes are traditionally viewed as consisting of a form and an interpretation. In Di Sciullo and Williams 1987, the fact that parts of morphological objects are associated with meaning takes the form of theta grids to which argument-structure calculus applies. I now consider the hypothesis that the semantic interpretation of morphological objects is derived from the meaning of their parts.

14. The bare output conditions (Theta Theory, Binding Theory, and so on) are not satisfied equally in words and phrases. The Theta Theory, including the Theta Criterion (Chomsky 1981), is not fully satisfied in words, since morphological objects are predicates, and so they must have at least one argument to saturate outside of D_M. According to the Binding Theory (Chomsky 1981), pronominals must be free locally, while anaphors must be bound in their binding domains. Considering word-internal pronouns and reflexives, the pronoun *him* in the complex anaphor *himself* has no independent reference, and the simplex anaphor *self* cannot be bound to the pronoun *him* within the M-domain, since the complex anaphor *himself* must have an antecedent in D_S. Furthermore, as observed in Di Sciullo and Williams 1987, while a syntactic subject must be part of the DP in (ia), and could also be assumed to be part of (ib), no syntactic subject is available in (ic), where *self-control* is interpreted as in (ib).

(i) a. They saw [$_{DP}$ PRO pictures of each other] on the wall.
    b. [PRO self-control] is no fun
    c. [self-control reactions] should be checked

Thus, the bare output conditions do not apply to the outcome of D_M as they do to the outcome of D_S.

Chapter 4

1. I proposed in Di Sciullo 1996b that Linking is part of the derivation of morphological objects. I defined this operation as follows. The specifier and complement positions are either argument (A) or nonargument (~A):

(i) ~A position must be A linked.

(ii) A position may be ~A linked.

M-Link, as defined in Asymmetry Theory, covers argument, aspect, and operator-variable linking relations, as discussed in this chapter and in chapters 5 and 6.

2. Blocking is a negative restriction on the derivation of semantically equivalent forms. As defined in Aronoff 1976, blocking is the nonoccurrence of a form because of the existence of another form with the same lexical category, the same meaning, and the same root. For example, *-ity* suffixation is blocked in (i) because of the blocking category *glory*.

(i) In a sequence ... $]_{X_1} + Suf_1]_Y + Suf_2]_{X_2}$,
   the adjunction of Suf_2 is blocked if X_1 and X_2 have the same lexical category, the same meaning, and the same root.

(ii) glory$]_{N_1}$ + ous$]_A$ + *ity$]_{N_2}$

In (i), blocking takes the form of a set of conditions on a Word Formation Rule. In (iii), the blocking rule relates to the notion of "competing suffixes"—affixes that could potentially apply to a same base.

(iii) Given the productive rule ... $]_X + Suf_1]_Y$,
   other rules with the same semantics are blocked if Suf_1 is a productive suffix for the class of words$]_X$

(iv) amputation, *amputament; admiration, *admirament

The examples in (iv) show successful application of the blocking rule, while the examples in (v) and (vi) are counterexamples to the rule.

(v) incitation, incitement

(vi) dislocatione, dislocamento   (It)

Shortcomings of morphological blocking are mentioned in Di Sciullo and Williams 1987 and elsewhere, including Scalise 1994. Scalise (1994) points out that the notions of "same meaning" and "productive affix" cannot be formal conditions on rules. Di Sciullo and Williams (1987) questioned the notion of productivity of certain affixation processes, or the lack thereof in morphology, as opposed to syntax.

3. Di Sciullo and Williams (1987) examined two ways the head could be related to the nonhead: the nonhead may satisfy an argument of the head in compounding, and Functional Composition applies in affixation. In this theory, there is a crucial difference between the external argument and the internal arguments. Considering the argument-structure properties of derived verbs, nouns, and adjectives, Di Sciullo and Williams showed that the external argument, be it the R argument of nouns and adjectives' or the AG/EX/TH argument of verbs, has a special status. Functional composition picks out the external argument of the affixal head, to become the external argument of the derived word, and takes the arguments to which the head (a functor) applies, to become arguments of the derived word.

For example, in Di Sciullo and Williams 1987, 32–33, the arguments of an affix are represented in terms of a structured list of theta roles, as in the morphological structures in (i).

(i) a.

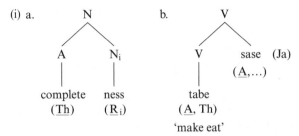

b.

'make eat'

In (ia) the nominal affix *ness* has an external R(eference) argument, and in (ib), the Japanese causative affix *sase* has an external A(gent) argument. Functional composition applies to these structures and compositionally derives the argument structure of the words from the argument structure of their parts. Basically, the external argument of the head of the word becomes the external argument of the derived word and the arguments of the nonhead becomes its internal arguments. The result of this operation is given in (ii) and (iii).

(ii) a.

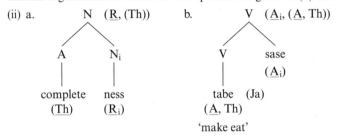

b.

'make eat'

(iii) a. the completeness of the proof$_i$
       (($\underline{Th}_i$) $\underline{R}$)
     b. John ga Mary$_i$ ni tabe   sase.   (Ja)
        ($\underline{A}_i$, Th) ($\underline{A}$)
     'John makes Mary eat.'   (Di Sciullo and Williams 1987, 35)

   Di Sciullo and Williams showed how the argument structure of a morphological object is determined by the argument structure of its head. Asymmetry Theory preserves the crucial difference between the external and internal arguments in the A-Shell, while the operations of Argument Satisfaction and Control of Di Sciullo and Williams 1987 are subsumed under the operation M-Link.

4. In parasynthetic constructions, such as *entrapment*, one of the arguments of the verbal projection is legible at PF. However, it is not a DP and it exhibits the typical genericity and referential opacity of word-internal nominal constituents.

5. The representations in (5) are minimal argument-structure configurations. A ditransitive head would fall under (5c), given restricted recursivity, as depicted in (i).

(i)

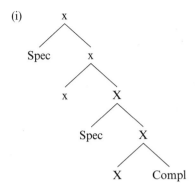

6. As observed by Marcin Morzycki (personal communication), argument-structure shift can be thought of as the semantic analogue of semantic shift. According to Morzycki, type shifts are more limited, however, in the sense that by definition they manipulate only the semantics, not the syntax. With flexible argument structure, type shifts essentially change the kind of arguments a predicate can take without changing the predicate fundamentally. The notion that argument structure is flexible is more conservative than assuming that it is not, since if one were to assume that semantic types are flexible but not syntactic argument structure, one would have to commit to the idea that semantic types and syntactic argument structure do not have to correspond closely. Thus, if one accepts the notion of type shifts, argument-structure flexibility might be the null hypothesis.

There are even some respects in which this leads to constraints on argument structure. Chierchia's (1998) principle according to which type shifts can be used only when there is no lexical item available to convey the intended meaning, could also be thought of as constraining argument-structure flexibility. Thus, *Floyd dreamt a beautiful dream* is better than *Floyd dreamt a dream*, possibly because *Floyd dreamt a dream* is blocked simply by *Floyd dreamt*, which expresses the same thing. So with Chierchia's principle, this fact about cognate objects could be subsumed under a kind of generalized blocking principle saying that it is impossible to resort to argument-structure flexibility (including type shifts) if there is a way of getting precisely the same meaning without doing so.

7. The hypothesis that argument structure should be construed as flexible might be useful in explaining some quasi-regular constructions, discussed in Construction Grammar works (see Fillmore et al. 2003 and related works), such as *Floyd danced his way out of the room*, *Greta sneezed her way to the doctor*, or *Fido barked his way through the shrubbery*. One could think of this as a situation in which a semantically odd kind of argument, *his/her way*, has trouble merging with a verb that normally does not take an object, but manages it only when flexibility of argument structure is allowed, and in order to do this, movement or locomotion has to be added to the meaning of the verb. Assuming that there is some limited flexibility in argument structure seems to provide a pretty natural understanding of the phenomenon. I thank Marcin Morzycki for discussion of this topic.

8. Interestingly, a syntactic head asymmetrically selects another head without requiring that the latter have a given argument structure. Thus a verb asymmetrically

selects the head of an NP, independently of the argument structure of that NP. For discussion, see Di Sciullo 2003b.

9. There is no additional derivational complexity that arises with morphological selection, because the search space for configurational selection has the same dimension as the search space for head-head selection. The search space of M-selection is the lower layer of the shell in (i) including β, H_2, and δ; the search space for S-selection is also the lower layer of (i) including H_2.

(i)

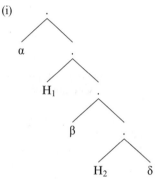

10. In Lieber 1992, verbs have both a lexical conceptual structure (LCS) and a predicate-argument structure (PAS), as in (i) for the verb *admire*. However, affixes such as the nominal affix *-er* have a subcategorization frame specifying the category of the left sister of the affix as well as the category of the immediate mother of the affix of the resulting complex noun—for example, the first line in (ii), and an LCS, the second line of (ii), but no PAS.

(i) admire V
        LCS: [x ADMIRE y]$_{ACTION}$
        PAS: x ⟨y⟩

(ii) -er]V____]N
        LCS: x[LCS of input V]   Lieber (1992, 136 (27))

(iii) admirer LCS: x[x ADMIRE y]
              PAS: ⟨y⟩   Lieber (1992, 136 (28))

According to Lieber (1992, 132), "*-er* in some sense 'links' the first argument of *admire*, which maps at PAS to the external argument; the PAS of *admire* therefore contains only the direct internal argument," as in (iii). See Pylkkänen 2002 for the problems related to multilayered lexical representations of argument structure, in particular the fact that additional linking rules are required for the mapping of the semantic interpretation onto the syntactic structure. No linking rule is required in the theory developed here, since the lexical (underivable) information on affixes and roots takes the form of minimal trees.

11. I assume that theta-role labels are not primitives but derived from configurations (see, among other works, Larson 1990; Levin and Rappaport Hovav 1995; Hale and Keyser 1993, 2002). That the so-called agentive affix *-er* does not necessarily give rise to agentive nominals provides further empirical support for the claim that theta-role labels are not part of the primitives of morphology. That this affix may combine with unergative verbs indicates that the restrictions

on M-Shift do not reside in the thematic labels, because the external argument of an unergative verb is not an agent. The nominals may refer not only to agents (e.g., *killer, baker, catcher, dealer, fighter*), but also to instruments (e.g., *opener, scraper, hanger, peeler, timer*), and to experiencers, (e.g., *dreamer, snorer, laugher, hater, sleeper*). The fact that this affix may combine with unergatives but not with unaccusatives, as shown above, indicates that the selectional restrictions imposed by the affix are based on canonical argument positions, which are available to D_M, given the asymmetric property of argument-structure relations.

12. It is worth noting that A-feature Distinctiveness is not the only restriction on the LF legibility of morphological domains. Aspect structure interacts with argument structure. For example, *-able* combines with predicates denoting activities but less optimally with predicates denoting states. This can be seen with predicates that may either denote states or activities (e.g., *John weighs a bag of apples, a bag of apple is weighable*; *John weighs 150 pounds, *150 pounds are weighable*). The differences follow if we assume a configurational representation of event structure and aspect (see Pustejovsky 1991; Tenny 1994; Di Sciullo 1993, 1995, 2003c, among other works), where states have a different asymmetric articulation than activities. See chapter 5 for Asp-feature Distinctiveness.

13. In Romance, the adverb may be covert; however, a simplex anaphor is obligatory, as seen in the following examples.

(i) a. Ce livre se   lit   facilement. (Fr)
        this book SELF reads easily
        'This book is easy to read.'
    b. Ce livre se   lit.
        this book SELF reads
        'This book is easy to read.'
    c. *Ce livre lit   facilement.
        this book reads easily
        'This book is easy to read.'
    d. *Ce livre lit.
        'This book reads.'

In the absence of the adverb, the clitic signals an argument-structure flexibility effect. A transitive verb, here the verb *read*, is used as an unaccusative. As expected, the auxiliary used with the middle variant is *be* and not *have*; the former is generally used with unaccusatives and the latter is generally used with transitives (see (ii)).

(ii) a. Ce livre s'est   lu   facilement.
         this book SELF is read easily
         'This book has been read easily.'
     b. Les enfants ont/*sont lu ce livre.
         'The children have/are read this book.'

These facts provide additional support for the notion of argument-structure flexibility and for the role of modifiers in the argument-structure type shifting.

Chapter 5

1. Aspect conveys a viewpoint on the situation or the event described by a sentence (among the more recent works, see Carlson 1977, 1999, 2003; Demirdache

and Uribe-Etxebarria 2000; Smith 1991; Verkuyl 1993, 1999). Aspect is generally discussed in relation to tense—for example, the progressive form of the verb, as opposed to the simple form, and the perfect form. It is also discussed in relation to temporal modifiers, such as *at noon*, *yesterday*, and *during the summer*. I take aspect to be analyzed in terms of spatial and temporal features, describing a situation or an event with respect to its beginning point, its internal structure, and its end point if there is one.

2. The properties of prepositional prefixes and particles have been discussed in various works, including Borer 1991; Di Sciullo and Klipple 1994; Di Sciullo 1997; Hale and Keyser 1993, 1998, 2002; Roeper 1999; Lieber 1992; Lieber and Baayen 1993; Marantz 1997; Mateu 2000a; Neeleman and Schipper 1992; Snyder 1995, 2001; Spencer and Zaretskaya 1998; Stiebels 1998; Talmy 1985, 1991; Walinska de Hackbeil 1986; Stiebels and Wunderlich 1992; Van Hout and Roeper 1998.

3. According to the Internal/External Prefix Hypothesis, the iterative affix is generated outside of the verbal argument-structure domain (see (ia)), whereas directional affixes are adjoined to the verb within the argument-structure domain (see (ib)), and they are adjoined to the nominal or adjectival root in denominal and deadjectival verbs (see (ic)).

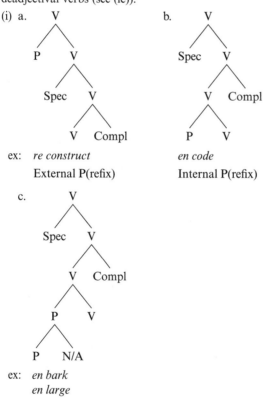

(i) a.
ex: *re construct*
External P(refix)

b.
ex: *en code*
Internal P(refix)

c.
ex: *en bark*
     en large
Internal P(refix)
(denominal and deadjectival verbs)   (Di Sciullo 1997, 54)

The Internal/External Prefix Hypothesis differs from Roeper and Keyser's (1992) Abstract Clitic Hypothesis. According to Roeper and Keyser's hypothesis, proposed on the basis of English data, each verb is associated with a category-neutral abstract clitic position, which also bears on prefixed verbs. The Abstract Clitic Hypothesis (see (ii)) covers five types of entities that can occupy the clitic position: the prefix *re-*, the abstract dative marker, particles, idiomatic nouns, and idiomatic adjectives. These entities may not co-occur.

(ii) *Abstract Clitic Hypothesis (ACH)*
   a. All verbs in English have an invisible clitic position that may be occupied by markers such as the ones we have called dative.
   b. *Re-*, like dative, is one such marker. (Roeper and Keyser 1992, 91)

According to the ACH, the prefix *re-* is an adjunct to a V^0 (Roeper and Keyser 1992, 103), as in (iii).

(iii)

Support for this hypothesis comes from the fact that in English, the prefix *re-* and the indirect object position are incompatible, as in **we regave him the money* and **he rethrew the ball*. This fact follows from the ACH, according to which the indirect object position and *re-* both occupy the same underlying position in verbal projections; thus they do co-occur. However, contrary to English, in Italian and in French, *ri-/re-* is compatible with an indirect object position. The prefix *re-* and the indirect object position are not incompatible in Romance languages. For example, *Il lui a redonné l'argent* (Fr) 'He regave him the money' and *Il a relancé la balle* (Fr) 'He rethrew the ball' are perfectly acceptable. Roeper and Snyder (forthcoming) argue that Romance languages do not have an abstract clitic position.

4. Particles may also provide an end point to the event (e.g., *to read up the paper*, *to read the paper up*). Particles generally occur to the right of the verb in English, and sometimes to the left as well (e.g., *to sleep over*, *to over sleep*). The status of particles is subject to debate (see, among other works, Den Dikken 1995; Svenonius 1996; Klipple 1997; Roeper 1999; Hale and Keyser 2002). I will assume that they are not derived in D_M.

5. A similar view is argued for in syntax for determiners in Sportiche 2002, for prepositions in Kayne 2003, and for adjectives in Carlson 2003.

6. The head of Ev-tree may be small v, as well as small n, as is the case for bare event nouns such as *event* or *fight*.

7. Languages generally include categories that may affect verbal projections from the outside or from the inside. Adverbs are generally thought of as belonging to the first sort and prepositions to the second. This categorial distinction does not hold across the board, however, because there are adverbs that are selected by verbs, as with the verbs *behave* and *word* (e.g., *he behaves well, he worded the letter *(carefully)*). There are also prepositions that are not selected by verbs, as is the case generally for temporal PPs.

8. The modification structure in M is isomorphic to the modification structure in S where, following Cinque 1999, adverbs and prepositions are generated in the Spec of functional projections. This similarity is the effect of the basic asymmetry of grammatical relations shared by M and S. However, there are differences—for example, in the distribution of adjuncts in M and S. ADVPs and PPs have a wider distribution than adverb- and preposition-like affixes. Thus, the parallelism in the modification structure does not lead to the derivation of M-structure in the S dimension of the computational space.

9. Supporting evidence from Romanian is found in the following examples:

(i) a. Vara   asta au   secat   toate lacurile. (unaccusative) (Ro)
       summer this have dried out all   lakes-the.
       'This summer, all the lakes have dried out.'
   b. Primaria   a desecat mlastinile de la marginea   orasului.
       city-hall-the has dried out swamps-the from at outskirts of city-the
       (transitive)
       'City hall has dried the swamps at the outskirts of the city.'

(ii) a. Apa   calda nu curge mereu. (unaccusative)
        water-the hot   not run   always
        'Hot water doesn't always run.'
    b. Multe consecinte   decurg (*din aceasta decizie).
        Many consequences follow from this decision.

(iii) a. Maria doarme. (unergative)
         Maria sleeps.
         'Maria is sleeping.'
     b. Maria adoarme copilul. (transitive)
         Maria a-sleeps the child
         'Maria is putting the child to sleep.'

10. In the case of motion verbs, A-structure modification can be seen as a consequence of the fact that the directional I-Asp affix adds a direction to the event denoted by the verb it adjoins, and a PP referring to a spatial end point is licensed, as in *correre* and *accorrere*.

11. In Hungarian, the affix on the predicate must be reduplicated by a PP for the telic (perfective) interpretation (see (ia)); such reduplication is not observed for the nontelic (imperfective) interpretation (see (ib)).

(i) a. Kati **be**-írta   a vers-et   a barátnő-je   **emlékkönyv-é-be**. (Hu)
       Kate into-wrote the poem-acc the girlfriend-her scrapbook-her-into
       'Kate wrote the poem into her girlfriend's scrapbook.'
   b. Kati épp írta   a vers-et   a barátnő-je   **emlékkönyv-é-be**, amikor
       Kate just wrote the poem-acc the girlfriend-her scrapbook-her-into when
       beléptem a szobába.
       entered-I   the room
       'Kate was just writing the poem into her girlfriend's scrapbook when I entered the room.'

12. Cases such as *redisembark* and *redisentangle* are similar in this respect. They are formed of one internal I-Asp affix *en-* and two E-Asp affixes, *re-* and *dis-*. The affix *dis-* must be E-Asp because it precedes the I-Asp affix *en-*, and there can only

be one I-Asp per projection. Furthermore, *re-* also precedes *dis-*, which could suggest that the former is more extended than the latter. However, the inverse E-Asp *dis-* is yet another sort of E-Asp different projection than the iterative E-Asp, and thus does not contravene to Asp-feature Distinctiveness. The fact that the iterative affix must have scope over the inverse affix (e.g., *#disreembark*) might be due to semantics.

Chapter 6

1. My proposal is compatible with asymmetry-based approaches to semantic and pragmatic categories, such as Diesing's (1992) analysis of the VP, Stowell's (1995) analysis of Tense, and Speas and Tenny's (2003) analysis of speech roles. These works further support the hypothesis that asymmetry is basic in the derivation of the formal and semantic properties of linguistic expressions.

2. In the case of *wh*-words and *th*-words, the specifier of the Op-Shell is legible at PF but not the head. This is congruent with the idea that generally, a variable has no PF features contrary to an operator. There are, however, nonovert operators, as in parasitic gap constructions (see Chomsky 1982; Engdahl 1983, 1985; Taraldsen 1981; Cinque 1990; Browning 1987), as well as overt variables, as in the resumptive pronoun strategy (see McCloskey 1991; Sells 1984).

3. Moreover, the conditions proposed on the Op-variable relation do not apply to the Op-Shell relations. The Bijection Principle (Koopman and Sportiche 1982, 146), according to which there is a bijective correspondence between variables and A-bar positions, has been questioned in Safir 1985. The Bijection Principle fails to account for cases of binding of multiple variables, as discussed in Aguero 2001 and Kratzer 1998, in expressions such as (i). Under the interpretation in which *local* refers to the region of *each president*, the quantifier is binding two variables: its own trace and the null variable in *local*.

(i) A local hero visited each president.

   Bijection may not be a principle of the grammar. According to the Minimal Match Condition (Aoun and Li 2003, 4), an operator must form a chain with the closest XP that it c-commands containing the same relevant features. The MMC is a representational mechanism that constrains the operator-variable relation by requiring that this relation be local and asymmetric. The MMC applies to representations as well as to the structures derived by Attract/Move. It does not apply in M, because there are no movement and no XP categories in D_M. Moreover, the Op and the variable are already in a local asymmetric relation in the Op-Shell. In addition, they share the relevant features given that they are related by Agree.

4. In Russian, *wh*-words are also bipartite constructs, not taking into consideration the case morpheme located in the extended projection of the constructs (see (i)).

(i) kto   Nom   chto   Nom
    kog-o   Gen   cheg-o   Gen
    kom-u   Dat   chem-u   Dat
    kog-o   Acc   chto-Ø   Acc
    kem   Instrum   chem   Instrum
    kom   Preposit   chom   Preposit
    'who'   'what'

The first part of the construct is spelled out by *k*- (ch- is a variant of *k*-); it can be analyzed as spelling out the Op-variable relation, and it is followed by a morpheme spelling out the restrictor. Russian is sensitive to the animate/nonanimate distinction in the form of *wh*-words; *k-to* (animate) differs from *ch-to* (inanimate).

(i) k-to   (Ru)   who   (animate)
    ch-to   what   (inanimate)
    k-uda   where   (direction)
    k-ogda   when   (time)
    k-ak   how   (manner)
    po-ch-emu   why   (reason)
    za-ch-em   why   (purpose)
    k-akoi   which   (part)

Furthermore, the forms *po-* and *za-* are part of an adjunct structure to the Op-Shell. They modify the stem *chto po-ch-emu* and *za-ch-em*, on a par with the Romance forms *pourquoi* (Fr) and *perche* (It). *Po-ch-emu* is used to ask about the reason for a situation (Olga Zavitnevich, personal communication), whereas *za-ch-em* is used to query the purpose of an action.

Evidence that *k*- is a *wh*-morpheme in Russian comes from the fact that most *wh*-words have their *th*-word counterparts, similar to the English pairs *where-there* and *when-then* (see (ii)).

(ii) chto   'what'   to   'that'   (Ru)
     kuda   'where'   tuda   'there'
     kogda   'when'   togda   'then'
     kak   'how'   tak   'so, this way'
     pochemu 'why'   potomu   'because'
     zachem   'why'   zatem   'because'

Thus, *th*-words are similar to *wh*-words. The *t*- spells out the *th*-component, the Op-variable relation, on a par with *k*-, which spells out the *wh*-component of the construct. The other affix spells out the Re relation.

5. In spite of being a morphologically different type of language, Turkish illustrates the same pattern in formation of *wh*-expressions as other languages.

(i) kim   (Tu)   'who'
    ne   'what'
    ne zaman   'when' (what time)
    ne vakit   'when'
    nerede   'where'
    niçin   'why' (what for)
    nasil   'how'
    ne kadar   'how much'

In this language, *wh*-words can appear as two separate words, as in *ne zaman/ vakit* 'what time?', instead of in a single functional form, as in English *when*. *Kim* 'who' does not seem to be decomposable into morphemes. However, Turkish has a personal suffix indicating possession, *-im*, which has the features: human, 1ˢᵗ p. sing., as in *elim* 'my-hand' (*el* 'hand'). The suffix form of the verb "to be" for 1ˢᵗ p. sing. is *-im*, as in 'I am at home'—*evde-y-im* (*evde* 'home'); thus the same features for 1st p. sing. are present. The derivational suffix *-im* used in the formation of nouns—many of which denote a single action, as in *dil* 'to slice', *dilim* 'a slice', *kim* 'who'—has the same set of features: human and singular. Thus, *-im* can be analyzed as the morphological spell-out of the restrictor.

6. The pronominal affix *o-* occurs in the forms of *who* and *where*, and the pronominal affix *é* occurs in the forms of *what*, *why*, and *how*, which indicates that they are not the spell-out of the restrictor.

(i) ó-vhá   who   (Ye)
    é-mè   what
    à-nè / ò bò   where (what place)
    ghì èrèghè   when (which time)
    á-bà   how (what manner)
    é-mézè   why (what happens)
    ghì   which
    é-kè   how many/much

Moreover, syntactic forms are observed instead of morphological forms (e.g., *ghi èrèghè* 'which time' instead of a single form equivalent to *when*) as is the case for Russian.

7. Yekhee operates on a system of complex demonstratives, including the definite determiner and a demonstrative element (double-definite system). Nouns entering into this construction must already be definite—that is, they must be accompanied by a definite article (see (i)).

(i) a. ọ̀nà ówà   ọ̀nà   (Ye)
       the house   this
       'this house'
    b. ọ̀nà ówà   ólì
       the house   that
       'that house'

8. In languages such as Japanese, particles are used to form questions (see (i)). The question particle *ka* has been claimed to move out of an indefinite in the derivation of a question (Hagstrom 1998). However, it is not clear whether the particle movement he proposes is cyclic, and why the movement is not meaning preserving.

(i) a. *John*-wa   **nani-o**   *tabe-masi-ta* **ka**?   (Ja)
       John −Top what-Acc eat-Past   Q-part
       'What did John eat?'
    b. *Dare-mo ga*   **nani-ka** o   *tabe-te-ir*u
       Everyone Nom something Acc eating
       'Everyone is eating something'.

According to Misa Hirai (personal communication), while *ka* is a question particle, it cannot be used alone, as an echo question. Rather, it is the indefinite with a question intonation that is used (e.g., *nani?*). When *ka* is part of an indefinite, it is in the domain of another operator; consequently it does not determine the features of the whole construct.

9. In Chomsky 1995 and 1998, the noninterpretable Op-feature Q and the interpretable [+wh] feature are part of the derivation of questions. While the first must be deleted in the syntactic derivation, the second cannot be, because its deletion would run counter to recoverability. In the morphological derivation of *wh*-words, however, neither the Q feature nor the +wh feature must be deleted, since they are interpretable features in the morphology.

10. A plausible idea is that every operator originally included under the scope of the *wh*-movement rule in Chomsky 1977 should in principle bear a [+wh] feature, including null operators of various kinds, such as the operators in parasitic gaps and tough/enough constructions. Exclamatives, relatives and free relatives, questions, comparatives, and null operator constructions of various kinds were treated by Chomsky (1977) as instances of the same phenomenon. The unifying feature in Chomsky's original proposal was taken to be the *wh*-feature; this is also the case in the typology I propose. (I thank Calixto Aguero for discussion of this topic.)

11. Den Dikken (2003) proposes the following typology of *wh*-words, using the features [±wh] and [±Focus]:

(i) a. regular question words   [+Wh, ±Focus]   single question
    b. echo-question words   [+Wh, +Focus]   [+Wh] not attractable
    c. indefinite *wh*-words   [+Wh, −Focus]   [+Wh] not attractable
    d. relative *wh*-words   [+Wh, −Focus]

(Den Dikken 2003; 84 (10))

This typology is based on syntactic properties of *wh*-words, assuming that *wh*-movement is a movement to Focus. In some languages, such as Somali, the Focus feature can be thought of as being part of the restrictor of the Op-Shell. Svolacchia et al. (1995) show that *wh*-elements in Somali incorporate a focus particle in their morphological structure; thus *muxuu* 'what' is made of *ma* (interrogative particle) + *wax* ('thing') + *aa* (contracted form of a Focus marker) + *uu* ('he'). The focus feature is part of the feature structure of *wh*-words. However, this is not the case with other languages, where focus is an independent morpheme.

12. See Hagstrom 1998, arguing that the same operator Q is part of the semantics for both *wh*-words such as *what* and indefinites such as *something*.

13. As pointed out by Calixto Aguero (personal communication), this is in line with the D feature that Chomsky has been using since the onset of minimalism. Under that implementation of the D feature, the proposed typologies in (30) and (31) are not mutually exclusive. That is, an item may have membership in both typologies, since an item may be specified with multiple features. Chomsky also takes *wh*-phrases to have a [+D] feature. This is necessary to account for the fact that *wh*-phrases can satisfy the EPP or OCC feature in sentences like the following.

(i) Who seems to his mother to have destroyed the city?

In this sentence *who* comes from the embedded clause: it is an argument of *destroy*. Since the sentence does not have the flavor of a WCO violation, the *wh*-phrase must have stopped in an A-position between the pronoun in the matrix clause and the matrix COMP position, the assumption being that A-movement prevents the WCO violation (a standard assumption since Mahajan 1990). The best candidate for that position would be the Spec IP, which was at some point taken to have an uninterpretable D feature. *Wh*-phrases were thought to stop at that position because they had interpretable D features.

14. The restrictor is assumed to range over categorial features, case, and argument/adjunct features. Tsai (1994), following Huang (1982), distinguishes nominal *wh*-phrases from nonnominal ones with respect to extraction.

15. Functional words such as *since* and *because* are subordinate conjunctions. They relate two propositions (see (i)). They can be viewed as conjunction operators, with the typical structure of the M-Shell (see Di Sciullo 2003b). If they relate two propositions, their Re layer relates two instances of the same semantic type. This would constitute a violation of the Distinctiveness Condition, which requires that pairs of features in the M-Shell be distinct.

(i) a. Gates left since David was bored with the meeting.
    b. Bill left because David came in.

The distinctiveness lies in the sequence of events that will impose an asymmetry between the two events denoted by the propositions.

Chapter 7

1. Crosslinguistic evidence for my proposal comes from Turkish, where the morphemes spell out the part of *n*-words in a more explicit way than in English; see (i).

(i) hiç bir   yerde   (Tu)
    no some where
    'nowhere'

The impossibility of reordering the constituents of the functional words observed in English and in Romance languages is also found in Hungarian, as in (ii), for example.

(ii) a. vala-ki   (Hu)
         some-who
         'someone'
     b. *ki-vala
         who-some

However, Russian and Polish exhibit variation: while Neg [+Indef] works the same way as in English (see (iii), (iv)), the existential quantifier [+wh] shows the reverse pattern ((v), (vi)). It must be added that other Slavic languages (Bulgarian, Serbian, Czech) seem to work like English in that there is no variation.

(iii) ni-kto   (Ru)
      Neg-wh
      'noone'

(iv) ni-gdzie   (Po)
     no-where
     'nowhere'

(v) kto-nibud   (Ru)
   wh-some
   'someone'

(vi) gdzie-ś   (Po)
   where-some
   'somewhere'

With respect to *whenever*, Hungarian exhibits the reverse order, as in (vii).

(vii) a. akár-ki   (Hu)
        ever-who
        'whoever'
     b. akár-hol
        ever-where
        'whereever'

I will not discuss the microvariation facts here, because they require a deeper understanding of the properties of Slavic and Finno-Ugric languages. I leave this area for further research.

2. wh+*ever* constructions (e.g., *whoever, whatever, whichever, wherever, whenever*) are interesting with respect to scope properties. Wh+*ever* may head a free relative (e.g., *he does whatever he wants to do*); it may also be the answer to an information question (e.g., Q: *What will he do now?* A: *Whatever*), and used as a *wh*-word (e.g., *Whatever happened to you?*). Given that *wh*-words and *th*-words can be structured on the basis of the feature structure defined in section 6.4.2, wh+*ever* can be analyzed as a relative pronoun (i.e., a [−D, +wh] element), as an indefinite (i.e., a [+D, −th]), and as a *wh*-word (i.e., a [+Q, +wh]) (see (i)).

(i) a. [$_{Op–D}$ wh- [$_{Fx+wh}$ - at [ever x [β y δ]]]]
    b. [$_{Op+D}$ wh- [$_{Fx–th}$ - at [ever x [β y δ]]]]
    c. [$_{Op+Q}$ wh- [$_{Fx+wh}$ - at [ever x [β y δ]]]]

There seems to be a relationship between *everywhere* (*every+where*) and *wherever* (*where+every*). In particular, *wherever* seems to have universal force suggesting that *ever* scopes over the *where*. According to Dayal 1997, Jacobson 1995, and von Fintel 2000, wh+*ever* includes universal quantification; for Tancredi 2004, the interpretation of wh−*ever* is not quantificational but has a plural interpretation. It might be the case that when *ever* is the morphological spell-out of *every*, it scopes over the *wh*-constituent; see (ii).

(ii) [$_{Op}$ α ever [$_{Op}$ wh- [$_{Fx}$ β here γ]]]

The linear order of the construction is derived by Flip in PF, where *ever* follows *where*, as in *wherever*, assuming that like the plural, the operator sits in the head position. I will leave this question for further research.

3. See also Boeckx and Stjepanović (2001) and Harley (2003) for the application of head movement in morphophonology. Head movement is part of L-syntax (Hale and Keyser 2002) under the assumption that L-syntax is immune to both Extension and Inclusiveness. It is also part of Distributed Morphology, where word-internal head adjacency relation can be obtained either in the course of the syntactic derivation by head movement or in the phonological derivation by head

lowering. Embick (2004) suggests that in languages such as English, where V does not raise to I in the syntax, I is lowered to V in the phonology, assuming that the phonology is immune to the Proper Binding Condition.

4. As observed by Marcin Morzycki (personal communication), the fact that this kind of adding structure does not look directly like building a tree upward could plausibly be due to how the trees are drawn rather than anything deeper.

5. Moreover, as observed by Calixto Aguero (personnal communication), this version of head movement violates cyclicity, since it skips the head position of the affix, and it may also predict additional scope possibilities for the remnants that are not attested.

6. Williams (2003) proposes a similar operation, which he also refers to as FLIP. The operation he proposes reverses two linearly ordered categories. It applies only to inflectional morphology.

(i) a. FLIP: if X = [A > B], A and B terminal or nonterminal,
       FLIP(X) = [B < A]
    b. REASSOCIATE; if X = [A > [B > C]]
       R(X) = [[A > B] > C] (Williams 2003)

The operation Flip proposed here applies to minimal S- and M-trees under different conditions. Furthermore, it applies to derivational as well as inflectional M-trees.

7. The fact that S-Flip is optional when the constituent in the specifier position is not "heavy," whereas M-Flip is obligatory, may be attributed to the following: M-Flip applies in the argument-structure layer and provides a way to reduce the complexity that would arise with the parsing of non-PF-legible specifier. The latter is either legible at PF or not. Thus M-Flip is obligatory. S-Flip applies to the modifier layer to reduce the complexity that would arise when the specifier includes too much structure, generating computational complexity. The specifier can be "heavy" or not; thus S-Flip is optional.

Chapter 8

1. A Minimalist approach to morphological variation contrasts with the traditional approaches that describe variation in terms of broad differences, either typological or parametric. According to the traditional typology, languages fall into one of the following morphological classes: isolating, agglutinative, inflectional, and polysynthetic. Chinese and Vietnamese are considered typical isolating languages, with very little affixation. Turkish and Hungarian are typical agglutinative languages, where each morpheme has a single grammatical function. Latin and Russian are inflectional languages—that is, typically polymorphemic and where more than one grammatical feature are fused into single morphemes. Mowack and Chukchee qualify as polysynthetic languages; they allow noun incorporation and thus express with single words what other languages express with long sentences.

The typological approach has been criticized in several works, including Spencer 1991. One reason for replacing the typological approach with morphological variation is that the typical differences between the morphological types of languages are not clearcut: properties of different morphological systems can be found in a single language. For example, while most affixation in Turkish is PF legible at the right periphery of the word, some affixes do occur at the left periphery. Turkish has prefixation in loanwords (e.g., *gayri*-müslim 'non-Muslim', *anti*-demokratik 'antidemocratic', *na*-tamam 'incomplete'). It also has reduplication of the (C)V of the initial syllable with one of the consonants /p/, /s/, /r/, /m/ added to it. This reduplication occurs with a subclass of adjectives, color- and shape-denoting adjectives (e.g., *sap*-sari 'bright yellow', *dos*-doğru 'absolutely straight', *ter*-termiz 'very clean', *bem*-beyaz 'extremely white') (Sebüktekin 1971).

2. In the Minimalist Program, syntactic variation has been attributed to a minimal difference in the strength of functional features (Chomsky 1995). However, in a truly minimalist framework, the notion of strength has no place, since it is a second-order feature—that is, a feature over a feature—and thus introduces complexity in the grammar. This notion has been dispensed with in Chomsky 2000a, 2000b, 2001. In a truly minimalist framework, specific cases of linguistic variation should follow from the operations of the grammar and independent properties of the languages.

3. Case Theory (Vergnaud 1980 and related works), which restricts the distribution of phrasal expressions to the properties of functional elements, and the hypothesis that language variation is limited to the realm of the lexicon (Borer 1986), contribute to the implementation of the uniformity principle.

4. The strong suffixing character of agglutinative languages such as Turkish can also be shown to follow from the theory. Turkish is an SOV agglutinative language of the South-West branch of the Turkic language family (Lewis 1967; Sebüktekin 1971; Kornfilt 2004). Turkish has five cases, as well as post-clitics and post-positions (e.g., *uyku-da* sleep at 'asleep', *sahil-de* shore at 'ashore').

Turkish is a strong suffixing language; however, some affixes occur at the left periphery in loan words (see note 1), and modifier-like affixes precede the root in derivations such as the following reported in Sebüktekin (1971, 62): *mukabele* 'response', *bilmukabele* 'in response, as a response', *isatisna* 'exception', *bilâistisna* 'without exception'. The fact that *wh*-morphemes also precede the rest of the *wh*-words, as evidenced in chapter 6, is also predicted by the theory, because operator-like affixes occupy the specifier position of their minimal tree. Thus, even in a language where most affixes occur to the right of the root, modifier-like and operator-like affixes precede the root.

The PF legibility of affixes to the right of the root can follow from an independent property of Turkish mophophonology: vowel harmony. Vowel harmony is based on the spreading of [+back] and [+round] features from stem initial vowel to the other stem vowels and to the suffix vowel, from left to right, root outward (Bakovic 2000). Turkish exhibits rightward backness and labial vowel harmony (VH) (Levi 2001). Interestingly, affixes do occur at the left periphery in loan words, but vowel harmony does not occur in loan words.

One way to derive the "strong suffixing" property in Asymmetry Theory is to assume that Turkish has a vowel harmony feature in the head position of cognate affixes and root trees. This feature is PF legible, and thus M-Flip applies in D_Φ to minimal tree headed with the vowel harmony feature. Consequently, affixes are ordered after the root. Loan affixes do not have the vowel harmony feature in the head position of their minimal tree. Consequently, the minimal trees of loan affixes and root do not undergo M-Flip, and thus loan prefixes precede the root. See Di Sciullo 2005 for discussion.

5. Talmy (1985) analyzes lexicalization patterns in English and Spanish, proposing that parts of meaning such as "direction of motion" and "fact of motion" are conflated in individual morphemes, and that these patterns differ crosslinguistically. Thus, the pattern conflating motion and manner exists in French though not in English. Talmy also claims that verbs conflating direction and motion are scarce in English, while they are more typical in Romance languages. He relates the existence of verb particles to the lexicalization patterns. He proposes that verb particles in languages such as English and German are grammatical satellites. In English-type languages, satellites carry the main predication, whereas in French-type languages, the main predication must be carried by the verb.

6. The nominal category they include expresses neither an entity nor a state undergoing change nor a resulting place or state; rather it expresses a separable instrument of the event. This can be seen in their related XP structures in (i) and (ii), where the prepositional *with*-phrase does not provide an end point to the event.

(i) segare/tagliare DP con una sega   (It)
    'to saw/to cut DP with a saw'

(ii) martellare/battere DP con un martello
     'to hammer/to hit DP with a hammer'

More generally, instrumental PPs do not express the location of an event or an entity undergoing change of place or state. According to Higginbotham and Ramchand (1997), an instrumental PP has the event as its external argument, and not the location where it occurred. This can be seen explicitly in *the cutting is (done) with a saw* and *the hitting was done with a hammer*. Thus, the nominal category enclosed in the related X^0 verbal structures is not in the sister-contain domain of an I-Asp head, and no P is visible at PF in these verbal structures.

7. In Di Sciullo 1999b, I expressed the variation in terms of the difference between Directional Asp (D/ASP) and Locational Asp (L/ASP), in the sense of Klipple 1997. The nominal related to D/ASP undergoes a change of place, whereas the nominal related to L/ASP is the terminus of the event denoted by the verbal predicate. Thus, denominal and deadjectival (N/A) verbs include an internal ASP projection c-commanding the prepositional P projection. The variation in the legibility of the prefixes is proposed to follow from a difference in the strength of the terminus [T] feature of ASP, where D/ASP=$_{def}$ P does not c-command N/A. L/ASP=$_{def}$ P c-commands N/A. The proposed parameter is the following.

(i) *[T] parameter*
    In Italian the [T] feature of D/ASP is strong; in French it is weak.

In Asymmetry theory the Asp-Shell is superior to the Ev-Shell. The difference between the languages under consideration in the legibility of Asp affixes follows from local linking, under asymmetric agreement. The proposed analysis is simpler than the one including the [T] parameter to the extent that no additional requirement is needed to account for this microvariation. In particular, it does not rely on second-order types of features, such as feature strength.

References

Abels, Klaus. 2001. On an alleged argument for the Proper Binding Condition. *MIT Working Papers in Linguistics* 43, 1–16.

Abney, Steven. 1987. The English noun phrase in its sentential aspect. Unpublished doctoral dissertation, MIT.

Adger, David. 2003. Stress and phasal syntax. GLOW abstract.

Aguero, Calixto. 2001. Cyclicity and the Scope of Wh-Phrases. Unpublished doctoral dissertation, MIT.

Aguero, Calixto. 2003. The DPBE and Its Exemption in Romance. Unpublished manuscript, UQAM.

Aguero, Calixto. 2004. Isolability at the Interfaces and the Notion of Binding Domain. Unpublished manuscript, UQAM.

Ambar, Manuela. 1983. Gouvernement et inversion dans les interrogatives Qu- en Portugais. *Recherches Linguistiques* (Paris) 16, 5–31.

Ambar, Manuela. 1988. *Para una sintaxe da inversao sujeto verbo en portuguès.* Doctoral dissertation. Lisbon: Colibi.

Ambar, Manuela. 2003. Wh-asymmetries. In Anna Maria Di Sciullo, ed., *Asymmetry in Grammar, Volume 1: Syntax and Semantics*, 209–251. Amsterdam: John Benjamins.

Ambar, Manuela, and Rita Veloso. 2001. On the nature of wh-phrases—word order and wh-in-situ. Evidence from Portuguese, French, Hungarian and Tetum. In Yves d'Hulst, Johan Rooryck, and Jan Schroten, eds., *Selected Papers from "Going Romance" 1999, Current Issues in Linguistic Theory* 221, 1–39.

Anderson, Steven. 1992. *A-Morphous Morphology.* Cambridge: Cambridge University Press.

Androutsopoulou, Antonia, and Manuel Español Echevarria. 2003. French definite determiners in indefinite contexts and asymmetric agreement. In Anna Maria Di Sciullo, ed., *Asymmetry in Grammar, Volume 2: Morphology, Phonology, Acquisition*, 11–27. Amsterdam: John Benjamins.

Aoun, Joseph, and Yen-Hui Audrey Li. 1993. *Syntax of Scope.* Cambridge, MA: MIT Press.

Aoun, Joseph, and Yen-Hui Audrey Li. 2003. *Essays on the Representational and Derivational Nature of Grammar.* Cambridge, MA: MIT Press.

Aronoff, Mark. 1976. *Word Formation in Generative Grammar.* Cambridge, MA: MIT Press.

Aronoff, Mark. 1983. Potential words, actual words, productivity and frequency. In Shiro Hattori, Kazuko Inoue, Tadao Shimomiya, Yoshio Nagashima, eds., *Proceedings of the 13th International Congress of Linguists, 1982, Tokyo.* Tokyo: Tokyo Press, 163–171.

Aronoff, Mark. 1994. *Morphology by Itself.* Cambridge, MA: MIT Press.

Arregi, Karlos. 2003. Nuclear stress and syntactic structure. Paper presented at the North American Syntactic Conference, Concordia University.

Bach, Emmon. 1996. On the grammar of complex words. In Anna Maria Di Sciullo, ed., *Configurations: Essays on Structure and Interpretation.* Somerville, MA: Cascadilla Press.

Baker, Mark C. 1988. *Incorporation: A Theory of Grammatical Function Changing.* Chicago: University of Chicago Press.

Bakovic, Eric. 2000. Harmony, Dominance, and Control. Unpublished doctoral dissertation, Rutgers University.

Barwise, Jon, and Robin Cooper. 1981. Generalized quantifiers in natural languages. *Linguistics and Philosophy* 4(1), 159–219.

Beard, Robert. 1988. The separation of derivation and affixation: Toward a lexeme-morpheme based morphology. *Quaderni di semantica* 5, 277–287.

Beard, Robert. 1995. *Lexeme-Morpheme Based Morphology.* Albany, NY: SUNY Press.

Bendor-Samuel, David. 1988. The ongoing use of vernacular literature. *Notes on Scripture in Use and Language Programs* 18, 3–20.

Bendor-Samuel, John T., and Rhonda L. Hartell, eds. 1989. *The Niger-Congo Languages: A Classification and Description of Africa's Largest Language Family.* Lanham, MD: University Press of America.

Binnick, Robert. 1998. *Time and the Verb.* Oxford: Oxford University Press.

Boeckx, Cedric. 2003. Symmetries and asymmetries in multiple checking. In Cedric Boeckx and Kleanthes K. Grohmann, eds., *Multiple Wh-Fronting*, 17–26. Amsterdam: John Benjamins.

Boeckx, Cedric, and Kleanthes K. Grohmann. 2003. *Multiple Wh-Fronting.* Amsterdam: John Benjamins.

Boeckx, Cedric, and Sandra Stjepanović. 2001. Heading toward PF. *Linguistic Inquiry* 32, 345–355.

Booij, Geert. 1989. On the representation of diphthongs in Frisian. *Journal of Linguistics* 25, 319–332.

Borer, Hagit. 1986. I-subjects. *Linguistic Inquiry* 17(3), 375–416.

Borer, Hagit. 1988. On the parallelism between compounds and constructs. *Yearbook of Morphology* 1, 45–66.

Borer, Hagit. 1991. The causative-inchoative alternation: A case study in parallel morphology. *Linguistic Review* 8, 119–158.

Borer, Hagit. 1994. The projection of arguments. In E. Benedicto and J. Runner, eds., *Functional Projections*, 19–47. Amherst: GLSA, University of Massachusetts.

Borer, Hagit. 1998. Morphology and syntax. In Andrew Spencer and Arnold Zwicky, eds., *The Handbook of Morphology*, 151–190. Oxford: Blackwell.

Bošković, Željko. 1997. *The Syntax of Nonfinite Complementation: An Economy Approach.* Cambridge, MA: MIT Press.

Brody, Michael. 2000. Mirror theory: Syntactic representations in perfect syntax. *Linguistic Inquiry* 31, 29–56.

Browning, Marguerite. 1987. Null operator constructions. Unpublished doctoral dissertation, MIT.

Burzio, Luigi. 1986. *Italian Syntax: A Government-Binding Approach.* Dordrecht: Reidel.

Bybee, Joan, Revere Perkins, and William Pagliuca. 1994. *The Evolution of Grammar: Tense, Aspect, and Modality in the Languages of the World.* Chicago: University of Chicago Press.

Carlson, Greg. 1977. Reference to Kinds in English. Unpublished doctoral dissertation, University of Massachusetts, Amherst.

Carlson, Greg. 1999. Event semantics and propositional semantics. Paper presented at the Thermi Conference on Tense, Aspect and Mood, Thermi International Summer School of Linguistics (TISSL).

Carlson, Greg. 2002. Weak indefinites. In Martine Coene and Yves d'Hulst, eds., *From NP to DP, Volume 1: The Syntax and Semantics of Noun Phrases*, 195–210. Amsterdam: John Benjamins.

Carlson, Greg. 2003. Interpretive asymmetries in major phrases. In Anna Maria Di Sciullo, ed., *Asymmetry in Grammar, Volume 2: Morphology, Phonology and Acquisition*, 301–315. Amsterdam: John Benjamins.

Chierchia, Gennaro. 1998. Reference to kinds across languages. *Natural Language Semantics* 6, 339–405.

Chierchia, Gennaro. 2001. A puzzle about indefinites. In Carlo Cecchetto, Gennaro Chierchia, and Maria Teresa Guasti, eds., *Semantic Interfaces: Reference, Anaphor and Aspect*, 51–89. Stanford, CA: Center for the Study of Language and Information.

Chierchia, Gennaro, and Sally McConnell-Ginet. 1990. *Meaning and Grammar: An Introduction to Semantics.* Cambridge, MA: MIT Press.

Chomsky, Noam. 1965. *Aspects of the Theory of Syntax.* Cambridge, MA: MIT Press.

Chomsky, Noam. 1970. Remarks on nominalizations. In R. Jacobs and P. Rosenbaum, eds., *Readings in Transformational Grammar*, 184–221. Boston: Ginn.

Chomsky, Noam. 1975. *Reflections on Language.* New York: Pantheon.

Chomsky, Noam. 1977. On wh-movement. In Peter Culicover, Thomas Wasow, and Adrian Akmajian, eds., *Formal Syntax*, 71–132. New York: Academic Press.

Chomsky, Noam. 1981. *Lectures on Government and Binding*. Dordrecht: Foris.

Chomsky, Noam. 1982. *Some Concepts and Consequences of the Theory of Government and Binding*. Cambridge, MA: MIT Press.

Chomsky, Noam. 1986. *Knowledge of Language*. New York: Praeger.

Chomsky, Noam. 1993. A minimalist program for linguistic theory. In Kenneth Hale and Samuel Jay Keyser, eds., *The View from Building 20*. Cambridge, MA: MIT Press.

Chomsky, Noam. 1995. *The Minimalist Program*. Cambridge, MA: MIT Press.

Chomsky, Noam. 1998. Minimalist inquiries: The framework. *MIT Occasional Papers in Linguistics* 15. (Revised version published as Chomsky 2000b.)

Chomsky, Noam. 1999. Derivation by phase. *MIT Occasional Papers in Linguistics* 18. (Revised version published as Chomsky 2001.)

Chomsky, Noam. 2000a. Beyond Explanatory Adequacy. Unpublished manuscript, MIT.

Chomsky, Noam. 2000b. Minimalist inquiries: The framework. In R. Martin, D. Michaels, and J. Uriagereka, eds., *Step by Step: Essays on Minimalist Syntax in Honor of Howard Lasnik*, 89–155. Cambridge, MA: MIT Press.

Chomsky, Noam. 2001. Derivation by phase. In Michael Kenstowicz, ed., *Ken Hale: A Life in Language*, 1–52. Cambridge, MA: MIT Press.

Chomsky, Noam, and Morris Halle. 1968. *The Sound Pattern of English*. New York: Harper & Row.

Chung, Sandra. 1998. *The Design of Agreement: Evidence from Chamorro*. Chicago: University of Chicago Press.

Cinque, Guglielmo. 1990. *Types of Ā-dependencies*. Cambridge, MA: MIT Press.

Cinque, Guglielmo. 1993. A null theory of phrase and compound stress. *Linguistic Inquiry* 24, 239–297.

Cinque, Guglielmo. 1999. *Adverbs and Functional Heads: A Cross-Linguistic Perspective*. New York: Oxford University Press.

Collins, Christopher. 1997. *Local Economy*. Cambridge, MA: MIT Press.

Collins, Christopher. 2002. Eliminating labels. In S. D. Epstein and T. D. Seely, eds., *Derivation and Explanation in the Minimalist Program*, 42–64. Oxford: Blackwell.

Comrie, Bernard. 1976. *Aspect: An Introduction to the Study of Verbal Aspect and Related Problems*. Cambridge Textbooks in Linguistics. Cambridge: Cambridge University Press.

Corver, Norbert. 1997. The internal syntax of the Dutch extended adjectival projection. *Natural Language and Linguistic Theory* 15, 289–368.

Dayal, Veneeta. 1997. Free relatives and ever: Identity and free choice readings. *Proceedings of SALT VII*, 99–116. Ithaca, NY: CLC Publications.

De Almeida, Roberto G., and S. Tesolin. 2004. Priming Arguments and Conceptual Fillers of Verbs. Unpublished manuscript, Concordia University.

Demirdache, Hamida, and Myriam Uribe-Etxebarria. 2000. The primitives of temporal relations. In R. Martin, D. Michaels, and J. Uriagereka, eds., *Step by Step: Minimalist Essays in Honor of Howard Lasnik*, 157–187. Cambridge, MA: MIT Press.

den Dikken, Marcel. 1995. *Particles—On the Syntax of Verb-Particle, Triadic and Causative Constructions*. Oxford: Oxford University Press.

den Dikken, Marcel. 1997. The syntax of possession and the verb "have." *Lingua* 101, 129–150.

den Dikken, Marcel. 2003. On the morphosyntax of *wh*-movement. In C. Boeckx and K. Grohmann, eds., *Multiple Wh-Fronting*, 77–98. Amsterdam: John Benjamins.

den Dikken, Marcel, and Anastasia Giannakidou. 2002. From *hell* to polarity: "Aggressively non-D-linked" wh-phrases as polarity items. *Linguistic Inquiry* 33, 31–61.

Diesing, Molly. 1992. *Indefinites*. Cambridge, MA: MIT Press.

Di Sciullo, Anna Maria. 1992. Deverbal compounds and the external argument. In I. M. Roca, ed., *Thematic Structure: Its Role in Grammar*, 65–78. Berlin: Foris.

Di Sciullo, Anna Maria. 1993. The complement domain of a head at morphological form. *Probus* 5, 257–290.

Di Sciullo, Anna Maria. 1994. Prefixes and suffixes. In Claudia Parodi, Carlos Quicoli, Mario Saltarelli, and Maria-Luisa Zubizarreta, eds., *Romance Linguistics in Los Angeles: Selected Papers from the 24th Linguistic Symposium on Romance Languages*. Washington, DC: Georgetown University Press.

Di Sciullo, Anna Maria. 1996a. Atomicity and relatedness in configurational morphology. In Anna Maria Di Sciullo, ed., *Configurations. Essays on Structure and Interpretation*, 17–40. Somerville, MA: Cascadilla Press.

Di Sciullo, Anna Maria. 1996b. X-bar selection. In J. Rooryck and Laurie Zaring, eds., *Phrase Structure and the Lexicon*, 77–108. Dordrecht: Kluwer.

Di Sciullo, Anna Maria. 1996c. X^0/XP Asymmetries. *Linguistic Analysis* 26, 1–26.

Di Sciullo, Anna Maria. 1997. Prefixed-verbs and adjunct identification. In Anna Maria Di Sciullo, ed., *Projections and Interface Conditions: Essays in Modularity*, 52–74. New York: Oxford University Press.

Di Sciullo, Anna Maria. 1999a. The local asymmetry connection. *MIT Working Papers in Linguistics* 35, 25–49.

Di Sciullo, Anna Maria. 1999b. Verbal structures and variation. In Esthela Treviño and José Lema, eds., *Semantic Issues in Romance Syntax*, 39–57. Amsterdam: John Benjamins.

Di Sciullo, Anna Maria. 2002. The asymmetry of morphology. In P. Boucher, ed., *Many Morphologies*, 1–28. Somerville, MA: Cascadilla Press.

Di Sciullo, Anna Maria. 2003a. Asymmetry in morphological objects and derivational complexity. In N. Callaos, A. M. Di Sciullo, T. Ohta, and T. K. Liu, eds., *SCI 2003 Proceedings*, 13–18. Orlando, FL: International Institute of Informatics and Systemics.

Di Sciullo, Anna Maria. 2003b. Morphological relations in asymmetry theory. In Anna Maria Di Sciullo, ed., *Asymmetry in Grammar, Volume 2: Morphology, Phonology and Acquisition*, 9–36. Amsterdam: John Benjamins.

Di Sciullo, Anna Maria. 2003c. Spatial relations in morphological objects. In Geert Booij, Janet DeCesaris, Angela Rali, and Sergio Scalise, eds., *Topics in Morphology: Selected Papers from the Third Mediterranean Morphology Meeting*, 29–50. Barcelona: Universitat Pompeu Fabra.

Di Sciullo, Anna Maria. 2004. Deriving Compounds. Unpublished manuscript, UQAM.

Di Sciullo, Anna Maria. 2005. Affixes at the edge. LSA handout. Oakland, CA.

Di Sciullo, Anna Maria. Forthcoming. On the asymmetrical nature of elementary operations: Evidence from codeswitching. In Jeff McSwam, ed., *Grammatical Theory and Bilingual Codeswitching*. Cambridge, MA: MIT Press.

Di Sciullo, Anna Maria, and Sandiway Fong. 2001a. Asymmetry, zero morphology and tractability. In *Proceedings of the 15th Pacific Asia Conference on Language, Information and Computation*, 61–72. Hong Kong: City University of Hong Kong.

Di Sciullo, Anna Maria, and Sandiway Fong. 2001b. Efficient parsing for word structure. In *NLPRS 2001, Proceedings of the 16th Natural Language Processing Pacific Rim Symposium*, 741–748. Tokyo: National Center of Sciences.

Di Sciullo, Anna Maria, and Dana Isac. 2003. Ways of agreeing, phases, and interfaces. Paper presented at the Workshop on Agreement, Universidade Nova de Lisboa.

Di Sciullo, Anna Maria, and Dana Isac. 2004. Possible extraction domains and AGREE as an asymmetric relation. Paper presented at the Interfaces Conference, Pescara, Italy.

Di Sciullo, Anna Maria, and Elisabeth Klipple. 1994. Modifying affixes. *WECOL* 6.

Di Sciullo, Anna Maria, and Roumyana Slabakova. Forthcoming. Quantification and aspect. In A. van Hout, H. de Swart, and H. Verkuyl, eds., *Aspect*. Dordrecht: Kluwer.

Di Sciullo, Anna Maria, and Edwin Williams. 1987. *On the Definition of Word*. Cambridge, MA: MIT Press.

Di Sciullo, Anna Maria, Dana Isac, Anne Bricaud, Marguerite Champagne-Desbiens, Laura Darche, Roseline Hebert, and Mara Simon. 2003a. Asymmetry-based lexicon. In N. Callaos, A. M. Di Sciullo, T. Ohta, and T. K. Liu, eds., *SCI 2003 Proceedings*, 7–12. Orlando, FL: International Institute of Informatics and Systemics.

Di Sciullo, Anna Maria, Ileana Paul, and Stanca Somesfalean. 2003b. The clause structure of extraction asymmetries. In A. M. Di Sciullo, ed., *Asymmetry in Grammar, Volume 1: Syntax and Semantics*, 279–300. Amsterdam: John Benjamins.

Dowty, David. 1979. Word meaning and Montague grammar: The semantics of verbs and times in generative semantics and in Montague's PTQ. In Jakko Hintikka and Stanley Peters, eds., *Synthese Language Library*. Dordrecht: Reidel.

Dresher, B. Elan. 2003. Contrast and asymmetries in inventories. In Anna Maria Di Sciullo, ed., *Asymmetry in Grammar, Volume 2: Morphology, Phonology, Acquisition*, 239–257. Amsterdam: John Benjamins.

Dressler, Wolfgang. 1986. Forma y funcion de los interfijos. *Revista Espanola de Linguistica* 16, 381–395.

Elugbe, Ben Ohi. 1989. Edoid. In John Bendor-Samuel and Rhonda L. Hartell, eds., *The Niger-Congo Languages: A Classification and Description of Africa's Largest Language Family*, 291–304. Lanham, MD: University Press of America.

Embick, David. 2000. Syntax and categories: Verbs and participles in the Latin perfect. *Linguistic Inquiry* 31, 185–230.

Embick, David. 2004. On the structure of resultative particles in English. *Linguistic Inquiry* 35(3), 355–393.

Embick, David, and Rolf Noyer. 2001. Movement operations after syntax. *Linguistic Inquiry* 32, 555–595.

Engdahl, Elisabet. 1983. Parasitic gaps. *Linguistics and Philosophy* 6, 5–34.

Engdahl, Elisabet. 1985. Parasitic gaps, resumptive pronouns, and subject extractions. *Linguistics* 23, 3–44.

Epstein, Samuel David. 1995. Un-principled syntax: The derivation of syntactic relations. In S. D. Epstein and N. Hornstein, eds., *Working Minimalism*, 317–347. Cambridge, MA: MIT Press.

Everaert, Martin, Arnold Evers, Riny Huybregts, and Mieke Trommelen, eds. 1988. *Morphology and Modularity*. Dordrecht: Foris.

Fabb, Nigel. 1984. Syntactic Affixation. Unpublished doctoral dissertation, MIT.

Filip, Hana. 2001. Prefixes and the delimitation of events. In Wayles Browne and Barbara Partee, eds., special issue of *Journal of Slavic Linguistics*, 55–101.

Fillmore, Charles, Paul Kay, Laura A. Michaelis, and Ivan A. Sag. 2003. *Construction Grammar*. Chicago: University of Chicago Press.

Fodor, Jerry. 1979. *The Language of Thought*. Cambridge: Harvard University Press.

Fox, Danny. 2000. *Economy and Semantic Interpretation*. Cambridge, MA: MIT Press.

Fox, Danny. 2002. Antecedent-contained deletion and the copy theory of movement. *Linguistic Inquiry* 33, 63–96.

Frank, Robert. 2002. *Phrase Structure Composition and Syntactic Dependencies*. Cambridge, MA: MIT Press.

Frank, Robert. 2004. Restricting grammatical complexity. *Cognitive Science* 28(5), 669–698.

Frank, Robert, K. Vijay-Shanker, and John Chen. 1996. Dominance, precedence and c-command in description-based parsing. In Carlos Martin-Vide, ed., *Proceedings of the 12th Congreso de Lenguajes Naturales y Lenguajes Formales*, 61–74. Barcelona: PPU.

Frege, Gottlob. [1891] 1952. On sense and reference. In P. Geach and M. Black, eds., *Translations from the Philosophical Writings of Gottlob Frege*, 56–78. Oxford: Blackwell.

Giannakidou, Anastasia. 2000. Negative concord and the scope of universals. In Paul Rowlet, ed., *Transactions of the Philological Society* 98(1), 87–120.

Gil, David. 2001. Quantifiers. In M. Haspelmath, E. Köning, W. Oesterreicher, and W. Raible, eds., *Language Typology and Language Universals*, vol. 2, 1257–1294. Berlin: Walter de Gruyter.

Gillon, Brendan. 1998. The autonomy of word formation: Evidence from classical Sanskrit. *Indian Linguistics* 56, 15–52.

Giorgi, Alessandra, and Giuseppe Longobardi. 1991. *The Syntax of Noun Phrases: Configuration, Parameters, and Empty Categories*. Cambridge: Cambridge University Press.

Giusti, Giuliana. 1991. The categorial status of quantified nominals. *Linguistische Berichte* 136, 438–454.

Greenberg, Joseph. 1963. Some universals of grammar with particular reference to the order of meaningful elements. In Joseph Greenberg, ed., *Universals of Language*, 73–113. Cambridge, MA: MIT Press.

Grevisse, Maurice. [1936] 1986. *Le bon usage*. Gembloux: Duculot.

Grimshaw, Jane. 1990. *Argument Structure*. Cambridge, MA: MIT Press.

Grimshaw, Jane. 1991. Extended Projections. Unpublished manuscript, Brandeis University.

Grimshaw, Jane. 1994. Minimal projection and clause structure. In B. Lust, M. Suner, and J. Whitman, eds., *Syntactic Theory and First Language Acquisition*, 75–83. Hillsdale, NJ: Erlbaum.

Gruber, Jeffrey. 1965. Studies in Lexical Relations. Unpublished doctoral dissertation, MIT.

Gruber, Jeffrey. 1997. Modularity in a configurational theta theory. In Anna Maria Di Sciullo, ed., *Projections and Interface Conditions. Essays in Modularity*, 155–200. New York: Oxford University Press.

Guasti, Teresa, and Luigi Rizzi. 1999. Agreement and Tense as Distinct Syntactic Positions: Evidence from Acquisition. Unpublished manuscript, University of Siena.

Guéron, Jacqueline. 1992. Types syntaxiques et types sémantiques: la phrase copulative comme palimpseste. *Revue Québécoise de linguistique* 1, 7–115.

Guéron, Jacqueline. 1994. Beyond predication. In Guglielmo Cinque, Jan Koster, Jean-Yves Pollock, and Raffaella Zanuttini, eds., *Paths Towards Universal Gram-*

mar: Studies in Honor of Richard Kayne. Washington, DC: Georgetown University Press.

Guéron, Jacqueline. 2001. On the aspectual functions of the verb BE. Paper presented at The Syntax of Aspect, Research Workshop of the Israel Science Foundation, Ben-Gurion University of the Negev.

Hagstrom, Paul. 1998. Decomposing Questions. Unpublished doctoral dissertation, MIT.

Hagstrom, Paul. 2002. Implications of child errors for the syntax of negation in Korean. *Journal of East Asian Linguistics* 11(3), 211–242.

Hale, Kenneth. 1986. Notes on world view and semantic categories: Some Warlpiri examples. In Peter Muysken and Henk van Reimsdijk, eds., *Features and Projections*, 233–245. Dordrecht: Foris.

Hale, Kenneth, and Samuel J. Keyser. 1993. On argument structure and the lexical expression of syntactic relations. In Kenneth Hale and Samuel J. Keyser, eds., *The View from Building* 20, 53–109. Cambridge, MA: MIT Press.

Hale, Kenneth, and Samuel J. Keyser. 1998. The basic elements of argument structure. In Heidi Harley, ed., *Papers from the Penn/MIT Roundtable on Argument Structure and Aspect, MIT Working Papers in Linguistics* 32, 73–118.

Hale, Kenneth, and Samuel J. Keyser. 2002. *Prolegomena to a Theory of Argument Structure.* Cambridge, MA: MIT Press.

Halle, Morris, and Alec Marantz. 1993. Distributed morphology and the pieces of inflection. In Kenneth Hale and Samuel J. Keyser, eds., *The View from Building* 20, 111–176. Cambridge, MA: MIT Press.

Hamblin, C. L. 1958. Questions. *Australian Journal of Philosophy* 36(3), 159–168.

Harley, Heidi. 2003. Merge, conflation, and head movement: The First Sister Principle revisited. Paper presented at NELS 34, Stony Brook, NY.

Harley, Heidi, and Rolf Noyer. 2000. State-of-the-article: Distributed morphology. *Glot International* 4(4), 3–9.

Haspelmath, M. 1997. *Indefinite Pronouns.* Oxford: Clarendon Press.

Hazout, Ilan. 1991. Verbal Nouns: Theta Theoretic Studies in Hebrew and Arabic. Unpublished doctoral dissertation, University of Massachusetts, Amherst.

Hazout, Ilan. 2000. Adjectival genitive constructions in Modern Hebrew: A case study in coanalysis. *Linguistic Review* 17, 29–52.

Heim, Irene, and Angelika Kratzer. 1998. *Semantics in Generative Grammar.* Oxford: Blackwell.

Higginbotham, James. 1985. On semantics. *Linguistic Inquiry* 16, 547–593.

Higginbotham, James. 1996. On events in linguistic semantics. In Fabio Pianesi, Achille Varzi, and James Higginbotham, eds., *Speaking of Events.* New York: Oxford University Press.

Higginbotham, James. 1999. Headedness and telicity. Paper presented at the University of Siena. Unpublished manuscript, University of Oxford.

Higginbotham, James, and Gillian Ramchand. 1997. The stage-level/individual-level distinction and the mapping hypothesis. *Oxford University Working Papers in Linguistics, Philology & Phonetics* 2, 53–83.

Hintikka, Jaakko. 1986. The semantics of "a certain." *Linguistic Inquiry* 17, 331–336.

Hiraiwa, Ken. 2001. Multiple agree and the defective intervention constraint in Japanese. *MIT Working Papers in Linguistics* 40, 67–80.

Hoeksema, Jack. 1985. *Categorial Morphology*. New York: Garland.

Hoekstra, Teun. 1988. Small clause results. *Lingua* 74, 101–139.

Holmberg, Anders. 2001. Expletives and agreement in Scandinavian passives. *Journal of Comparative Germanic Syntax* 4, 85–128.

Huang, C.-T. James. 1982. Logical Relations in Chinese and the Theory of Grammar. Unpublished doctoral dissertation, MIT.

Hulst, Harry van der. 2002. *Word Prosodic Systems in the Languages of Europe*. Berlin: Mouton de Gruyter.

Hulst, Harry van der, and Nancy Ritter. 2003. Levels, constraints and heads. In Anna Maria Di Sciullo, ed., *Asymmetry in Grammar, Volume 2: Morphology, Phonology, Acquisition*, 147–188. Amsterdam: John Benjamins.

Jackendoff, Ray. 1972. *Semantic Interpretation in Generative Grammar*. Cambridge, MA: MIT Press.

Jackendoff, Ray. 1975. Morphological and semantic regularities in the lexicon. *Language* 51, 639–671.

Jackendoff, Ray. 1983. *Semantics and Cognition*. Cambridge, MA: MIT Press.

Jackendoff, Ray. 1990. *Semantic Structures*. Cambridge, MA: MIT Press.

Jackendoff, Ray. 1997. *The Architecture of the Language Faculty*. Cambridge, MA: MIT Press.

Jacobson, Pauline. 1995. On the quantificational force of free relatives. In Emmon Bach, Eloise Helinek, Angelika Kratzer, and Barbara Partee, eds., *Quantification in Natural Languages*, 451–486. Dordrecht: Kluwer.

Johnson, Kyle. 1991. Object positions. *Natural Language and Linguistic Theory* 9, 577–636.

Joshi, Aravind K. 1985. Tree-adjoining grammars: How much context sensitivity is required to provide reasonable structural descriptions? In D. Dowty, L. Karttunen, and A. Zwicky, eds., *Natural Language Parsing*, 206–250. Cambridge: Cambridge University Press.

Joshi, Aravind K., Leon S. Levi, and Masako Takahashi. 1975. Tree adjunct grammars. *Journal of Computer and System Sciences* 10(1), 136–163.

Julien, Marit. 1996. *Syntactic Word Formation in Northern Sámi*. Oslo: Novus Press.

Kalluli, Dalilna. 1995. Clitics in Albanian. Unpublished master's thesis, University of Durham.

Karttunen, Lauri. 1977. Syntax and semantics of questions. *Linguistics and Philosophy* 1, 3–44.

Kayne, Richard. 1985. Principles of particle constructions. In Jacqueline Guéron, Hans-Georg Obenauer, and Jean-Yves Pollock, eds., *Grammatical Representation*, 101–140. Dordrecht: Foris.

Kayne, Richard. 1994. *The Antisymmetry of Syntax*. Cambridge, MA: MIT Press.

Kayne, Richard. 1998. Person Morphemes and Reflexives. Unpublished manuscript, New York University.

Kayne, Richard. 2000. *Parameters and Universals*. Oxford: Oxford University Press.

Kayne, Richard. 2001. Prepositions as Probes. Unpublished manuscript, New York University.

Kayne, Richard. 2003. Antisymmetry, adpositions and remnant movement. Paper presented at the Approaching Asymmetry at the Interfaces Conference, UQAM.

Keyser, Samuel J. 1968. Review of Sven Jacobson, *Adverbial Positions in English*. *Language* 44, 357–375.

Keyser, Samuel J. and Tom Roeper. 1997. Anti-symmetry and leftward movement in morphology. Unpublished manuscript, MIT and University of Massachusetts.

Kiefer, Ferenc. 1992. Compounding in Hungarian. *Rivista di Linguistica* 4(1), 61–78.

Kiparsky, Paul. 1982. Lexical morphology and phonology. In In-Seok Yang, ed., *Linguistics in the Morning Calm*, 1–91. Seoul: Hanshin Publishing Co.

Kiss, Katalin. 1991. Logical structure in linguistic structure: The case of Hungarian. In C.-T. James Huang and Robert May, eds., *Logical Structure and Linguistic Structure*, 111–147. Dordrecht: Kluwer.

Klipple, Elisabeth. 1997. Prepositions and variation. In Anna Maria Di Sciullo, ed., *Projections and Interface Conditions: Essays on Modularity*, 74–108. New York: Oxford University Press.

Koopman, Hilda. 1984. *The Syntax of Verbs: From Verb Movement Rules in the Kru Languages to Universal Grammar*. Dordrecht: Foris.

Koopman, Hilda, and Dominique Sportiche. 1982. Variables and the bijection principle. *Linguistic Review* 2(3), 139–160.

Koopman, Hilda, and Dominique Sportiche. 1991. The position of subjects. *Lingua* 85(1), 211–258.

Koopman, Hilda, and Anna Szabolcsi. 2000. *Verbal Complexes*. Cambridge, MA: MIT Press.

Kornfilt, Jaklin. 2004. *Turkish*. London: Routledge.

Kratzer, Angelika. 1996. Severing the external argument from its verb. In Johan Rooryck and Laurie Zaring, eds., *Phrase Structure and the Lexicon*. Dordrecht: Kluwer.

Kratzer, Angelika. 1998. Scope or pseudoscope? Are there wide scope indefinites? In S. Rothstein, ed., *Events in Grammar*, 163–196. Dordrecht: Kluwer.

Krifka, Manfred. 1990. Boolean and non-boolean "and." In László Kálman and László Polos, eds., *Papers from the Second Symposium on Logic and Language*, 161–188. Budapest: Akadémiai Kiadó.

Kroch, Anthony, and Aravind Krishna Joshi. 1985. *The Linguistic Relevance of Tree Adjoining Grammar.* Report MS-CIS-85-16. Department of Computer and Information Science, Moore School, University of Pennsylvania, Philadelphia.

Ladusaw, William. 1992. Expressing negation. In Chris Barker and David Dowty, eds., *SALT II*, 237–259. Ithaca, NY: CLC Publications.

Ladusaw, William. 1994. Thetic and categorical, stage and individual, weak and strong. In Mandy Harvey and Lynn Santelmann, eds., *Proceedings from SALT IV*, 220–229. Ithaca, NY: CLC Publications.

Lapointe, Steven. 1979. A theory of Grammatical Agreement. Unpublished doctoral dissertation, MIT.

Larson, Richard. 1987. Missing prepositions and the analysis of English free relative clauses. *Linguistic Inquiry* 18(2), 239–266.

Larson, Richard. 1988. On the double object construction. *Linguistic Inquiry* 19, 335–391.

Larson, Richard. 1990. Double objects revisited: Reply to Jackendoff. *Linguistic Inquiry* 21, 589–632.

Lasnik, Howard. 1999. *Minimalist Analysis.* Malden, MA: Blackwell.

Lasnik, Howard. 2002. Feature movement or agreement at a distance? In Artemis Alexiadou, Elena Anagnostopoulou, Sjef Barbiers, and Hans-Martin Gärtner, eds., *Dimensions of Movement*, 189–208. Amsterdam: John Benjamins.

Lebeaux, David. 2003. A subgrammar of contructions with reflexive clitics in Polish. In Anna Maria Di Sciullo, ed., *Asymmetry in Grammar, Volume 2: Morphology, Phonology and Acquisition*, 285–301. Amsterdam: John Benjamins.

Legate, Julie. 2003. Some interface properties of the phase. *Linguistic Inquiry* 34, 506–516.

Levi, Susannah. 2001. Glides, laterals, and Turkish vowel harmony. *CLS* 37, 379–393.

Levin, Beth, and Malka Rappaport Hovav. 1995. *Unaccusativity: At the Syntax–Lexical Semantics Interface.* Cambridge, MA: MIT Press.

Lewis, G. L. 1967. *Turkish Grammar.* Oxford: Oxford University Press.

Liberman, Mark, and Allan S. Prince. 1977. On stress and linguistic rhythm. *Linguistic Inquiry* 8, 249–336.

Lieber, Rochelle. 1980. On the Organization of the Lexicon. Unpublished doctoral dissertation, MIT.

Lieber, Rochelle. 1992. *Deconstructing Morphology: Word Formation in Syntactic Theory.* Chicago: University of Chicago Press.

Lieber, Rochelle, and R. Harald Baayen. 1993. Prefixes in Dutch: A study in lexical conceptual structure. In Geert Booij and Jaap van Marle, eds., *Yearbook of Morphology*, 51–78. Dordrecht: Kluwer.

Mahajan, Anoop. 1990. The A/A-bar Distinction and Movement Theory. Unpublished doctoral dissertation, MIT.

Mahajan, Anoop. 2000. Eliminating head movement. *GLOW Newsletter* 44, 44–45.

Manzini, Maria Rita, and Leonardo M. Savoia. 1999. The syntax of middle-reflexive and object clitics: A case of parametrization in Arberesh dialects. In M. Mandalà, ed., *Studi in onore di Luigi Marlekaj*, 283–328. Bari: Adriatica.

Marantz, Alec. 1984. *On the Nature of Grammatical Relations*. Cambridge, MA: MIT Press.

Marantz, Alec. 1997. No escape from syntax: Don't try to do morphological analysis in the privacy of your own lexicon. In A. Dimitriadis, I. Siegel, C. Surek-Clark, and A. Williams, eds., *Proceedings of the 21st Annual Penn Linguistics Colloquium 201–225, Pennsylvania Working Papers in Linguistics* 4(2). Philadelphia: University of Pennsylvania.

Marantz, Alec. 2003. Pulling words up by the root. Handout for presentation at McGill University.

Mateu, Jaume. 2000a. Paths and telicity in idiomatic constructions: A lexical syntactic approach to the *way* construction. Paper presented at the 2000 ESSLLI Workshop on Paths and Telicity in Event Structure, University of Birmingham.

Mateu, Jaume. 2000b. Syntactically-based lexical decomposition. Paper presented at the 26th Annual Meeting of the Berkeley Linguistics Society (BLS 26), University of California, Berkeley.

Matushansky, Ora. Forthcoming. Going through a phase. In Martha McGinnis and Norvin Richards, eds., *Proceedings of the MIT Workshop on EPP and Phases*. Cambridge, MA: MITWPL.

May, Robert. 1977. The Grammar of Quantification. Unpublished doctoral dissertation, MIT.

May, Robert. 1985. Syntactic rules and semantic rules: Their relation in *wh*-constructions. In J. Guéron, H.-G. Obenauer, and J.-Y. Pollock, eds., *Grammatical Representation*, 187–201. Dordrecht: Foris.

May, Robert, and James Higginbotham. 1981. Crossing, pragmatics, markedness. In A. Belletti, L. Brandi, and L. Rizzi, eds., *Theory of Markedness in Generative Grammar: Proceedings of the Third GLOW Colloquium*, 423–444. Pisa: Annali della Scuola Normale Superiore, Classe de Lettere e Filosofia.

McCarthy, John. 1982. Prosodic structure and expletive infixation. *Language* 58, 574–590.

McCloskey, James. 1991. There, it, and agreement. *Linguistic Inquiry* 22, 563–567.

McGinnis, Martha. 2001. Variation in the phase structure of applicatives. In J. Rooryck and P. Pica, eds., *Linguistic Variation Yearbook*. Amsterdam: John Benjamins.

Merlo, Christian and Pierre Vidaud. 1967. *Unité des langues négro-africaines*. Paris: G.-P. Maisonneuve et Larose.

Montague, Richard. 1970. Universal grammar. *Theoria* 36, 373–398.

Montague, Richard. 1973. The proper treatment of quantification on ordinary English. In J. Hintikka, J. Moravcsik, and P. Suppes, eds., *Approaches to Natural Language*. Dordrecht: D. Reidel. (Reprinted in Montague 1974.)

Montague, Richard. 1974. *Formal Philosophy: Selected Papers of Richard Montague*. Ed. Richmond H. Thomason. New Haven, CT: Yale University Press.

Montague, Richard, and Donald Kalish. 1959. That. *Philosophical Studies* 10, 54–61.

Moro, Andrea. 1997. *The Raising of Predicates*. Cambridge: Cambridge University Press.

Moro, Andrea. 2000. *Dynamic Antisymmetry*. Cambridge, MA: MIT Press.

Moro, Andrea, Marco Tettamanti, Daniela Perani, Catarina Donati, Stefano F. Cappa, and Ferruccio Fazio. 2001. Syntax and the brain: Disentangling grammar by selective anomalies. *Neuroimage* 13(1), 110–118.

Muysken, Pieter. 1981. Quechua word structure. In F. Heny, ed., *Binding and Filtering*. London: Croom Helm.

Muysken, Pieter. 1988. Affix order and interpretation: Quechua. In M. Everaert, A. Evers, R. Huybregts, and M. Trommelen, eds., *Morphology and Modularity*. Dordrecht: Foris.

Neeleman, Ad, and Joleen Schipper. 1992. Verbal prefixation in Dutch: Thematic evidence for conversion. In G. Booij and J. Van Marle, eds., *Yearbook of Morphology*, 57–92. Dordrecht: Kluwer.

Nissenbaum, Jon. 2000. Covert movement and parasitic gaps. In M. Hirotani, A. Coetzee, N. Hall, and J.-Y. Kim, eds., *Proceedings of the 30th Annual Meeting, North East Linguistics Society* 30. Amherst, MA: GLSA, University of Massachusetts.

Obenhauer, Hans. 1994. Aspects de la syntaxe A-barre. Thèse de doctorat d'Etat, Université de Paris VIII.

O'Keefe, John. 1995. The spatial prepositions in English, vector grammar, and the cognitive map theory. In Paul Bloom, Mary A. Peterson, Lynn Nadel, and Merrill F. Garrett, eds., *Language and Space*. Cambridge, MA: MIT Press.

Olsen, Mari Broman. 1997. *A Semantic and Pragmatic Model of Lexical and Grammatical Aspect*. New York: Garland.

Partee, Barbara H., Alice Ter Meulen, and Robert Wall. 1990. *Mathematical Methods in Linguistics*. Dordrecht: Kluwer.

Perlmutter, David M. 1987. Impersonal passives and the unaccusative hypothesis. In J. Jaeger et al., eds., *Proceedings of the Fourth Annual Meeting of the Berkeley Linguistic Society*, 159–189. Berkeley: University of California at Berkeley.

Pesetsky, David. 1985. Morphology and logical form. *Linguistic Inquiry* 16, 193–245.

Pesetsky, David. 1989. The earliness principle. Paper presented at *GLOW* 1989.

Pesetsky, David. 1995. *Zero Syntax*. Cambridge, MA: MIT Press.

Pesetsky, David, and Esther Torego. 2001. T-to-C movement: Causes and consequences. In Michael Kenstowicz, ed., *Ken Hale: A Life in Language*. Cambridge, MA: MIT Press.

Philips, Colin. 2003. Linear order and constituency. *Linguistic Inquiry* 34(1), 37–90.

Piggott, Glyne. 2003. Obstruent neutrality in nasal harmony. In Anna Maria Di Sciullo, ed., *Asymmetry in Grammar, Volume 2: Morphology, Phonology and Acquisition*, 189–215. Amsterdam: John Benjamins.

Pollock, Jean-Yves. 1989. Verb movement, universal grammar, and the structure of IP. *Linguistic Inquiry* 20, 365–424.

Potsdam Eric, and Maria Polinsky. 2001. Long-distance agreement and topic in Tsez. *Natural Language and Linguistic Theory* 19, 583–646.

Przepiorkowski, Adam, and Anna Kupsc. 1997. Negative concord in Polish. *Technical Report* 828. Polish Academy of Sciences, Institute of Computer Science, Warsaw.

Pulleyblank, Douglas George. 1983. Tone in lexical phonology. Unpublished doctoral dissertation, MIT.

Pustejovsky, James. 1988. The geometry of events. In Carol Tenny, ed., *Studies in Generative Approaches to Aspect. Lexicon Project Working Papers* 24, 19–39. Cambridge, MA: MIT Press.

Pustejovsky, James. 1991. The syntax of event structure. *Cognition* 41, 47–81.

Pustejovsky, James. 1995. *The Generative Lexicon: A Theory of Computational Lexical Semantics*. Cambridge, MA: MIT Press.

Pylkkänen, Liina. 2002. Introducing Arguments. Unpublished doctoral dissertation, MIT.

Raimy, Eric. 2000a. *The Phonology and Morphology of Reduplication*. Berlin: Mouton de Gruyter.

Raimy, Eric. 2000b. Remarks on backcopying. *Linguistic Inquiry* 3, 541–552.

Raimy, Eric. 2003. Asymmetry and linearization in phonology. In Anna Maria Di Sciullo, ed., *Asymmetry in Grammar, Volume 2: Morphology, Phonology and Acquisition*, 129–146. Amsterdam: John Benjamins.

Ralli, Angela. 1992. Compounds in Modern Greek. *Rivista di Linguistica* 4(1), 143–174.

Ralli, Angela, and Maria Raftopoulou. 1999. Compounding as a diachronic phenomenon of word formation. *Studies in Greek Linguistics*, 389–403. Thessaloniki: Aristotle University of Thessaloniki.

Reichenbach, Hans. 1947. *Elements of Symbolic Logic*. New York: Free Press.

Reinhart, Tanya. 1983. *Anaphora and Semantic Interpretation*. London: Croom Helm.

Reinhart, Tanya. 1997. Interface economy and markedness. In C. Wilder, H. Gärtner, and M. Bierwisch, eds., *The Role of Economy Principles in Linguistic Theory*, 146–170. Berlin: Akademie Verlag.

Reinhart, Tanya. 2000. Strategies of anaphora resolution. In H. Bennis, M. Everaert, and E. Reuland, eds., *Interface Strategies*, 295–324. Amsterdam: Royal Academy of Arts and Sciences.

Reuland, Eric. 1998. Structural conditions on chains and binding. In *Proceedings of NELS* 28, 341–356. Amherst, MA: GLSA, University of Massachusetts.

Rice, Keren. 1998. Salve (Northern Athapaskan). In Andrew Spencer and Arnold Zwicky, eds., *The Handbook of Morphology*, 649–689. Oxford: Blackwell.

Ritter, Elisabeth. 1991. Two functional categories in noun phrases: Evidence from modern Hebrew. In S. Rothstein, ed., *Syntax and Semantics* 26, 37–62. San Diego: Academic Press.

Rizzi, Luigi. 1990. *Relativized Minimality*. Cambridge, MA: MIT Press.

Roeper, Thomas. 1998. Compound syntax and head movement. *Yearbook of Morphology* 1, 187–228. Dordrecht: Foris.

Roeper, Thomas. 1999. Leftward Movement in Morphology. Unpublished manuscript, University of Massachusetts.

Roeper, Thomas, and Samuel J. Keyser. 1992. Re: The abstract clitic hypothesis. *Linguistic Inquiry* 23, 89–125.

Roeper, Thomas, and William Snyder. 2005. Language learnability and the forms of recursion. In A. M. Di Sciullo, ed., *UG and External Systems*, 155–169. Amsterdam: John Benjamins.

Rohrbacher, Bernhard. 1994. The Germanic VO Languages and the Full Paradigm: A Theory of V to I Raising. Unpublished doctoral dissertation, University of Massachusetts, Amherst.

Ross, John R. 1967. Constrains on Variables in Syntax. Unpublished doctoral dissertation, MIT.

Rumelhart, David E., and James L. McClelland. 1986. On learning the past tense of English verbs. In J. L. McClelland, D. E. Rumelhart, and the PDP Research Group, eds., *Parallel Distributed Processing: Explorations in the Microstructure of Cognition, Volume 2: Psychological and Biological Models*, 216–271. Cambridge, MA: MIT Press.

Safir, Kenneth. 1985. *Syntactic Chains*. Cambridge: Cambridge University Press.

Scalise, Sergio. 1984. *Generative Morphology*. Dordrecht: Foris.

Scalise, Sergio. 1994. *Morfologia*. Bologna: Il Mulino.

Sebüktekin, Hikmet. 1971. *Turkish-English Contrastive Analysis*. The Hague: Mouton.

Selkirk, Elisabeth. 1982. *The Syntax of Words*. Cambridge, MA: MIT Press.

Sells, Peter. 1984. Syntax and Semantics of Resumptive Pronouns. Unpublished doctoral dissertation, University of Massachusetts.

Shibatani, Masayoshi, and Taro Kageyama. 1988. Word formation in a modular theory of grammar: A case of post-syntactic compounds in Japanese. *Language* 64, 451–484.

Smith, Carlotta. 1991. *The Parameter of Aspect*. Dordrecht: Kluwer.

Smolensky, Paul, Michael C. Mozer, and David E. Rumelhart, eds. 1996. *Mathematical Perspectives on Neural Networks*. Mahwah, NJ: Erlbaum.

Snyder, William. 1995. A neo-Davidsonian approach to resultatives, particles, and datives. In J. Beckman, ed., *Proceedings of NELS 25*. Amherst, MA: GLSA, University of Massachusetts.

Snyder, William. 2001. On the nature of syntactic variation: Evidence from complex predicates and complex word-formation. *Language* 77, 324–342.

Speas, Margaret. 1990. *Phrase Structure in Natural Language*. Dordrecht: Kluwer.

Speas, Margaret. 1994. Null arguments in a theory of economy of projection. *UMass Occasional Papers in Linguistics*.

Speas, Margaret, and Carol Tenny. 2003. Configurational properties of point of view roles. In Anna Maria Di Sciullo, ed., *Asymmetry in Grammar, Volume 1: Syntax and Semantics*, 315–345. Amsterdam: John Benjamins.

Spencer, Andrew. 1991. *Morphological Theory*. Oxford: Blackwell.

Spencer, Andrew. 1998. The redundancy of lexical categories. In *If You See What I Mean ... Essays on Language*. Presented to Keith Brown on the Occasion of His Retirement in 1998. (ERRL special issue, May 1998.)

Spencer, Andrew, and Marina Zaretskaya. 1998. Verb prefixation in Russian as lexical subordination. *Linguistics* 36, 1–39.

Spencer, Andrew, and Arnold M. Zwicky. 1998. *The Handbook of Morphology*. Oxford: Blackwell.

Sportiche, Dominique. 2002. Movement types and triggers. *GLOW Newsletter* 48, 116–117.

Stiebels, Barbara. 1998. Complex denominal verbs in German and the morphology-semantics interface. In Geert Booij and Jaap van Marle, eds., *Yearbook of Morphology 1997*, 265–302. Dordrecht: Kluwer.

Stiebels, Barbara, and Dieter Wunderlich. 1994. Morphology feeds syntax: The case of particle verbs. *Linguistics* 32, 913–968.

Stowell, Timothy. 1995. What do the present and past tenses mean? In P. Bertinetto, V. Bianchi, J. Higginbotham, and M. Squartini, eds., *Temporal Reference, Aspect, and Actionality, Volume 1: Semantic and Syntactic Perspectives*, 381–396. Torino: Rosenberg and Sellier.

Svenonius, Peter. 1996. The Verb-Particle Alternation in the Scandinavian Languages. Unpublished manuscript, University of Tromsö.

Svenonius, Peter. 2003. Phases at the interface. Handout. IAP Workshop on EPP and Phases.

Svolacchia, Marco, Lunella Mereu, and Annarita Puglielli. 1995. Aspects of discourse configuration in Somali. In K. Kiss, ed., *Discourse Configurational Languages*, 65–98. New York: Oxford University Press.

Talmy, Leonard. 1985. Lexicalization patterns: Semantic structure in lexical forms. In Timothy Shopen, ed., *Language Typology and Syntactic Description, Volume 3: Grammatical Categories and the Lexicon*, 57–149. Cambridge: Cambridge University Press.

Talmy, Leonard. 1991. Path to realization: A typology of event integration. *Buffalo Working Papers in Linguistics* 91-01.147-87.

Talmy, Leonard. 2000. *Toward a Cognitive Semantics, Volume 1: Concept-Structuring Systems; Volume 2: Typology and Process in Concept Structuring.* Cambridge, MA: MIT Press.

Tancredi, Christopher. 2004. Wh-mo NPs in Japanese: Quantifiers, plurals, or a different beast altogether. Unpublished manuscript.

Taraldsen, Tarald. 1981. The theoretical interpretation of a class of marked extractions. In A. Belletti, L. Brandi, and L. Rizzi, eds., *Theory of Markedness in Generative Grammar.* Pisa: Scuola Normale Superiore.

Tenny, Carol. 1988. The Aspectual Interface Hypothesis. *Lexicon Project Working Papers* 31. Center for Cognitive Sciences, MIT.

Tenny, Carol. 1994. *Aspectual Roles and the Syntax-Semantics Interface.* Dordrecht: Kluwer.

Toman, Jindrich. 1998. Word-syntax. In Andrew Spencer and Arnold Zwicky, eds., *Handbook of Morphology*, 306–321. Oxford: Blackwell.

Travis, Lisa. 1984. Parameters and the Effects of Word Order Variation. Unpublished doctoral dissertation, MIT.

Treiman, Rebecca. 1985. Onsets and rimes as units of spoken syllables: Evidence from children. *Journal of Experimental Child Psychology* 39(1), 161–181.

Tsai, Dylan Wei-Tien. 1994. On nominal islands and LF extraction in Chinese. *Natural Language and Linguistic Theory* 12, 121–175.

Tsapkini, Kyrana, Gonia Jarema, and Anna Maria Di Sciullo. 2004. The role of configurational asymmetry in the lexical access of prefixed verbs: Evidence from French. *Brain and Language* 90, 143–150.

Ura, Hiroyuki. 1995. Towards a theory of "strictly derivational" economy condition. In Robert Pensalfini and Hiroyuki Ura, eds., *Papers on Minimalist Syntax.* Cambridge, MA: MIT Press.

Uriagereka, Juan. 1999. Multiple spell-out. In S. D. Epstein and M. Hornstein, eds., *Working Minimalism*, 251–283. Cambridge, MA: MIT Press.

Van Hout, Angeliek, and Tom Roeper. 1998. Event semantics and aspectual structure in derivational morphology. In Heidi Harley, ed., *Papers from the Penn/MIT Roundtable on Argument Structure and Aspect, MIT Working Papers in Linguistics* 32, 175–200.

Van Riemsdijk, Henk. 1989. Movement and regeneration. In Paola Benincà, ed., *Dialect Variation and the Theory of Grammar: Proceedings of the GLOW Workshop on Linguistic Theory and Dialect Variation*, 105–136. Dordrecht: Foris.

Vendler, Zeno. 1967. *Linguistics in Philosophy.* Ithaca, NY: Cornell University Press.

Vergnaud, Jean-Roger. 1980. Dépendances Formelles en Syntaxe. Thèse de Doctorat d'État, Université de Paris 7.

Vergnaud, Jean-Roger, and Maria Luisa Zubizarreta. 1992. The definite determiner and the inalienable construction in French and English. *Linguistic Inquiry* 23(4), 595–652.

Verkuyl, Henk. 1993. *A Theory of Aspectuality. The Interaction between Temporal and Atemporal Structure.* Cambridge Series in Linguistics 64. Cambridge University Press.

Verkuyl, Henk. 1999. *Aspectual Issues. Studies on Time and Quantity.* CSLI Publications. Center for the Study of Language and Information. Stanford, California.

Von Fintel, Kai. 2000. Whatever. In Brendan Jackson and Tanya Matthews, eds., *Proceedings of SALT 10.* Ithaca, NY: CLC Publications.

Walinska de Hackbeil, Hanna. 1986. The Roots of Phrase Structure: The Syntactic Basis of English Morphology. Unpublished doctoral dissertation, University of Washington.

Wechsler, Stephen. 1990. Accomplishments and the prefix re-. In J. Carter and R.-M. Déchaine, eds., *Proceedings of the North Eastern Linguistic Society* 19, 419–434. Amherst, MA: University of Massachusetts.

Williams, Edwin. 1980. Predication. *Linguistic Inquiry* 11, 203–238.

Williams, Edwin. 1981a. Argument structure and morphology. *Linguistic Review* 1, 81–114.

Williams, Edwin. 1981b. On the notions "lexically related" and "head of a word." *Linguistic Inquiry* 12, 245–274.

Williams, Edwin. 2003. *Representation Theory.* Cambridge, MA: MIT Press.

Wurmbrand, Susi. 2003. A-movement to the point of no return. In Makoto Kadowaki and Shigeto Kawahara, eds., *Proceedings of the North Eastern Linguistic Society Annual Meeting* (NELS 33), 463–474. Amherst, MA: University of Massachusetts, GLSA.

Zamparelli, Roberto. 1995. Layers in the Determiner Phrase. Unpublished doctoral dissertation, University of Rochester.

Zubizarreta, Maria Luisa. 1998. *Prosody, Focus, and Word Order.* Cambridge, MA: MIT Press.

Zwarts, Joost. 1992. X'-syntax–X'-semantics: On the Interpretation of Functional and Lexical Heads. Unpublished doctoral dissertation, Utrecht University.

Index

Abney, Steven, 41
Adger, David, 37, 40, 48
A-feature Distinctiveness, 60, 62–63, 72
A-features, 27, 41, 44–45, 55, 58, 60, 63, 90
Affix, 14, 41
  aspectual, 84, 158, 159
  causative, 14, 28, 39, 44–45, 65, 68
  comparative, 28, 138–139
  derivational, 58, 62, 64–69
  diminutives, 14, 188n6
  inflectional, 25, 43–44, 129, 132, 139, 151,
    154–156
  iterative, 5, 76–79, 85, 90, 92, 96, 199n12
  modifier, 25, 32, 132
  operator, 25, 32, 138
  predicate, 24–25, 32, 60, 63, 69, 132
  sequential, 5, 25, 76, 79, 84
  spatial, 5, 78–79, 83–84, 149
Agree, 30, 32, 46, 47, 63, 117, 189n10. *See
  also* Asymmetry Theory
Aguero, Calixto, 190n12, 199n3
Ambar, Manuela, 99, 106
Anderson, Steven, 65
Androutsopoulou, Antonia, 53
Aoun, Joseph, 99, 123, 199
Argument structure, 5, 24–25, 55–58, 62,
    76, 78, 93–94, 139–140, 182n4, 184n8,
    190n13, 191n3, 193n8, 194n10, 195n12
  flexibility, 54–55, 58–59, 65–66, 70, 90, 93,
    139, 184n7, 193nn6–7, 195n13
  projection, 78–79, 192n5, 195n2, 205n7
  relations, 24, 56–57, 195n11
  shift, 59, 65, 67, 69, 71, 73–74, 90, 187n4,
    196n6
  structural types of, 65–57
Aronoff, Mark, 55
Arregi, Karlos, 48–49
A-Shell, 55, 59, 172
A-Shell Hypothesis, 59–60
Aspect, 19, 24–25, 53, 75, 195n1
  external, 25, 79–80, 93 (*see also* E-Asp)

internal, 25, 27, 79–80, 91, 93 (*see also*
  I-Asp)
  structure, 59, 79, 195n12
Aspectual selection, 87, 88–89
  classes, 76
  features, 61, 75–77, 103
  heads, 79
  modification, 75–76, 79, 91, 93–94, 160
  modifiers, 25, 79, 94
Asp-feature Distinctiveness, 82–83, 93, 94–
  96, 199n12
Asp-features, 76–77, 80–84, 90, 93–96,
  195n12, 198n12
Asp-Shell, 26, 76, 79–85, 89, 90–92, 93, 97,
  103, 160, 170, 172
Asp-Shell Hypothesis, 79–80, 83–94, 91–92
Asymmetry, 1–8, 11, 13, 15–16, 18–19, 21–
  24, 28, 31, 33–37, 39, 46, 48–49, 53–55,
  57–59, 61, 63, 65, 67, 69, 71, 73–74, 76,
  78, 79, 81, 83–84, 87, 89, 91, 93, 95, 96–
  97, 99, 101, 107, 109, 115, 117–119, 121–
  124, 129, 131, 144. *See also* Relation
Asymmetry Hypothesis, 1–2, 4–5, 166, 169,
  180n14
Asymmetry Theory, 21–23, 24, 27–29, 33–
  34, 46, 48, 50–53, 55, 57–59, 76, 78, 84,
  97, 99, 103, 108, 122–124, 128, 130–131,
  135, 138–139, 144–147, 150, 154, 158,
  160, 169, 173–175, 180n14, 181n1, 183n4,
  185n13, 186nn17–18, 191n1, 192n3,
  206n4, 20 7n7
Atomicity Thesis, 21, 33, 187n18

Baayen, Harald, 196n2
Bach, Emmon, 182n2
Baker, Marc, 10, 129, 184, 195n11
Bakovic, Eric, 206n4
Barwise, Jon, 101
Bendor-Samuel, David, 73, 154
Binnick, Robert I., 75
Blocking, 55, 182n2, 191n2, 193n6

Ramchand, Gillian, 207n6
Rappaport Hovav, Malka, 59, 62, 184n7, 194n11
Reinhart, Tanya, 3, 123, 179n12
Relation, 17–20
  antisymmetric, 7, 18
  asymmetric, 2, 3, 18
  asymmetric c-command, 8, 20
  c-command, 8
  contain, 20
  dominance, 1, 19
  irreflexive, 18
  precedence, 1, 19
  reflexive, 18
  sister-contain, 1, 20
  sister of, 19
  symmetric, 2, 18
Remnant movement, 31, 133–134, 138, 147, 157
Reuland, Eric, 20
Rice, Keren, 184n10
Right Hand Rule, 41, 127, 188n6
Ritter, Elizabeth, 53
Rizzi, Luigi, 177n1
Roeper, Thomas, 4, 38, 62, 178n8, 185n12, 196n2, 197nn3–4
Rohrbacher, Bernhard, 182n2
Romanian, 198n9
Ross, John, R., 3, 177n1
Rumelhart, David E., 182n2
Russian, 72, 73, 110, 199n4, 203n1

Safir, Ken, 199n3
Sag, Ivan, A., 53
Savoia, Leonardo M., 53
Scalise, Sergio, 191n2
Schipper, Joleen, 196n2
Scope
  affixal, 128–129
  ambiguity, 3, 7, 123, 125–126, 172, 174
  inverse, 15, 127
  narrow, 3
  properties, 27
  relations, 10, 23, 79, 84, 123–124, 127–128, 172
  wide, 3
  word-internal, 124–125
Selkirk, Elizabeth, 38
Sells, Peter, 199n2
Semantic type, 24–25, 50–51, 59, 101–102, 106–107, 119–121, 184n8, 193n6, 203n15
Shell
  M-, 36–39, 41, 43, 46–48, 50, 51, 53, 170
  Op-, 102, 106–108, 114, 116, 118, 121–122, 138, 172
  VP, 58, 187n2
Shibatani, Masayoshi, 182n2, 186n18

Shift, 29–30. *See also* Asymmetry Theory
Slabakova, Roumyana, 84
Smith, Carlotta, 196n1
Smolensky, Paul, 182n2
Snyder, William, 166
Somesfalean, Stanca, 167, 177n1
Speas, Margaret, 25, 174
Spencer, Andrew, 182n4
Sportiche, Dominique, 26, 56, 197n5, 199n3
Stiebels, Barbara, 196n2
Stjepanović, Sandra, 204n3
Stowell, Timothy, 199n1
Strict Asymmetry, 33–34, 36, 39, 61, 103, 170, 187n19
Strict asymmetry of morphology, 13, 15, 23–24, 34, 127, 169, 172
Strict Scope, 124–127, 147, 172
Subset, 17
Svenonius, Peter, 40, 48, 164
Svolacchia, Marco, 202n11
Syllable structure, 4
Szabolcsi, Anna, 130

Takahashi, Masaka, 187n17
Talmy, Leonard, 159
Tancredi, Christopher, 204n2
Taraldsen, Tarald, 199n2
Tenny, Carol, 75, 87
Ter Meulen, Alice, 16
Transfer, 22–23, 48, 51, 114, 124, 131, 141, 145, 169, 176, 181n1,182n4, 183n5, 187n18
Transportability convention, 31, 141
Travis, Lisa, 10, 129
Tree Adjoining Grammar, 186n17
Treiman, Rebecca, 5
Tsai, Dylan Wei-Tien, 107
Tsapkini, Kyrana, 5
Turkish, 110, 113, 200n5, 203n1, 206n1, 206n4
Type-theoretical semantics, 50, 101, 184n8

Uniformity Condition, 123–124, 149–150, 206n3
Universal Base Hypothesis, 23, 77, 124, 131, 183n6
Ura, Hiroyuki, 99
Uriagereka, Juan, 4, 21, 40
Uribe-Etxebarria, Myriam, 196n1

Van Hout, Angeliek, 196n2
Van Riemsdijk, Henk, 25
Variation, 9, 80, 99, 112, 122–123, 139, 149–161, 163, 165–167, 173, 188n7, 203n1, 204n1, 205n1. 206n2, 206n3, 207n7
Veloso, Rita, 106